SO-AWP-211

Restaurants of San Francisco

The definitive guide to the Bay Area's Best

Patricia Unterman
Stan Sesser

A Comstock Edition

Sausalito • California

Copyright © 1981, by Patty Unterman and Stan Sesser

All rights reserved under International and
Pan-American Copyright Conventions

Printed in the United States of America

ISBN: 0–89174–040–6

Cover art by Bill Yenne

Some of these reviews are derived from articles
previously published in the *San Francisco Chronicle*
and are used with permission.

COMSTOCK EDITIONS, INC.
3030 Bridgeway
Sausalito, CA 94965

CONTENTS

INTRODUCTION

Paris may have better French food, Taipei better Chinese food, Florence better Italian food. But few locations in the world combine the wide variety of eating experiences that are available in the San Francisco Bay Area. You can have a marvelous meal, night after night, without repeating the same ethnic type twice. You can sample some of the world's finest produce, picked fresh from nearby California farms; you can feast on fish caught that morning in the Pacific Ocean; you can drink some of the world's greatest wines, produced in the Napa Valley just a couple of hours away. When you add it up, San Francisco and the surrounding environs could well be the world's premier area for dining out.

Bay Area residents love to eat, and they're not at all stuffy in their choice of restaurants. People will happily dress up one night for a fancy French establishment and wear blue jeans the next night to a Chinese hole in the wall. One of the first subjects of conversation when two people meet is: What new restaurants have you discovered? Here, new restaurants pop up all over the place—and generally do very well.

In this sort of atmosphere, being a restaurant critic is a joy. In this book we've tried to capture the wide variety of eating experiences that are available. You'll read about expensive French restaurants, but also where to get the best hamburgers, hot dogs, and burritos. You'll see reviews of San Francisco's world-famous spots for dining out, but also of little neighborhood restaurants that have a handful of tables and a family running the whole operation. We take seriously the preparation of French sauces, but we're equally interested in the quality of ice cream and hot dog rolls.

First, a few words of advice about some of the different styles of Bay Area restaurants. Then, you're on your own. We wish you lots of good eating!

French Restaurants

"Is everything satisfactory, monsieur et mademoiselle?" Well, frankly, not always. The pretentious French restaurants with the red banquettes, the dim lighting, and the tuxedoed waiters inquiring every five minutes about the food frequently have more of an

1

impact on your wallet than on your dining pleasure. If you often feel uncomfortable in these places, you're not alone.

Fortunately, the Bay Area is filled with French restaurants that are friendly and informal, but that take their food very seriously. This is just the way it is in the best eating spots in France. With today's prices, even a bill in a relatively inexpensive French restaurant can add up. For your money, you're entitled not only to a first-rate meal, but also to the feeling that you're not being intimidated.

Light French food, with lots of vegetables and purees and fewer heavy sauces based on butter and cream, is in vogue today, the leading practitioner being Chez Panisse. But some of the more traditional French restaurants, like Maurice et Charles and La Mirabelle, do an excellent job with classic French cooking. Try both styles—they're equally to be treasured.

The freshness of the ingredients counts a lot in French cooking. That's why you should always inquire closely about what on the menu came from where—and when. Ignore the standard French dishes like snails (which often come from a can) or onion soup (which often is terrible), and ask about the chef's specialties. Concentrate on those dishes that seem unique to that particular restaurant. And if you don't like the food, send it back. At French restaurant prices, you're entitled to go away satisfied.

A Word About Wine

Many restaurants, particularly those that offer French food, make most of their money on an overpriced and often mediocre wine list. Others choose their wine lists very carefully, making sure there's always a selection of excellent but low-priced wines, as well as more expensive, older vintages.

Don't feel you have to be victimized when you encounter a restaurant of the first type. If you're not satisfied with the caliber of the wine list, make do with the house wine, which will be substantially less expensive and might not be worse than more pricy wines that have been poorly chosen. Remember that while great French wines can be superb, inexpensive California wines are often of higher quality than mediocre wines from France. And the best California chardonnays and cabernet sauvignons rival the best French white Burgundies and Bordeaux, frequently at a much lower price. Finally, Italian red wines, particularly those with some age on them, are often extraordinary values.

Because the weather is less variable in California, vintages aren't as important. Young white wines can be fresh and delightful; there's no particular need to look for age. But for red wines, the zinfandels and cabernet sauvignons of a recent vintage can be overwhelmingly heavy and tannic, not nearly ready to drink. Be sure to consult the waiter closely about these; a less expensive California wine might be a better choice than a higher-priced cabernet that is years away from maturity. For California whites, Chalone, Freemark Abbey, Hanzell, Mayacamas, Spring Mountain, and Sterling generally produce wines of high quality. For reds, look for Conn Creek, Freemark Abbey, Heitz, Mayacamas, Montevina, Joseph Phelps, and Ridge. These wineries comprise only a handful of dozens of great California producers, but their wines tend to be consistently good.

If you're ordering a French wine, remember that prices of Bordeaux and Burgundies have soared in recent years, particularly for the great 1978 vintage. And Beaujolais, while much cheaper, are too often mediocre. You might want to look for a red Rhone, which can be an excellent wine and a good value, or for a white from a district outside Burgundy, like Sancerre, Muscadet, or Vouvray. In recent years, white Bordeaux have been improving, and they also tend not to be very expensive.

For older French wines, some of the greatest vintages include: Bordeaux: 1961, 1966, 1970, 1971, 1975, and 1978. Red Burgundies: 1961, 1964, 1966, 1969, 1971, 1972, 1976, and 1978. White Burgundies: 1969, 1970, 1973, 1976, and 1978.

Most San Francisco restaurants offer corkage privileges, meaning that you can bring your own wine and pay something, often around $5 a bottle, for the privilege of drinking it there. Ask about this when you make reservations; if you have the time and the will, it's fun to choose your own wine. Two wine shops in San Francisco that have an excellent selection of older vintages, particularly of French wines, are Connoisseur Wine Imports, 462 Bryant Street, 433–0825, and Draper & Esquin, 655 Sutter Street, 855–4885.

Italian Restaurants

It's hardly like eating in Italy, where each district has its own special regional cuisine. Unlike the more specialized Italian restaurants of Boston and New York, Bay Area Italian food tends to be more of a mish-mash of ''California Favorite Italian Dishes.'' You can still eat very well if you simply follow some basic rules.

First, stay away from veal, unless it's Provimi veal from Wisconsin. California veal tends to be tough and tasteless, a far cry from the fork-tender, milk-white veal of Provimi. If you're eating at one of San Francisco's many family-style Italian restaurants, chances are the veal isn't going to be good.

Second, the more exotic the pasta dish sounds, the better it's likely to be. Too many Bay Area Italian restaurants make huge pots of spaghetti and meatballs or ravioli in advance rather than to order, and you tend to get a gloppy, overcooked mess. Ask which pasta noodles are made fresh at the restaurant, and which pasta dishes aren't prepared in advance.

Third, avoid antipastos and desserts unless we especially recommend them. In Italy antipastos are a wonderful mixture of such things as grilled yellow peppers, spinach soufflés, grilled zucchini, and toast covered with chopped olives. Here an antipasto is more often a few slices of luncheon meat with a couple of olives and canned peppers.

Finally, beware of pizza, except at the few restaurants where we recommend it. (Greens, Tommaso Famous Pizzeria, and Chez Panisse Cafe are among the best.) No one knows why, but the pizza in San Francisco tends to be several leagues below pizza you can get in New York, Chicago, or Boston.

Chinese Restaurants

Like Italian food, the lines between different styles of Chinese cooking tend to be blurred in San Francisco restaurants. Cantonese food, which predominates, is what most people normally think of as Chinese food. It includes such things as egg rolls, wonton soup, sweet-and-sour pork, spareribs, and chow mein. When cooked by a skilled chef, Cantonese food can be highly unusual and tasty. The Cantonese are particularly skilled in chicken and fish dishes, and preparations that are steamed or cooked in a clay pot are generally more successful than those that are stir-fried in a wok.

Deem sum (Chinese tea pastries) is one variety of Cantonese food for which San Francisco is a mecca. Only two cities in the world offer such a wide choice of excellent *deem sum* parlors: San Francisco and Hong Kong. So, if you can only have one Chinese meal in San Francisco, make it *deem sum* for brunch or lunch, at Tung Fong or Asia Garden.

The cooking at northern Chinese or Peking restaurants tends to be spicier, and wheat as well as rice is used as an ingredient in some dishes. Some of the best known northern dishes include Peking duck, hot-and-sour soup, twice-cooked pork, and *mu shi* pork with pancakes. Here the stir-fried dishes, including duck, red meat, and all sorts of vegetables, tend to be excellent.

Then there are the Szechuanese and Hunanese restaurants, the spiciest yet, where many dishes include red-hot chili peppers. Since the Chinese community in the Bay Area is largely Cantonese, so are most of the cooks, and excellent Cantonese dishes are frequently included at restaurants specializing in other types of cooking. Confused? So are we, when we try to determine what a restaurant's distinguishing style is. Just pick up your chopsticks and enjoy it.

Other Asian Restaurants

The Japanese food in San Francisco and the Bay Area could be the best Japanese food in the world. When eating in Japan, we've discovered that many key ingredients, including some of the fish, come from California. You can get it fresh here, at one-quarter the price.

Japanese food is far more than sukiyaki and teriyaki. Types of service include sushi bars, with their exquisite preparations of raw fish of every type, and noodle joints, where you can get an enormously satisfying bowl of noodles in a rich broth, accented with meat, fish, or vegetables. And, in the best restaurants, the menu includes some special dishes that you'll rarely see on another Japanese menu.

Then there's Thai food. The number of Thai restaurants in San Francisco seems to increase almost by the week, and the more we eat it, the more we like it. Many Thai dishes are hot, but the chili peppers never overwhelm the exotic bouquet of flavors. And like other Oriental cuisines, Thai food tends to be very reasonably priced.

Vietnamese food is also growing by leaps and bounds, with the stream of Vietnamese refugees arriving in the Bay Area. When you add to this some excellent Indian restaurants and a Korean restaurant or two, you can see that weeks of exploring are necessary to experience the delights of Asian cooking in the San Francisco Bay Area.

Latin Restaurants

Everyone knows that San Francisco's Mission District is lined with inexpensive and often first-rate Mexican restaurants. It's not the elaborate, almost continental food you get in Mexico itself, but rather the "Tex-Mex" variety: the tacos, burritos, enchiladas, and the like that predominate in Texas and California.

Less well known is the wide variety of other sorts of Latin restaurants, such as Cuban, Salvadoran, Peruvian, and Spanish. They also generally have Mexican food on their menu, but skip that and try their homeland's cuisine. Latin restaurants seem to do particularly well with fish, one food that Mexican restaurants largely ignore.

Miscellaneous Advice

San Francisco might be famous for its fish, but most fish restaurants sadly fail to live up to their calling. We've never had a good meal on Fisherman's Wharf, where everything seems to be frozen, overcooked, or have some defect. Before you order fish, always ask what's fresh. Stay away from sauces; a simple, broiled piece of fish will generally come out best. If you find

5

yourself in a fish restaurant that caters to tourists, make sure you ask for the fish to be cooked rare. It might sound funny, but it will bring you a much better meal.

Stay away from hotel dining rooms. In a city filled with fine food, no one has to experience the horrors of hotel eating—and no one should have to pay those kinds of prices for what most hotels trot out. Even late at night, there will always be a little restaurant open that offers a better alternative.

By all means, take advantage of the lower prices at lunch in sampling some of the more expensive French and Italian restaurants. Frequently they offer the same dishes, but at half the price.

Restaurant Selection

The Bay Area is noted for its many places to eat; San Francisco probably has more restaurants per capita than any other city in the United States. We haven't tried to include every restaurant in and around San Francisco. Rather, we offer a sampling of the uniquely wide variety that has helped to give the Bay Area its reputation for fine cuisine. (Actually, we've gone beyond the Bay Area, and written about some of the restaurants we've run across while traveling in Central and Northern California.) Basically, we've written about our favorites, because we feel that this should be a guide to pleasurable dining experiences. We have included our comments on some restaurants because they are currently well known and you may very well end up at them. If a major restaurant is not listed in this book, it's because we didn't feel it was exceptional—one way or the other.

In this era of inflation, we didn't dare give exact prices, since the book would practically be out of date the week it came off the presses. Instead, we characterize the prices as inexpensive, moderate, expensive, or somewhere in-between. These prices are relative to the kind of cuisine we're talking about—a moderate French restaurant might not be a moderate anything else.

Patty Unterman, in addition to reviewing restaurants for the *San Francisco Chronicle*, is part-owner of Hayes Street Grill, a San Francisco fish restaurant. To avoid any appearance of conflict of interest, Stan Sesser has written the reviews of all the fish restaurants.

PATTY UNTERMAN
STAN SESSER

Spring, 1981

KEY TO RESTAURANT RATINGS

★★★ **The greatest**

★★ **Excellent; well worth going out of your way for**

★ **Very good**

THE TEN VERY BEST RESTAURANTS

1. Chez Panisse ★★★
2. Ernie's ★★★
3. Gaylord ★★★
4. Khan Toke ★★★
5. Maurice et Charles ★★★
6. Miramonte ★★★
7. Modesto Lanzone's ★★
8. La Mirabelle ★★
9. Greens ★★
10. Akasaka ★★

THE TEN BEST LOW-PRICED RESTAURANTS

1. Alejandro's ★★
2. El Tazumal ★★
3. Hana ★★
4. Tung Fong ★★
5. Sears ★★
6. Ocean ★★
7. Wim's ★★
8. Little Joe's ★
9. Golden Turtle ★
10. Bill's Place ★

AND THE BEST OF THE REST

American: Great American Meat & Potatoes ★
Bread: Greens ★★
Burritos: La Cumbre ★
       Taqueria Morelia ★
Chef: Alice Waters, at Chez Panisse ★★★
Chinese: Chin Szchawn ★★
Crêpes: Millard's on Fillmore ★
Deem Sum: Tung Fong ★★
Duck: Mandarin (Smoked Tea Duck)
Favorite Dishes: Beef Tongue at El Tazumal ★★
       Paella at Alejandro's ★★
       Squab at Ernie's ★★★
Fish: Hayes Street Grill ★★
   Tadich Grill ★★
French: Chez Panisse ★★★
Hamburgers: Original Joe's
Ice Cream: Vivoli's ★
Indian: Gaylord ★★★
Italian: Modesto Lanzone's ★★
Japanese: Akasaka ★★
Late Night: Kinokawa ★★
      La Rondalla ★
      Original Joe's
      Vanessi's ★
Latin American: El Tazumal ★★
Pasta: Orsi's ★★
Pastry Cart: Andalou
Pie: Sears ★★
Pizza: Calzone at Tommaso ★
Russian: George's ★★
Salads: Greens ★★
Soup: Minestrone at Vanessi's ★
Steak: Alfred's ★★
Sunday Brunch: Doidge's ★★
Sushi: Kinokawa ★★
Thai: Khan Toke ★★★
Vegetarian Dishes: Greens ★★
Vietnamese: Golden Turtle ★
Wine List: Bay Wolf

The Restaurants
of
San Francisco
and the
Bay Area

Abalonetti ★

Monterey Fisherman's Wharf
Monterey
408/373–1851

Abalonetti does for squid what Alfredo did for fettucine, Caesar did for salad, and the Cordon Bleu did for veal. Twenty tons of squid a year are pounded, sauced, sautéed, and stewed in this Monterey wharf restaurant.

Monterey happens to be one of the largest squid ports in the United States. It exports hundreds of tons of squid to Europe, Greece, and the Philippines. Squid is almost pure protein with practically no fat, and is exceptionally nutritious. Yet, squid is still one of California's most underfished and underconsumed seafoods. Abalonetti justifiably purveys its squid with missionary zeal.

The name of the restaurant comes from the method of preparing squid by flattening out the body and pounding it into tenderness. The resulting filet, much like an abalone steak, is called an *Abalonetti*. It is then breaded and used in a number of different dishes on the menu. The beauty of squid is that it is cheap and mild tasting, taking on the flavors of the food it's cooked with. The problem with squid is that it has a rubbery texture, although, if it is prepared properly, it will be tender. Abalonetti has squid cleaning and cooking refined to a practical art.

Marty's Special is the dish to order if you are not sure you like the idea of eating squid. Breaded filets of squid on eggplant slices are baked in the oven with a good Italian tomato sauce and Parmesan cheese. The ingredients heartily complement each other. Served on a metal platter that's piping hot from the oven, the squid is meltingly tender and tastes much like abalone. The eggplant is creamy. The tomato sauce has not been simmered too long, so it retains a fresh, nonacidic quality. Everyone loves this dish.

Fried Calamari, Sicilian Style has rings of unpounded squid quickly sautéed in wine, butter, and garlic, with a lovely sprinkling of finely chopped parsley. *Squid Abalonetti* is pounded filets, lightly breaded and sautéed in butter. These simple pieces of seafood need only a few squirts of lemon to be a delectable treat. *Squid Cutlets* are filets with a spicy Italian breading. A similar mixture of raisins, bread crumbs, grated Parmesan cheese, chopped parsley, and herbs is used in *Stuffed Squid*. The whole

13

squids are then baked with tomato sauce to make a gorgeous-looking, amazingly light dish.

You can begin your meal with a choice of beautifully fresh shellfish and, although you'd be missing out on something great if you did so, you can order other sorts of seafood besides squid as your main course. Skip the mediocre *Boston Clam Chowder* and the *Iceberg Lettuce*; they just aren't worth eating.

Until the last couple of years, Abalonetti used to be housed in a tiny room behind the Liberty Fish Market. As a hole-in-the-wall restaurant run by an Italian family, it had the ambience and personal service lacking in every other Fisherman's Wharf restaurant, be it in Monterey or San Francisco. Now, alas, Abalonetti is in much larger quarters and looks as much like a tourist trap as any of the others. But fortunately, the squid still makes the experience worthwhile.

PRICE RANGE: Inexpensive to moderate
HOURS: 11:00 A.M.–9:00 P.M. Wed.–Mon.
RESERVATIONS ACCEPTED FRI.–SUN.
BEER AND WINE
NO CREDIT CARDS

Agadir Moroccan Restaurant ★★

746 Broadway
San Francisco
397–6305

As people who would just as soon dispense with knife and fork, we always love a Moroccan feast—and Agadir offers some of the best Moroccan food this side of North Africa. The restaurant imports both its spices and its chefs directly from Morocco, and you can taste the difference in the cooking: The food is authentic, exotic, and very alive.

The small dining area is a tent constructed of Moroccan textiles and rugs, lit by candles, and filled with Moroccan music. Seating is on cushions on a low bench along the wall or on the floor on ottomans. Either way, the placement of my knees has not been so critical since ballet class, if I want to keep them free of falling food. We wear loose, washable clothing for carefree tent dining.

The meal's opener, *Charba*, is an explosively hot, spicy red vegetable soup—cumin and red pepper being only two of the myriad spices we could identify. With a squeeze of lemon served with it, the soup foreshadows the range of seasoning to follow.

Then you get a platter of *Diced Cucumbers, Green Peppers, and Carrots*, and a *Cold Stew of Eggplant and Tomato*, all dressed in lemon juice, olive oil, and cumin, a brilliant palette of colors. Scooped up with lettuce leaves or crusty anise-flavored white bread, these Moroccan salads are alternately crunchy, juicy, and creamy.

Next, *B'stilla*, the festive Moroccan pigeon or chicken pie, arrives. At Agadir, chicken has been ground up with almonds, onions, and saffron, layered with hard-cooked egg, and wrapped in paper-thin filo-pastry glazed with cinnamon and powdered sugar. It looks like a flat pancake, but it is as light as a feather.

You get to choose your main course from a list of ten dishes, one of which is *Tajine with Prunes*, made with lamb and a broth infused with the flavors of prunes and toasted sesame seeds. The ingredients cook slowly in the clay *tajine*, giving them a slightly earthy taste and allowing the lamb to get tender without falling apart.

Chicken Mqualli, really a Cornish game hen braised in the crockery *tajine* and stuffed with pickled lemon wedges, is our favorite. The lemons used in this dish are soaked in a brine composed of salt, cumin, and exotic spices. They give the sauce a fruity, piquant, currylike flavor. We also like *Rabbit Braised in a Paprika-rich Broth*, the meat gloriously moist, and the sauce intense and spicy. This is one of the best rabbit dishes of any nationality that we've tasted.

Perhaps the best-known North African dish, *Couscous*, is light and airy here, with the grains of steamed semolina melting in your mouth. The mounded *Couscous* is scattered with a colorful assortment of chopped vegetables, raisins, nuts, and chunks of lamb.

Refreshing peeled *Orange Slices Sprinkled with Cinnamon*, tiny triangles of *Deep-Fried Filo-Pastry Filled with Ground Nuts*, and weak *Mint Tea* finish off your meal.

The Algerian red wines are full, fruity, and very drinkable, but they have been marked up almost 300 percent here. Expect half of your bill to be for wine. The menu prices, in contrast, are reasonable, considering the high quality of the food. Someone in the back of the tent really knows how to cook.

PRICE RANGE: Moderate to expensive
HOURS: 6:00 P.M.–midnight Tues.–Sat.
RESERVATIONS ACCEPTED
BEER AND WINE
MASTERCARD, VISA

Akasaka ★★

466 Bush Street
(near Grant Avenue)
San Francisco
981—0780

Every type of foreign cuisine in the United States makes some sort of concession to American tastes. Try finding sukiyaki in Japan, chop suey in China, or even bagels and lox in Israel, and you'll realize that these are largely American dishes.

But Akasaka, named after a district in Tokyo with lots of restaurants, is uncompromising. Even to someone who has been to dozens of Japanese restaurants in the Bay Area, two-thirds of its menu is totally unfamiliar. Great concern is taken not only with the quality of the food, but also with how it looks on the plate. And—this is the negative side of the authenticity—portions are small, so you'll probably want to eat more than one dish per person if you're ordering a la carte.

Akasaka has brought to San Francisco a Japanese tradition that can provide you with one of the most spectacularly interesting meals ever, if you're willing to splurge. If you reserve one of the two Japanese-style rooms upstairs, you get served the $25 *Chef's Special Dinner*. This is simply whatever the chef feels like making, and the courses can be totally different on two different nights. It doesn't take a large party to reserve; we did it with just three people.

Our banquet left us gasping; never before have we encountered food like this. Every dish was so splendidly presented, we didn't know whether to eat it or take it home to frame. Fortunately, they proved as satisfying to the palate as they did to the eye.

Imagine, for instance, a perfectly formed pink rose served on a tray to each person. When you look more closely at it, you realize it's not a rose at all, but thin slices of *Sashimi* (raw tuna) sculpted into a rose shape. To the left is a dollop of *wasabe*, the horseradish you mix into your soy sauce, placed on a slice of carrot that has been carved to look like a daisy. To the right is a mum blossom (a real one). And behind are slices of *Raw Albacore Tuna*, with pureed taro root on top, and slivers of green onion on top of that, again in a flower shape.

No sooner is this consumed than an equally breathtaking dish arrives. Each person gets a *Conch Shell, Filled with Slices of Conch Meat, Egg, and Green Onions* poached in a lovely broth.

The plate around the conch shell is heaped with salt, the salt doused with alcohol, and the alcohol lit. So the conch shell arrives at your table in a circle of flames.

These are two of just nine courses we were served. The various delicacies included a tiny *Cake Made from Sea Urchin Roe and Egg*, *Salmon Roe on a Slice of Taro Root*, a *Whole Baby Rock Cod* perfectly poached in a broth with mushrooms, *Tofu and Scallions*, and *Alaska King Crab Meat Wrapped in Cucumber Slices* served in a rice vinegar and lemon dressing. There were two kinds of soup, one at the beginning of the meal and one at the end. It appeared that one waitress did nothing the whole evening but tend to us, and each time she entered the room she shyly said, "Excuse me," before sliding open the rice-paper panel. When we asked her why all but one of the courses was fish, she replied, "Because the Japanese didn't start eating meat until 100 years ago."

All in all, it was an extraordinary dinner, bought at a price less than that of many fancy French restaurants. We wouldn't have traded it for a French dinner for anything.

If you eat at the tables downstairs, you can order two smaller varieties of the *Chef's Dinner*, one at $13 and one at $17. Or you can treat yourself to a host of interesting a la carte dishes. The *Baked Japanese Eggplant*, tender but without a drop of grease and served with a rich soybean-paste sauce on top, is our favorite. There are also pork, beef, and fish dishes that have been marinated for several days in special sauces. Also, you can sample *Broiled Eel*, *Sea Urchin Roe*, and *Shimeju Mushrooms*.

This is an extraordinary restaurant, and a delightful variation from the uniformity of most Japanese menus.

PRICE RANGE: Expensive
HOURS: 11:30 A.M.–2:00 P.M. Mon.–Fri.
       6:00–10:30 P.M. Mon.–Sat.
RESERVATIONS ACCEPTED
FULL BAR
AMERICAN EXPRESS, MASTERCARD, VISA

A La Carte ★★

Berkeley, just a decade ago a relative gastronomic wasteland, now seems to support an almost endless number of French restaurants. While most are less expensive than their counterparts in San Francisco, they still in general share the same problems: uninspired menus combined with uninspired cooking. A food critic probably experiences more bad French meals than any other type of cuisine.

But, oh, the exceptions! Two Berkeley French restaurants stand head and shoulders above the pack. One, Chez Panisse, already has an international reputation. The other, A La Carte, is virtually unknown.

A La Carte has had its ups and downs, and changes of ownership, over the years. But when the current owner, Annette Esser, took over the cooking in the fall of 1979, things began to move in one direction only—up. Like Alice Waters at Chez Panisse, she has an instinct for great cooking that allows her to keep learning and improving as she goes along. Also, like Alice Waters, she can't tolerate set menus. At A La Carte, the menu changes every day, generally with two or three appetizers, two main courses, and a couple of desserts being offered. Sometimes the menu isn't set until that morning, depending on what's fresh that day.

Usually, one of the main courses is a fish dish, and we've never had fish at A La Carte that's been less than perfect. If the fish is poached, you can be sure it won't be overcooked; whatever the sauce, you can be sure it will be interesting. And if you're lucky enough to pick a day when a fish mousse is being served, count your blessings. We once had a light, fluffy *Scallop Mousse with a Creamy Lobster Sauce* that was memorable; while the mousse was so light it almost floated off our plates, it still managed to taste distinctly of scallops, and the lobster sauce clearly smacked of its lobster origins.

Any appetizer or main course with pastry crust is also not to be missed. A La Carte has perfected one of the lightest, flakiest pastry crusts this side of France. We've had marvelous *Goat Cheese and Mushroom Tarts* as appetizers, and a *Boned Chicken Breast en Croute*, stuffed with cream cheese and herbs, was nothing less than spectacular. The cheese melted into a tangy sauce that coated the juicy chicken, while the crust remained flaky and dry. The main course generally comes with vegetables and rice, with the vegetables usually sautéed in butter and never, ever overcooked.

Desserts are generally as innovative as the rest of the menu. The fruit tarts are consistently freshly made with perfect crusts, and the rich layer cakes are always moist and satisfying. A La Carte's wine list is small, but most wines are reasonably priced and well selected.

A La Carte is a tiny restaurant tucked in alongside some stores in a largely residential neighborhood, and from the outside it looks like the proverbial hole in the wall. The atmosphere is cozy and informal, with a real brick fireplace, intimate, handmade wooden booths, and slow-burning antique lamps. If you want a relaxing evening of first-rate French food at relatively moderate prices, this is the perfect place to go.

PRICE RANGE: Moderate
HOURS: 6:00–9:30 P.M. Tues.–Sun.
RESERVATIONS NECESSARY
BEER AND WINE
NO CREDIT CARDS

Alejandro's Sociedad Gastronomica ★★

1840 Clement Street
(between 19th and 20th Avenues)
San Francisco
668–1184

"Just what we need," we thought when we saw Alejandro's going up in a Clement Street neighborhood already jammed with restaurants. "A fancy Mexican restaurant with a weird name."

That is, until we ate there. It turns out that Alejandro's Sociedad Gastronomica serves some of the best Spanish and Latin American food to be found anywhere in the Bay Area. The people who work there are sometimes overwhelmed by the crowds—you might find yourself waiting despite a reservation, and the service might be erratic. But the food makes it all worthwhile.

If you're a paella fan, constantly disappointed by the overcooked chicken, canned peas, and greasy rice that passes as paella in so many restaurants, you've come to the right place. At Alejandro's, the *Paella Valenciana* looks like a *Gourmet* magazine centerfold. This classic Spanish rice dish loaded with mussels, cracked crab, Spanish sausage, chicken, pork, peas, green beans, and tomatoes is plenty for dinner plus lunch the next day. Miracle of miracles: The vegetables are fresh, and nothing is overcooked. Each ingredient has been added to the woklike paella pan at just the right moment. The rice itself, golden from saffron, absorbs all the cooking juices, yet each grain stays separate. If there's better paella in San Francisco, we have yet to taste it.

But you don't have to wait for the main course to find food filled with life and spirit. Once you taste those hors d'oeuvres called *Alejandrinos*, you'll order them every time. They're bite-sized, deep-fried pastry filled with cheese, eggs, and *jalapeños* peppers, with an oniony mayonnaise dipping sauce. In addition, the *Ceviche*, a white fish marinated raw in lime juice with slices of sweet onion and fresh coriander, is the best version of this dish we've ever tasted. The same for the *Gazpacho*, a russet-colored beef consommé augmented by cucumbers, tomatoes, and spices.

Paella isn't the only marvelous entree. Another Spanish entree, *Trucha "Meson de Candido,"* is a boned whole trout topped with paper-thin slices of Serrano ham and ingeniously sauced by swirling a little butter into the juices of the cooking pan. The *Ragout of Rabbit*, called *Conejo en Salsa de Mani*, features a singularly thick sauce redolent of ground peanuts and cumin. Even the short Mexican side of the menu is superb, with sauces of unusual depth and refinement.

Many of the dishes are asterisked by an "SG" symbol, indicating that they have been recommended by the mysterious Sociedad Gastronomica. The most information we could garner about this society is that it is a group of Latin American epicures to which the owner of the restaurant belongs. After eating at their outpost in San Francisco, we're eager to join.

PRICE RANGE: Inexpensive to moderate
HOURS: 5:00–11:00 P.M. Sun.–Thurs.
　　　　5:00–12:00 P.M. Fri.–Sat.
RESERVATIONS RECOMMENDED
FULL BAR
MASTERCARD. VISA

Alfred's ★★

886 Broadway
San Francisco
781–7058

Going out for steak dinner carries memories for us of childhood "reward dinners." Those meals in dim, smoky restaurants, sitting in big, slippery booths, attempting to eat gargantuan slabs of sizzling meat and seemingly basketball-sized baked potatoes are as ingrained in our youth as walking the same blocks to school every day. Then, they symbolized being American and affluent—if only for a night—and having a good time.

Now, it seems, there aren't many restaurants around that can serve only steaks—and salads and potatoes—and survive. Prime beef is too expensive, too hard to get. Tastes have changed. Appetites are smaller.

Alfred's, at the top of Broadway right where the tunnel begins, is the one restaurant in San Francisco where you can have that old-fashioned steakhouse experience, one that Alfred's has provided since 1928. The obligatory steakhouse menu blurb shows a picture of an Alfred's truck pulling out of the Chicago stockyards. "Even though the Union Stockyard of Chicago is no longer operative," it reads, "Alfred's still receives weekly shipments of Prime Eastern corn-fed beef." A number of old-time San Franciscan steak eaters told us that Alfred's is the only place left in town that serves exclusively prime beef. Our recent experiences there led us to conclude that Alfred's serves the best steak we've had in California.

At Alfred's, you sit in real red leather banquettes, patched in a few places, but nonetheless luxurious. A real crystal chandelier drips from the red ceiling and real flames flicker in table lamps on white linen. At one end of the dining room, by the kitchen, is a glassed-in room displaying hunks of aging beef. The waiters in black and white half-tuxedos complete the scene. Most of them have been working at Alfred's for many years and they are models of their profession. Your meal unfolds without a hitch.

The wine list, though not terribly exciting, is genuinely serviceable, with red wines that go well with meat at reasonable prices. We were happy to see numerous half-bottles available, one of the better aspects of steakhouse dining.

We began one evening with Alfred's celebrated *Antipasto*, a relish tray of perky kidney-bean vinaigrette, rubbery calamari vinaigrette, chewy pickled pig's feet, olives, crisp, raw vegetables and thin slices of good Italian salami, *coppa*, and bologna. Not bad, but we gather from reports of long-time Alfred's diners, not as spectacular as it used to be.

Actually, everything on Alfred's menu pales in comparison to the steaks, which is why you come to this restaurant in the first place. The *Porterhouse* is our favorite, a luxuriously thick cut that gives you a large filet section and a vast New York section bifurcated by a succulent bone. No meat is more tender, juicy, and flavorful than meat closest to the bone, and the *Porterhouse* has a big one. The steak is buttery and tender but full of flavor.

The *T-Bone* is basically the same steak but a little smaller. For those who prefer the meat from one side of the short loin or the other, you can get *Corn-fed Filet Mignon*, *Corn-fed New York Cut*, or the *Delmonico Steak*, which is the New York with the bone.

What makes the steaks at Alfred's so succulent and tasty is that the beef is prime; it comes from young, specially fed cattle. The texture of prime beef is fine and the fat content is high. Also, the beef is aged for at least a week at cool temperatures, allowing the flesh to relax and the flavor to mellow. Finally, Alfred's cooks its steaks over a hot mesquite fire that immediately sears in the juices. When you order a rare steak at Alfred's, it is warm all the way through but blood red in the center, the best way to enjoy this delicacy.

PRICE RANGE: Expensive
HOURS: 11:30 A.M.–2:00 P.M. Mon.–Fri.
   5:30–11:00 P.M. Mon.–Sat.
   5:30–10:30 P.M. Sun.
RESERVATIONS ACCEPTED
FULL BAR
ALL MAJOR CREDIT CARDS

Alta Mira Hotel

125 Bulkeley Avenue
Sausalito
332–1350

Sunday brunch at the Alta Mira, a lovely old Sausalito hotel perched in the hills with an outdoor terrace and panoramic views of the bay, is on the top of most tourists' lists of things to do. And it's not a bad item, especially if you prepare yourself for the hour-and-a-half wait, even with reservations, and the lack of a place to sit while you are waiting. Watery *Ramos Fizzes*, the customary whipped egg white, lime juice, and gin drinks put out by the bar to smooth your wait, don't help that much. However, once you have a table, matters improve a lot. You can enjoy the fabulous views and the appointments of this well-kept California hotel, while eating a festive brunch.

While Alta Mira's kitchen is solidly in the hotel vein, which means that none of the food is exceptional, they do put out an honest *Eggs Benedict* with real hollandaise sauce on top of correctly runny poached eggs, toasted English muffin, and Canadian bacon. *Eggs Princess* puts the hollandaise sauce and poached eggs on top of a bed of creamed chicken, which isn't bad if you're in the mood for tearoom-type dishes. *Shirred Eggs*, which are eggs baked in molds in the oven and served with sautéed chicken livers, are a bit overdone, but not disastrously. You can also get salty *Scotch Kippers*, which are great with scrambled eggs.

A hint: The Alta Mira serves a very similar menu on weekdays as breakfast for its hotel guests. Then, it's possible to enjoy the splendors of the surroundings without the wait and the crowds, and the less-pressured kitchen crew does a better job on the food.

PRICE RANGE Moderate
HOURS: 8:00–11:00 A.M. Mon.–Sat. (breakfast)
        11:00 A.M.–5:00 P.M. Mon.–Sat. (lunch)
        8:00 A.M.–3:00 P.M. Sun. (brunch)
RESERVATIONS RECOMMENDED
FULL BAR
AMERICAN EXPRESS. DINER'S CLUB. MASTERCARD. VISA

Andalou

3rd and E Streets
San Rafael
454–4900

Andalou calls itself a California restaurant because it serves the best local products on a seasonally changing menu. We think of it as a California restaurant because its style of cooking is untraditional, fearless, and disarmingly simple. It's run by a large group of young owner-chefs, owner-waiters, owner-maître d's, and we suspect owner-dishwashers, who see their restaurant as more than a livelihood. They refurbished and lovingly decorated a Victorian house in downtown San Rafael, creating three uncluttered, elegant dining rooms that make you want to linger. From the moment you walk through the door, you are treated with graciousness and enthusiasm. You are guided through the meal, not waited upon, the staff gently participating in each decision—and this strikes us as a California phenomenon as well.

The short, handwritten menu emphasizes fresh fish, seafood, and light meals. All items are a la carte, and you will not overorder by trying an appetizer like their *Green Salad* crowned by a perfectly ripe avocado half, or *Spinach Salad*, both of which taste and look as if they had just been plucked from the garden. *Smoked Trout Filet*, a Japanese arrangement of a small strip of slightly dry smoked fish next to two cucumber slices in a creamy dressing, is a bit too effete for us. Just the opposite is *Bar-B-Q Oyster Brochette*, which consists of meaty Inverness oysters that have been skewered and cooked over charcoal and topped with a thick tomato sauce. A slice of homemade *Pâté* is always available, as is soup, often an unusual combination like *Apple-Celery Soup*. The soups are not quite as hot as they should be, a common problem of conscientious restaurants, because overheating destroys delicate flavor.

Most of the entrees are cooked over Mexican mesquite charcoal, which not only gives them a marvelous smoky flavor, but also sears in juices and leaves the flesh moist and tender. Andalou's philosophy about cooking is to do it as little as possible, and many of the entrees have been barely grazed over the fire, like *Ginger Snapper*, a recurring special that succeeds because the fish is absolutely fresh. Shreds of red pickled ginger, soy sauce, and garlic work well against the mild taste of the snapper, without overwhelming it. This is not the case with the fresh rosemary and apricot sauce on *Grilled Chicken Breasts*, but the two huge boned breasts are some of the finest chicken we've tasted. They deserve a lesser sauce.

The same impressive raw materials distinguish *Fresh Scallops in Gin and Tarragon*, a ramekin of plump, sweet scallops in a smoky, lightly creamed sauce. These flown-in eastern scallops are a true delicacy, and Andalou does them justice. We were not so enamored with the preparation of *Eastern Oysters*, sautéed with garlic and mushrooms, which we split one evening as an appetizer. The sauce was unrealized, the oysters neither raw nor cooked, and the whole thing would have been improved by further cooking.

All the entrees come with a brown rice pilaf and a fresh vegetable, like crisp asparagus sprinkled with sesame seeds or a delicious carrot custard.

Dessert is an event at Andalou, and you should save a little room for it. An elegant glass serving cart is wheeled over to your table that has a changing array of gorgeous-looking pastries.

Not everyone will like the type of cooking Andalou is developing. First of all, it's experimental, playing around with startling flavor combinations that some will love and others will find jarring. Second, the theory of fast minimal cooking may leave more than the food slightly cold. We happen to like it that way, because the natural flavors and textures of the food come through. Yet, Andalou is absolutely traditional in the high-quality purchasing by the kitchen, the attentive service, and the gracious ambience in the dining room.

PRICE RANGE: Moderate to expensive
HOURS: 11:30 A.M.–2:00 P.M. Tues.–Fri.
6:00-10:00 P.M. Tues.–Sun.
11:00 A.M.–3:00 P.M. (brunch)
RESERVATIONS RECOMMENDED
BEER AND WINE
MASTERCARD, VISA

Archil's ★

3011 Steiner Street
San Francisco
921–2141

Archil's is a young-hearted Russian restaurant in the Union Street area that serves food that could be eaten in grandmother's kitchen. The setting, however, couldn't be further removed. Archil's is formal, almost austere, with elegant decor touches. Two intimate dining rooms have stark, white walls scattered with a few well-placed paintings and authentic old Russian travel posters. Finely finished pine tables are set with quilted brown place mats, large white napkins, and sparkling goblets. Guests are greeted at the door by Archil, the dark-eyed young owner and son of Alexis, the Nob Hill restaurateur. He graciously takes your coat and sees you to your table, carefully keeping an eye on the whole operation.

From the decor and ambience alone, you expect beluga caviar and champagne. Instead, you get basic Russian fare—an aristocratic presentation of peasant food at pleasantly bourgeois prices. All dinners begin with a steaming tureen of *Cabbage Borscht*,

25

a tomato-based broth with firm strips of cabbage and cubes of potato, served, of course, with a crock of thick sour cream. The next course of *Fresh Romaine Tossed in Vinaigrette Dressing* is more French than Russian, but just what you want from a salad.

There are numerous entrees to choose from, many of them simple and hearty, such as *Bitki Smetana*, beef cutlets topped with pan-fried onions and sour cream, or *Fish Kutlety*, tasty pancakes of ground fish breaded and fried in butter, and served with a sweet mustard sauce. *Golubsty*, beef-stuffed cabbage rolls in a tomato sauce, and *Lamb Tongue Provençale*, our favorite dish at Archil's, have their own distinctive sauces made of roughly chopped fresh tomatoes and carrots. The *Tongue* is fork-tender and slightly smoky, cooked to perfection.

So is *Chicken Kiev*, shells of thinly pounded chicken breasts stuffed with herbed butter, breaded, and deep fried. As you cut into them, the melted butter gloriously squirts out. All the entrees are served with rice pilaf and crisp, fresh vegetables, such as gently garlicked zucchini slices. The plates are whimsically garnished with radish roses that look like carved ivory, and delicate carrot butterflies.

Dessert is included in the dinner price. The most interesting dessert is a *Fruit Kisel*, which is warm, jellied, sugared, and spiced red wine in a goblet.

Our only criticism of Archil's, and it's a personal one, is that in the effort to be tonier, the food loses some of its inherent heartiness, the rough edge that makes the country cooking of all cultures so appealing. Many of the dishes tend to taste alike. They need an infusion of energy, some contrasting flavors. However, high quality is present on all levels at Archil's, even if the spirit is a bit timid.

PRICE RANGE: Moderate
HOURS: 5:30–10:30 P.M. Tues.–Sun.
RESERVATIONS RECOMMENDED
BEER AND WINE
MASTERCARD. VISA

Arinell Pizza

2109 Shattuck Avenue
Berkeley
841—4035

2525 Dwight Way
Berkeley
841—7171

Arinell Pizza serves strictly take-out pizza by the slice or by the whole pie. The slice is better, because you get it fresh from the oven. Once Arinell pizza cools off, it can taste pretty boring.

We're talking New York-style pizza here, which means crust, tomato sauce with dried herbs, and a lot of cheese. That's it. A thick crust cut in rectangles is called *Sicilian*. A thin crust cut in wedges is *Neopolitan*. It's up to you to season it with the flakes of hot red pepper, oregano, fennel seed, salt, and pepper, put out on the utility counter with the napkins.

We were addicted to Arinell pizza for a year. At first, we didn't think very much of it, because there wasn't very much there. If we wanted mushrooms, sausage, or peppers, they were plunked on top of an already cooked slice and reheated in the oven to, we must say, bad effect.

Then the simplicity of the Arinell *Neopolitan* began to work on us. The crust is always crisp on the edges and tender without being soggy, thin enough to fold, and in perfect proportion to the cheese and sauce. The cheese, laid on with a liberal hand, melts completely into the pie. No annoying strings of rubbery cheese mar an Arinell pizza, and the tomato sauce, though commercial, serves as a good moistener. It barely peeks out from the covering of cheese.

Don't worry about the lines in front of Arinell. This means that the slices are moving at the usual breakneck pace and will be hot and fresh. The line moves fast, and the pizza makers have it timed so that, as one pizza gets sold, another is just coming out of the oven.

This is street pizza. It's meant to be eaten while walking. It loses its charm and quality if you take it home.

PRICE RANGE: Inexpensive
HOURS: 11:00 A.M.–9:00 P.M. Mon.–Fri.
Noon–9:00 P.M. Sat.
2:00–9:00 P.M. Sun.

Asia Garden ★★

772 Pacific
(near Stockton)
San Francisco
398–5112

Nine years ago, a rumor spread through Chinatown that a grand, new *deem sum* parlor was about to open, featuring one of the best *deem sum* chefs from Hong Kong, who had been lured away with a princely salary. (For those not schooled in the vocabulary of *deem sum*, see our review of Tung Fong.) A few weeks later, Asia Garden appeared and, thanks to a Chinese friend who had heard about it, we first ate there on opening day. Although the restaurant is so large you could put sod on the floor and use it as a football field, it was jammed from the very beginning.

Here is *Deem Sum* exactly as done in Hong Kong. Young women roll two-level carts from the kitchen, each with one or two types of dishes on it. They walk down the aisles, singing out the names of their wares in Chinese. If you want something, you point to it and they stop. At the end of the meal, a waitress counts the number of empty plates on the table to determine the bill. (Some of the more expensive things are served on a stack of two or more plates, not exactly the world's most energy-efficient system, since they all wind up in the dishwasher.)

While the food is a little less subtle than Tung Fong's, particularly in the over-sugaring of a few of the meat fillings and pastries, Asia Garden is still leagues ahead of many of its *deem sum* competitors. The little steamed pastries filled with *Shrimp* (*Har Gow*), *Pork* (*Su Mai*), *Black Mushrooms*, or *Vegetables* are particularly good, with the wrappings so thin they're almost transparent. The *Egg Rolls* are the best anywhere—crisp, greaseless, and filled with shrimp and an unusual variety of vegetables. Don't fail to have a *Custard Tart* for dessert; the crust is one of the flakiest this side of France.

PRICE RANGE: Inexpensive
HOURS: 10:00 A.M.–3:00 P.M. Mon.–Fri.
        9:00 A.M.–3:00 P.M. Sat.–Sun.
NO RESERVATIONS
NO BEER OR WINE
NO CREDIT CARDS

Auburn Hotel

853 Lincoln Way
Auburn
916/885–8132

Sometimes, after a long day of skiing, it seems like you just can't get enough food into your stomach. If that's the case, and you're coming back from the mountains on Interstate 80, stop at Auburn, a historic town in the foothills. The old Auburn Hotel has a Basque restaurant that serves portions so huge it's impossible to finish everything, no matter what the state of your stomach.

The courses come out one after the other until you wave the white flag. Main courses include such things as *Sautéed Sweetbreads*, *Chicken Cacciatore*, and *Roast Beef*. There's a huge tureen of soup, green salad, French bread and butter, pasta, etc., etc., etc. The food isn't wonderful, but it's better than that of most Sierra restaurants. Instead of being a plastic place set up to lure skiers, the Auburn Hotel has pleasant service in an Old West atmosphere, and it's filled with local families enjoying a night out.

PRICE RANGE: Inexpensive
HOURS: 5:00–10:00 P.M. Tues.–Sun.
RESERVATIONS ACCEPTED FOR FOUR OR MORE
FULL BAR
MASTERCARD, VISA

Basta Pasta

1268 Grant Avenue
San Francisco
434–2248

Basta Pasta does just enough things right to appeal to an enormous number of people, who queue up on the corner of Grant and Vallejo to get a table. It's relatively inexpensive. It serves the new popular combination of fish and pasta, and it has a prime North Beach location that appeals to tourists and San Franciscans alike, with valet parking for those whose block-circling patience has run out.

We don't like Basta Pasta, because in our experience it serves bland formula food that appeals to a low common denominator of palates. The problem is both with the food and with the surroundings, the latter being of North Beach ersatz—vinyl walls, polyurethaned tables, industrial carpeting, squeezed-in seating. Added to these minuses, when we've been there, we've had slapdash, uninformative service. We sense that a lot of corners are being cut, and we just don't feel satisfied after eating there.

When Basta Pasta first opened, there was much hoopla about "freshness," "natural flavors," "selection of vegetables each day," "fish fresh from the restaurant's own boat," and "simplicity of preparation," all passwords to gain the patronage of people who care about what they eat. Initial reports were that the restaurant was delivering. Now we get the feeling that the kitchen is not dedicated to anything of the sort. The vegetables are not that fresh; the pasta is not *al dente*; and much of the fish is nothing special.

What we find so frustrating about this restaurant is that it promises more than it delivers. If you made a meal of the house-cured *Prosciutto and Melon*, the "*Basta Pasta*" *Spaghettini*, and the *Grilled Whole Sole*, you would be dining very well. But if you stray from these few items, you may encounter a squarely mediocre dinner, hardly worth the wait to get in.

PRICE RANGE: Inexpensive to moderate
HOURS: 11:30 A.M.–2:00 A.M. daily
NO RESERVATIONS
BEER AND WINE
AMERICAN EXPRESS, MASTERCARD, VISA

Bay Wolf

3853 Piedmont Avenue
Oakland
655–6004

In many ways, Bay Wolf makes for a pleasant dining experience. Located in a comfortable, renovated old house near Kaiser Hospital in Oakland, it offers personal, caring service, a small French menu that changes each day, and a California wine list so expertly put together it's second to none in the Bay Area. Lots of people enjoy their meals here, and constantly recommend it to us.

Over the years, we've gone to Bay Wolf again and again, hoping for an outstanding meal. Each time we leave disappointed. Nothing is actually bad, but it seems that for almost every dish something in the preparation is lacking. We've never had a dish at Bay Wolf we could describe as "excellent."

Take our most recent meal there as an example. A *Cream of Pumpkin Soup* was acceptable, but the pumpkin taste was almost completely killed off by a puree of pimento on top. A *Mediterranean Salad* included a piece of albacore that was, by the kitchen's own admission, from the previous day.

The two main courses, sole and pork, both suffered severe problems from being overwhelmed by heavy sauces. The *Sole* was in a *Mushroom, Cream, and Vermouth Sauce* so thick and heavily reduced you couldn't tell you were eating fish underneath it; the sauce itself would have been delicious served alone to be mopped up by bread. The *Port and Wine Sauce* that accompanied the *Sliced Tenderloin of Pork* was just plain bad; a distinct burned taste came through.

Such experiences—including a *Chocolate Torte* for dessert so sweet it almost couldn't be eaten—have left us disappointed with Bay Wolf. It's too bad, because with just a little more skill in the cooking, the restaurant would have everything else going for it.

PRICE RANGE: Moderate
HOURS: 11:30 A.M.–2:00 P.M., 6:00–9:30 P.M. Wed.–Mon.
10:00 A.M.–3:00 P.M. Sat.–Sun. (brunch)
RESERVATIONS NECESSARY
BEER AND WINE
MASTERCARD. VISA

Bill's Place ★

2315 Clement Street
San Francisco
221–5262

Bill's Place is San Francisco's premier hamburger restaurant. Bill's grinds its own chuck, pats the meat into fat, six-ounce burgers, grills them to order, slathers on grilled onions by request, and serves them on soft, toasted buns. It's the great *All-American Hamburger*, and you can even get it rare. The other area of Bill's expertise is the shakes, made with hand-scooped ice cream and real milk in tall, silver containers, which you get at the table along with your glass.

Bill's also puts out a winning plate of *Cole Slaw* with freshly cut cabbage in a good sweet-and-sour dressing. Our only disappointment with Bill's Place is the *Fries*, which are pale and soggy. Stick with the potato chips that come with the burgers.

We particularly like to go to Bill's for our hamburgers because it's a full-scale restaurant. You can sit at the long counter, at tables, or in the garden in the back. A crew of uniformed waitresses, many of whom have worked at Bill's for years, efficiently take your orders and accommodate special requests, a far cry from the regimentation of fast-food places. Also, Bill's makes a point of catering to children. There are highchairs as well as booster seats, and the sound level is so high anyway at this usually full restaurant that noisy kids go unnoticed. It's rare to see anyone unhappy at Bill's Place. Mostly there are contented sighs as young and old alike bite into Bill's juicy hamburgers.

PRICE RANGE: Inexpensive
HOURS: 11:15 A.M.–9:00 P.M. daily
NO RESERVATIONS
NO BEER OR WINE
NO CREDIT CARDS

Bruno's

2389 Mission Street
(near 20th Street)
San Francisco
824–2258

Bruno's has been in business for forty-one years. It has the traditional open kitchen behind a long counter with stools, booth seating, and a separate bar room. A gallery of caricatures of long-time regulars is strung along a brick wall, and there's an honest-to-goodness piano bar in the next room. A few doors away, beneath a defunct movie marquee, is the entrance to Bruno's attended parking lot.

Ordering requires the same selectivity as it does at Original Joe's, a restaurant that's similar in style, but there's more opportunity here to wander astray. At one lunch we chose from the daily specials listed on a blackboard. *Filets of Sole*, dipped in egg

32

and pan fried, were watery, soggy, and none-too-fresh tasting. *Swiss Steak* reminded us of dishes from a school cafeteria line. The *Dinner Salad*, a large plate of head lettuce with chickpeas and kidney beans, did have a good, vinegary dressing.

We returned with our Lunch Adviser, who scanned the menu like a contract. "You ordered the worst possible items," he told us, and then proceeded to order *Chicken Liver Sauté with Mushrooms*, rare. They arrived soft and tender, though hardly rare, with a lively, peppery red wine sauce, lots of mushrooms, and some chicken hearts thrown in. He ordered *"Bruno's Own" Canneloni a la Romana*, because it was written in the biggest type on the menu. It was stuffed with a heavily allspiced mixture of ground veal, chicken, and pork, with both tomato and cream sauces and Monterey Jack cheese melted on top. Though hardly sublime, the concoction was satisfying, better than what you expect from "Joe's-type" pastas. We both agreed that the food at Bruno's is basically honest if not very special.

PRICE RANGE: Moderate
HOURS: 11:00 A.M.–2:00 A.M. Mon.–Sat.
        4:00 P.M.–midnight Sun.
RESERVATIONS ACCEPTED
FULL BAR
MASTERCARD. VISA

Bud's

1300 Castro Street
San Francisco
647–2573

For years people have lined up outside Bud's tiny corner ice cream store, rain or shine, for top-heavy *Cones of Bittersweet Chocolate, Honey Date*, or *Fresh Strawberry Ice Cream*, among others. Several years ago, however, Bud's started wholesaling, and ever since, the quality of the ice cream has gone downhill. We have found the once-perfect ice cream to be grainy with ice crystals from careless refrigeration, and at other times, gooey.

We still like Bud's for milkshakes, made mostly from ice cream with a splash of milk added to smooth them out. We also like Bud's well-known *Hot-Fudge Sundaes*, layered with banana slices, Howard Johnson's hot fudge sauce, and topped with real whipped cream and nuts. For straight cones, Bud's has been

33

eclipsed by the richer, creamier ice creams made by Double Rainbow, Vivoli's, and Gelato.

PRICE RANGE: Inexpensive
HOURS: Noon–11:00 P.M. Sun.–Thurs.
Noon–midnight Fri.–Sat.

Burton's

2223 Market Street
San Francisco
621–0441

Burton's is a relatively small place that is hidden away in a distinctly San Francisco neighborhood. It is meticulously designed and decorated, and is both intimate and sophisticated. The menu is short and uncomplicated, featuring hearty fresh foods. The service is gracious and well organized. There's an active bar worked by friendly bartenders who mix perfect drinks. The tunes of Cole Porter, Rogers and Hart, and Gershwin pour out of a resonant baby grand played by an emotive cafe pianist. You can't find the telephone number in the yellow pages and you can't get a table after 6:30 without a reservation.

We've had some disappointing experiences in gay restaurants, specifically regarding the food. Too often, the way the food looks on the plate takes precedence over the way the food is prepared. Canned hollandaise sauce looks perfect, but it tastes like library paste. So we tend to write off those pretty restaurants with cleverly placed plants and indirect lighting, which seem to open and close at a dizzying pace, as being mostly show and little substance.

Burton's, however, is no flash in the pan. The chef-maître d' partnership originally started Fanny's, a popular restaurant nearby in the Castro Street area, and sold it to open Burton's, where they've created an unfussy, stylish restaurant that delivers on all levels. It's a good place to have a drink and listen to the piano, but it's an even better place to go for a satisfying meat-and-potatoes meal at an affordable, though not cheap, price.

There are ten entrees to choose from, mostly meat, and a few different preparations of red snapper. The special, a modest-sized slice of rare *Roast Beef*, is served without the bone. The meat is tender and juicy and you can get it rare. A baked potato and buttered broccoli, cauliflower, and carrots, cooked a minute or so beyond crispness, fill out the plate. Generous bowls of horserad-ish and sour cream are laid on the table for use as you want them.

Another recommended entree is *Roast Loin of Pork*, a thick alabaster slice that is succulent and moist without being fatty. Sweet brandy-nutmeg sauce comes on the side and slices of fresh apple are a nice touch. The potatoes on this dish are boiled and tossed in Parmesan cheese and cream. You get either soup or salad for the price of the entree, and the soup, usually hearty and well seasoned, is the better choice.

There's not much for dessert, but my cup never stayed unfilled with good restaurant coffee.

We find it hard to leave Burton's. It's one of the best-planned restaurants in operation—everything flows smoothly along, even when the place is packed. A sincere effort is made by all to take care of you and make you feel welcome. The ambience is so total you feel as if you've entered another world where pleasure is taken very seriously. Burton's is a tour de force. Nothing about it is spectacular, but everything about it is pleasing. It's one of the few gay restaurants that focuses on the customers, rather than on itself.

PRICE RANGE: Moderate
HOURS: 6:00–11:00 P.M. daily
        11:00 A.M.–3:00 P.M. Sun. (brunch)
RESERVATIONS NECESSARY
FULL BAR
MASTERCARD. VISA

Cadell Place

524 Union Street
San Francisco
391–4343

Music and food are an age-old combination—the lyres and flutes of Homeric repasts, the string quartet in Don Giovanni's dining room, the supper clubs of the fifties—that sort of thing. Of late, due to specialization, styles, and economics, live music and food are seldom available together, outside of a few pricy hotel opera-tions. However, a timeless little jazz club in North Beach called Cadell Place offers food and music that are just right for each other. There's nothing trendy or chic about any of it, but Cadell Place is run by people who care about what they are doing.

Dinner is served in a pleasant back room with a working fireplace, North Beachy oil paintings of San Francisco scenes on the walls, fresh flowers on the tables, and candle light. The sounds from a jazz ensemble that filter in from the club, separated from the dining room by a hallway, are at just the right pitch—not so loud as to deter conversation, but noticeably and enjoyably there.

The food has its highs and lows. The *Mushroom Soup* that comes with dinner is a tour de force, a velvety, sherry-spiked, creamy broth full of crisp, quickly cooked, fresh mushrooms. However, a *Romaine Salad*, correctly made with crunchy, torn greens, labors under a vinaigrette dressing that tastes mostly of harsh vinegar.

A nightly special, *Fresh Trout*, is boned and fileted, and strewn with buttery toasted almonds, but the sauce tastes of raw cooking sherry. A plump *South Carolina Quail* is split and skillfully grilled, but it is painted with a sweet-and-sour barbeque sauce that we feel doesn't do it justice. The plates come with crisp slices of yellow and Italian squash, tossed with butter and bits of red pepper, and tender, but not mushy, boiled new potatoes.

The simplest items on the menu are always good. The tasty, huge *Top Sirloin Steak* is rubbed with herbs and olive oil. The *Half Chicken* is marinated with rosemary and thyme, and cooked slowly on the grill until its skin is crisp and its meat succulent.

Service is a bit amateurish, but everything will get to you eventually, especially with a little reminding.

After dinner you can have a drink in the club while you listen to the music. This arrangement makes for a nice evening out. You only need to park once and you don't pay a cover charge when you go in for dinner. Cadell Place also serves some of the best *Eggs Benedict* in town for Sunday brunch.

It's one of the few local places that has figured out how to offer both food and music and do it well. When we think of all the dry hamburgers and soggy spaghetti we've eaten at clubs where the kitchen is only an afterthought, we appreciate Cadell Place all the more. They're working hard and staying alive in two of the most difficult games in town.

PRICE RANGE: Moderate
HOURS: 6:00–11:00 P.M. Wed.–Mon.
          11:00 A.M.–3:00 P.M. Sun. (brunch)
RESERVATIONS ACCEPTED
FULL BAR
MASTERCARD, VISA

Cafe Central

14th Street and South Van Ness
San Francisco

Cafe Central is an authentic Mexican restaurant much frequented by locals in an old corner storefront that's "resplendent" with peeling paint, cracked windows patched up with tape, and a handwritten list of lunch specials. However, once you're inside you see why this restaurant is so good. The open kitchen is clean, well organized, and full of cooks at work boning chicken and chopping fresh vegetables. An old woman pats out homemade tortillas, while her daughter does most of the other cooking, and she's a *real* cook.

The meats for the various enchiladas and burritos have been long simmered and deliciously seasoned. The cooked tomato sauces have body and flavor while still tasting fresh. The beans, which stay whole and separate, have character. When you order a Mexican meal at Cafe Central, each item comes to you individually composed and each dish tastes distinctively different. The style here is a far cry from the mish-mash of sauce-laden food of undistinguishable nature stuck under the salamander right on the serving plate that you get in most Mexican restaurants.

The house specialty, *Tacos de Carne Asada*, are made with two soft corn tortillas, chopped, grilled round steak, and *salsa cruda*, which is chopped raw tomato, raw onion, and big leaves of fresh coriander. They are as beautiful to look at as they are good to eat. Both the *Quesadillas* and the *Chile Rellenos* are notable for the high-quality Jack cheese used inside them. *Bistec Ranchero*, another first-rate special, is a thin grilled steak cut into slices and tossed with green peppers and a hearty tomato sauce. It comes with the flavorful beans and rice.

Our favorite dish at Cafe Central is the *Chicken Enchiladas*. The chicken wrapped inside is redolent of garlic, onion, and chilis, a departure from the usual dry, strawlike chicken you get in most other Mexican restaurants. The *Tostados*, which are layered with grilled-to-order beef, the excellent beans, freshly cut tomatoes and lettuce, and a sprinkling of dry, white, aged Mexican cheese, make you look at this dish with new understanding.

We particularly recommend Cafe Central for lunch when the kitchen is in full swing. By late afternoon some items are gone.

37

PRICE RANGE: Inexpensive
HOURS: 7:30 A.M.–9:00 P.M. Mon.–Sat.
          7:30 A.M.–3:00 P.M. Sun.
NO RESERVATIONS
BEER
NO CREDIT CARDS

Cafe at Chez Panisse ★★

1517 Shattuck Avenue
Berkeley
548–5525

There are now two restaurants at Chez Panisse, the dining room downstairs that serves the original prix fixe menu Tuesday through Saturday, and a new cafe upstairs. The cafe is open continuously from 11 A.M. to midnight, performing the humanitarian service of providing a place to eat in the late afternoon and after movies, theater, and concerts. The menu, which changes daily, offers a variety of foods from light to substantial to fit the hour and your appetite, and allows you to sample the fresh, inventive food this restaurant is famous for in a less expensive, more informal way.

The upstairs portion of the restaurant has been lengthened and skylighted, and a beautiful, new open kitchen, including a wood-burning pizza-and-bread oven, has been installed in the center of the cafe. It provides decor in motion. You see the pizza maker throwing the dough, the pasta being cooked, and salads being tossed. Capacious wooden booths run adjacent to the kitchen, and dining areas with small cafe tables are at either end.

You can be as daring or as conventional as you like when ordering, which makes the cafe a unique meeting ground for people with different palates. The unifying philosophy of the food is the dedication to freshness, the variety of ingredients, and a stylish simplicity in presentation and cooking that always serves to reveal the foods rather than mask them.

The menu always offers three salads, oysters, a soup, two or three different pizzas, and some daily specials.

The *Tossed Salads* come in glass bowls, easily serving two. A *Fresh Garden Salad* is literally that—hand-picked, Berkeley-grown leaves of tangy roquette and baby red lettuce, sprinkled with Italian bacon. Unless you have a garden of your own, you will never taste a salad like this. Belgian endive is often used. The slightly bitter spears are dressed with an anchovy vinaigrette sauce, or tossed with walnuts and walnut oil, or served as a vegetable on a platter with asparagus and green beans accompanied by an herbed dipping sauce.

Another item always on the menu is local *Oysters from Pigeon Point*. These are crossbred, farmed oysters, small and delicate, and just an hour or two out of the sea.

Then there are the pizzas, which taste different from most other pizzas you've eaten, because the crusts are crisper, the ingredients all fresh, and the combinations unusual. *Calzone* is a fold-over pizza filled with mild goat cheese, mozzarella, fresh herbs, and prosciutto. It's very rich and cheesy, plenty for two people. The *Flat Pizzas* come with fresh tomatoes, green peppers, the best-tasting herbs, and Parmesan cheese. Another combination might be Italian bacon, tomatoes, red onions, garlic, and herbs.

The daily specials include a homemade pasta. Other daily specials might be a *Brochette of Salmon, Halibut,* and *Scallops in Tarragon Butter*, employing the freshest of fish, or a thin *New York Steak* encrusted with cracked black pepper and served with new potatoes.

By all means save a little of your appetite for dessert—all you need for one of the refreshing, homemade *Sherbets* that taste like the essence of the fruits they were made from. Excellent *Espresso* and *Cappuccino*, aperatifs, mineral waters, beers, and a select little wine list fill out the menu.

Chef Alice Waters deserves yet more praise for putting together a cafe that stays open thirteen hours a day, yet maintains the specialness that we have come to associate with her.

PRICE RANGE: Moderate
HOURS: 11:00 A.M.–midnight Mon.–Sat.
NO RESERVATIONS
BEER AND WINE
NO CREDIT CARDS

Café Lido

373 Broadway
San Francisco
391–7524

Longtime North Beach residents will probably remember Café Lido as André's, once one of the finest bars in San Francisco.

André went home to Canada, and the building went through a series of unsuccessful and largely disastrous restaurants. Now, judging from the long lines outside Café Lido for weekend brunch, a permanent occupant may have at last been found.

The long wooden bar, going across one side of the room, is still there, but this time it displays elaborately constructed *Fruit Tarts* and other tempting-looking desserts. There are two different brunch menus, one for weekdays, when the restaurant is uncrowded and a delightful place to sit for a couple of hours and sip some excellent *Cappuccino*, and the other for weekends.

The clear standouts of both menus are the *French Toast* and the *Ricotta Soufflé Pancakes*. You can get either with fresh fruit on top, an attractive alternative to the usual sugar syrup, and on weekends you can have your *French Toast* topped with steamed apples, whipped cream, and walnuts. The *Ricotta Pancakes* are light, fluffy, and moist, and don't leave you feeling at all leaden. On weekdays, there's a stuffed, delicate *Ricotta Blintz with Fresh Fruit Salad*. The *Omelettes* sound interesting, but turn out to be disappointingly bland.

PRICE RANGE: Moderate
HOURS: 8:30 A.M.–3:00 P.M. Tues.–Fri.
       10:00 A.M.–3:00 P.M. Sat.–Sun.
NO RESERVATIONS
FULL BAR
AMERICAN EXPRESS, MASTERCARD, VISA

Cafe Potpourri

Stanford Court Hotel
905 California Street
San Francisco
989–2500

The Cafe Potpourri in the Stanford Court is bright and gay in a fancy ice-cream-parlorish way. It's always bustling, noisy, and public. Page boys in full uniform pace the aisles with belled message boards summoning people to the phone.

You are dazzled by huge glass bowls of *Fresh Blueberries, Raspberries, Melons, and Peeled Oranges* on display as you enter from the hotel lobby, and then you run into one of the grandest carts of pastries in San Francisco. No breakfast fare these, but elaborate French constructions that require an afternoon appetite to demolish.

The *Eggs Benedict* are sheer perfection, poached to split-second doneness. The yolks swirl out into tart, warm hollandaise sauce. Cold sandwiches like *Tuna Fish with Chopped Cucumber and Watercress*, have the bright, clear taste of food that has just been prepared. A generous portion of equally well-made coleslaw, noteworthy for crunchy cabbage lightly tossed in vinegar-thinned mayonnaise, comes with it.

California Fruit Salad, a mélange of melon, strawberries, pineapple, and apple, marinated in lemon juice, comes with cottage cheese. Though unimaginative, this salad is impeccably fresh, and a boat of sour cream with caraway seeds is correctly served on the side.

For dessert, try the *Dacquoise* from the cart, a hazelnut meringue with mocha cream filling that literally melts in your mouth. Other selections might be a fresh *Mirabelle Plum Tarte*, a dramatic *Raspberry and Strawberry Tarte with Custard*, *Napoleon Slices*, a thick, crumbly *Cheesecake*, or a sweet-looking *Black Forest*.

PRICE RANGE: Moderate
HOURS: 7:00 A.M.–6:00 P.M. daily
RESERVATIONS ACCEPTED FOR LUNCH
FULL BAR
AMERICAN EXPRESS, MASTERCARD, VISA

Cafe Riggio ★

4112 Geary Boulevard
San Francisco
221–2114

Cafe Riggio is a relatively small, new San Francisco restaurant that exemplifies the ever-evolving "California restaurant sensibility," which emphasizes local products simply prepared though imaginative, cheerful decor, and service by people who are personally involved in the restaurant. It's always fun to go to Cafe Riggio, not because you'll be getting the best food in town, but because everything works together in a personable, comfortable, stylish way to make your experience pleasant.

The carefully planned menu offers a selection of foods that are interesting but not overly ambitious, the right formula for a restaurant in which tables turn over constantly. For starters, there are

41

Chiocciole, shell-less snails in a rich sauce of red wine and garlic, and *Formaggio al'Argintera*, fried cheese in a sizzling pool of olive oil and lemon juice. On the lighter side, there are *Carciofi*, fresh, not canned, marinated artichoke hearts sprinkled with parsley and lemon and imported *niçoise* olives, and a sensational *Calamari Salad* with capers, celery, pimento, and green peppers in a tart vinaigrette dressing. The homemade *Minestrone Soup* is loaded with fresh chard, chickpeas, crisp vegetables, and plenty of garlic, a bright-tasting interpretation.

The pastas aren't as good as the salads and appetizers. They are overcooked and their sauces lack punch, but we can highly recommend the fish and seafood main courses. *Pesce al Griglia Napoletana* is a filet of fresh snapper topped with tomato sauce and Parmesan cheese, something akin to a fish parmigiana. It works because the sauce is light and herby and the fish is not overcooked. The same unponderous touch goes into *Vongoli al Fiorentina*, which is a large bowl of steamed clams highlighted by fresh tomatoes, sweet basil, and garlic. *Cioppino*, that usually cooked-to-death San Francisco favorite, takes on new appeal here. It's thick with a sturdy fresh fish, crab in the shells, prawns, and clams in a hearty tomato sauce fragrant with fresh basil.

Forget the desserts: they're heavy-handed. Finish with an *Amaretto* and some *Espresso*. Take advantage of Cafe Riggio's good bar. In cafe tradition, wines are offered at reasonable prices, and the changing list of Italian wines is one of the best in town.

PRICE RANGE: Moderate
HOURS: 5:00–11:00 P.M. daily
NO RESERVATIONS
FULL BAR
MASTERCARD, VISA

Caffe La Botte ★

1166 Geneva Avenue
San Francisco
334–3292

A taxi-driving, food-aficionado friend of ours took us to Caffe La Botte for lunch one day, and we were immediately hooked. La Botte cooks Sicilian soul food, huge portions of heavy, spicy food that stays with you all day. You have to be in the mood for it to like it, and you have to know how to order or you can come away with a mundane meal. Yet, every time we've been to La Botte, we've eaten something special and authentic that's not to be found in other Italian restaurants around town.

Ruby, the cab driver, claims he discovers these neighborhood places from his fares. He, in turn, is very possessive of his information. It was only because of a fit of noontime hunger induced by a long discussion about Chicago-style pizza that he took us to La Botte, and then we had to ply him wih *grignolino* to get him to agree to let us write about it. We ate an emotional meal in a restaurant that serves emotional food.

We started off slowly with a plate of *Tomatoes Strewn with Anchovies and Capers*. We weren't impressed. The tomatoes weren't ripe enough, but the bottles of wine vinegar and real olive oil served with it and the fat, moist anchovies indicated better things to come. When *Fettucine with Pesto* arrived, we were won over. The thick, round-edged noodles were tossed in a fresh-basil sauce loaded with aromatic olive oil and garlic. The basil had been roughly chopped and added to order, so you could taste it in all its fresh, perfumy glory.

Then the *Calamari Fritti* arrived, and we knew a kindred soul was in the kitchen. Rings of squid had been lightly breaded and sautéed momentarily in butter. They melted in our mouths, tender and sweet, just the way pan-fried calamari should taste. Even better were the house-made *Italian Sausages*, smothered in red and green bell peppers, and sautéed in a little oil and vinegar. The texture of these extraordinary sausages was almost buttery—juicy without being fatty—and their seasoning was subtle—a little hot, a little allspicy, a little garlicky.

For dessert we forced down a piece of *Zuppa Inglese*, an Italian version of English trifle, with rum-soaked cake, custard laced with dried fruits, and whipped cream.

The dinner menu is much larger and more expensive. There are many more opportunities to go astray on it. However, you will not make a mistake by ordering *Bucatini alla Amatriciana*, a spaghetti-like pasta cooked past *al dente* texture, and served with a disarmingly simple combination of freshly chopped scallions, prosciutto, and butter. There's a spectacular *Calamari Sauté*, this time cooked in a thick, hot, spicy tomato sauce alive with bits of green peppers, onions, and capers, and an excellent *Sicilian Antipasto Plate* that has slices of cold beef tongue in a piquant dressing, finely chopped calamari with onions, and firm marinated mushrooms, a far cry from the usual antipasto plates of sliced lunch meat and canned olives.

For main courses there is a glistening, russet-brown *Chicken alla Diavola* that's just as crisp and succulent as it looks, and a *Chicken Cacciatora*, smothered in red and green peppers, mushrooms, and tomatoes.

The veal dishes are all disappointing, because they're coated with gummy flour. It's too bad, because La Botte uses the best white Provimi veal.

Portions are huge. All the main courses get sautéed peppers, Swiss chard cooked in butter and garlic, and rice pilaf with vermicelli. For a dollar more you can also get minestrone or an iceberg lettuce salad. We recommend ordering a la carte so that you can sample more of the restaurant's Sicilian dishes.

Tony, the owner and creator of many of the dishes, makes a point of introducing himself to you at the door. He's gregarious, effusive, and very Italian. He tells you what to order, but his taste and yours may not coincide. He wants to participate in your meal. He may even end up sitting down at your table if you're not careful. He's passionate about his restaurant, and that's what makes it a "find."

PRICE RANGE: Moderate
HOURS: 11:00 A.M.–2:00 P.M. Tues.–Fri.
        5:00–10:00 P.M. Tues.–Fri. and Sun.
        5:00–11:00 P.M. Fri.–Sat.
RESERVATIONS RECOMMENDED ON WEEKENDS
BEER AND WINE
MASTERCARD, VISA

Caffe Roma

414 Columbus
San Francisco
391–8584

What makes a good pizza comes down to personal preference. Pizza is a bastard dish of unknown parentage and there are no right or wrong ways to make it. When we hanker after pizza, we think of Pizzaria Uno or Due in Chicago, and their extraordinary thick-crust pizzas carpeted in crumbled Italian sausage and served in black cast-iron pans. Then our stomachs drift to southern France, where the pizzas are cooked in crock ovens over fragrant wood fires laced with branches of herbs. There the pizzas are dressed with anchovies, fresh tomatoes, onions, and tiny black olives.

44

Lately, several pizza aficionados have told us how much they like Caffe Roma, on Columbus above Broadway. We must have passed the place a thousand times and never ventured in. We're glad we finally did, because Caffe Roma not only bakes a light-crusted, cheesy pizza lavishly topped with fresh ingredients, but also serves excellent *Espresso* and *Cappucino*, good, inexpensive bottles of California and Italian wine, and carefully chosen commercial pastries.

The cafe is located in a high-ceilinged, old North Beach building, the interior of which has been painted with cherubs and clouds—authentic San Francisco baroque. The choice tables are set against plate-glass windows that front Columbus Avenue. In true cafe style, you can sip foamy *Cappucino* and aromatic *Espresso* while watching the passing parade on the street.

The Caffe Roma crowd is cosmopolitan, an urbane mixture of North Beach denizens and Europeans. The friendly staff seems to know most of them. You order everything at the counter and pay when you're ready to leave—probably because you tend to keep ordering more and more. Some customers sit all day, loyal to the talent behind the espresso machine.

One afternoon, we started with *Salads*, oval platters of chilled, crunchy iceberg lettuce with fat anchovies, tomatoes, Italian black olives, dill pickles, and hot, vinegary *pepperoncini* thrown on top. We had a couple of *Heinekens* with it. Then two of us stuffed ourselves on a medium *Combination Pizza*, certainly large enough for three normal eaters. The pizza must have weighed three pounds, a crusty yeast dough laden with mushrooms, olives, fresh tomatoes, mozzarella, pepperoni, Italian salami, Italian sausage, green peppers, and onions. Then we had *Cappucino*, and some freshly baked Italian pastry from the excellent Victoria Bakery a few blocks away, and then a couple of *Espressos* to wash everything down. It didn't turn out to be your basic cheap lunch, but we couldn't imagine a better one.

PRICE RANGE: Moderate
HOURS: 7:45 A.M.–midnight Sun.–Thurs.
        7:45 A.M.–1:30 A.M. Fri.–Sat.
NO RESERVATIONS
BEER AND WINE
NO CREDIT CARDS

Caffe Sport ★★

574 Green Street
(near Columbus)
San Francisco
981–1251

Caffe Sport is a masterpiece of contemporary Sicilian rococo. Layers of glittering junk are glued to the walls, hang from the ceiling, are Varathaned on the tables, and plastered to the beams, surrounding you in a wacky world of trinkets, empty panettone boxes—and garlic fumes. The paparazzi play football at the front. The bohemians drink cappuccinos and espressos in the middle of the room, and the diners are sent to the black hole of Palermo, a cave room lined with aquariums and an air purifier in the depths of the Sport.

The kitchen is a miracle, a steaming closet where owner-chef Antonio in his undershirt, his body displaying the effects of many meals of pasta, delivers forth his gutsy (very) southern Italian dishes. The *Pasta Rustica alla Carrettierra*, like all the pasta served at the Sport, is rigatoni-style hollow noodles cooked to the correct *al dente* doneness, over which Parmesan cheese, cream, small bay shrimp, and a circle of thick, rich tomato sauce are lavished. *Pasta con Melanzane* is tossed with cheese, olive oil, and tomato sauce, and topped with rounds of sautéed eggplant baked with Parmesan cheese and garlic that melt in your mouth. A plate of *Fresh Clams in the Shell* come with the *Pasta con Vongole*.

The other category on the Sport menu is seafood. We had *Scaloppe all' Antonio*, big white bay scallops, barely cooked so that they retained their delicate flavor and juiciness, that were served in an appropriately thin tomato sauce and topped with slivered almonds. This was a magnificent dish—simple, respectful of the superior scallops, but also an interesting combination of texture and flavor. *Scampi all' Antonio*, a plate of deliciously underdone prawns, is prepared the same way. *Sautéed Calamari* and *Fried Calamari* once again show off Antonio's talent—the pieces of squid are cooked quickly in lots of garlic and olive oil. Nothing is worse than calamari turned to rubber by overcooking. The calamari, prawns, and clams in the shell that make up the *Combination Plate* are also sautéed in garlic and olive oil, with a bit of white wine thrown in.

All portions are very generous and serve two to three people, depending on how many dishes are ordered. As in a Chinese restaurant, huge platters of food are brought to the table and everyone gets an empty plate, so you get your best value by bringing a group to the Sport.

The Caffe Sport is not for the namby-pamby eater, the timid of stomach, the skimpy of appetite. The sauces *all' Antonio* are laced with raw pieces of garlic, the aftermath of which could put an unsuspecting diner into garlic shock. Olive oil and good Italian Parmesan cheese are thrown around with a generous hand, though not a heavy one. Each time you eat at the Sport, the food is slightly different. Some days the garlic is cooked; some days the tomato sauce is thin. Sometimes it takes twenty minutes for the meal to come, sometimes five, depending on how Antonio decides to prepare a dish. It's the type of place where the olives on your antipasto might be eaten by the waiter on the way to the table.

The Sport is one of the few restaurants that serves dinner late. Go on a weeknight; it's crazy on the weekends.

PRICE RANGE: Moderate
HOURS: Noon–2:00 P.M., 6:30–11:00 P.M. Tues.–Sat.
NO RESERVATIONS
FULL BAR
NO CREDIT CARDS

California Culinary Academy

215 Fremont Street, 7th Floor
San Francisco
543–2764

Eating at the California Culinary Academy, San Francisco's first and only school for professional chefs and one of the few in the United States, can be hit or miss. All the meals are prepared by the students, and depending on who the chef/instructor is, you can get a very good meal for a bargain price. When Jeremiah Tower, former Chez Panisse chef, was teaching, the California Culinary Academy was the best place to eat in town. When some of the other more traditional, hotel-oriented chefs are at the helm, the food can be disappointing. Also, the ''Grand Buffet'' set up on the weekends should be avoided at all costs. The emphasis is on presentation and no one cares whether the food is edible.

The dining room set-up itself is fun. It's a huge, sunlit room with colorful cloth baffles hanging from the ceiling. You can watch the horde of white-hatted students at work through the glassed-in kitchen, which somehow stays immaculately neat and clean despite all the activity. Your waiters are students, and most of them are so inexperienced and sweet that they welcome your suggestions.

Your best bet is to call ahead and ask who is teaching and what his or her background is. If it sounds interesting, give the school a try. You might be a winner.

PRICE RANGE: Moderate
HOURS: Seatings at 6:00, 6:30, and 7:00 P.M. Mon.–Wed.
RESERVATIONS RECOMMENDED
BEER AND WINE
MASTERCARD, VISA

Capri ★

101 East Napa Street
Sonoma
707/996–3866

The best restaurant meals happen by surprise. You wander in because it's convenient, and the restaurant turns out to be good beyond your expectations. These serendipitous occurrences have been happening to us in the wine country lately, where there has been an explosion of new restaurants.

We spent a day in Sonoma at a friend's house working up some ravenous sleeping-in-the-sun appetites. Not knowing where to go, we asked around in nearby Glen Ellen. The consensus from shop owners and gas station attendants was that the best restaurant in the area was a tiny place right in downtown Sonoma called the Capri.

We knew this restaurant had the right idea when we were served a basket of *Sonoma French Bread*, a local delicacy that is softer and more finely grained than the San Francisco sourdough, but with more character.

The fourteen entries of "fresh country cuisine" listed on the menu all come with appetizer, soup, and salad. This particular evening we were each served a thin slice of finely textured *Pâté* made with three kinds of liver. It was moist, fresh, and nicely seasoned, making a good companion for that wonderful bread.

48

A thick *Puree of Butternut Squash* was an honest presentation of that nutty tasting vegetable. A *Salad* of good-looking greens in vinaigrette dressing made with olive oil and good vinegar also pointed to a conscientious kitchen. Often, the openers of a meal can show finesse, but when it comes to the more complicated main courses, the kitchen fizzles out. Such was not the case at the Capri.

The restaurant truly believes in serving fresh local products, such as the *Sonoma Quail Stuffed with Pâté*. It was one of the most successful preparations of its kind we have tasted. Not only were the quail gently cooked, allowing them to show off their delicate, meaty flavor, but the miniscule amount of creamy textured stuffing added flavor without being distracting.

In *Poulet Sauté Jerusalem*, the fowl was again cooked to the point at which the flesh was firm but still moist and juicy. It sported a rich sour cream sauce studded with artichoke hearts and mushrooms.

The sautéeing of locally grown *Fresh Rabbit*, however, had gone too far. The flesh had dried out, although its red wine and mushroom sauce probably benefited from the longer cooking.

Both a *Chocolate Mousse* and a *Crème Caramel*, standard French restaurant fare, transcended cliché by their skillful preparation.

One of the major attractions of the Capri Restaurant is a remarkable Sunday brunch, an absolute ''must'' for all brunch fans. Imagine perfect *French Toast* made even better by thick slices of Sonoma French bread, and accompanied by homemade fresh fruit preserves. *Eggs Benedict* might be a standard item on every Sunday brunch menu, but at the Capri they're done perfectly, something you rarely find. The muffins are well toasted, not mushy; the egg yolks are runny but not watery; the hollandaise sauce is as good as you'll ever eat. And the Capri makes a magnificent *Oysters Rockefeller*, a welcome change from the traditional brunch fare. All this comes accompanied by a bowl of fresh fruit, fresh-squeezed orange juice, and homemade blueberry muffins. This brunch alone is well worth the drive from San Francisco.

The two chef-owners, sticking to high-quality fresh foods, have created an unpretentious, serviceable country restaurant. What the menu lacks in innovation is made up for in execution. The food is attractive and you can taste the individual effort behind it.

PRICE RANGE: Moderate
HOURS: 5:30–9:30 P.M. Tues.–Fri. and Sun.
       5:30–10:00 P.M. Sat.
       10:00 A.M.–2:00 P.M. (brunch)

RESERVATIONS RECOMMENDED
BEER AND WINE
MASTERCARD, VISA

Caravansary

310 Sutter Street
San Francisco
362–4640

2268 Chestnut Street
San Francisco
921–3466

Ersatz is the word to describe Caravansary, and it's not a word that goes over well in San Francisco, where there are so many authentic restaurants representing dozens of different cuisines of the world. Caravansary to our mind tries to cook Middle Eastern food to satisfy people who hang out in "continental" restaurants—restaurants that don't claim to be French but have a vaguely French cuisine. Part of the menu itself is continental: *Sautéed Scallops with Shallots and Marsala Wine, Charcoal-Grilled Trout,* and *Quiche* aren't exactly Middle Eastern specialties. And what is Middle Eastern tends to be inappropriately seasoned.

Take, for instance, the *Chicken Tabaka,* described on the menu as "boneless breast of chicken marinated in pomegranate juice, then pressed and baked in lemon butter, garlic, and herbs." It sounds good, but the sauce that emerges tastes overwhelmed by vinegar and oregano. The chicken is juicy and tender, but the sauce is not only badly done, it has none of the characteristic flavors of the Middle East.

Even the three Middle Eastern salads that come with the dinners as appetizers taste bland and uninteresting. The tabouleh seems at least half chopped parsley, the hummus is much too pasty, and the pureed eggplant cries out for Middle Eastern spices.

All this is too bad, because the Caravansary, although fairly high priced for what you get, is a fun place to eat. You walk through a cookware store to get to a pleasantly decorated back room that serves as the restaurant. The basic meats seem of high quality, too, particularly the tender, fat-free *Lamb Shanks,* which would make a first-rate dish if only the yogurt sauce were spiced up. Someone should buy a few bottles of coriander, cumin, mustard seed, and the like from the shop up front and make a present of them to the chef.

PRICE RANGE: Moderate
HOURS: 11:00 A.M.–3:00 P.M., 5:00–10:00 P.M. Mon.–Sat.
Chestnut Street location: 11:00 A.M.–3:00 P.M. Sun. (brunch)
RESERVATIONS ACCEPTED
BEER AND WINE
ALL MAJOR CREDIT CARDS

Carnelian Room

Bank of America Building
555 California Street
San Francisco
433–7500

A maxim heard in the restaurant-reviewing business, and one that we have yet to disprove, is that the higher up the restaurant, the worse the food. The Carnelian Room, on the fifty-second floor of the Bank of America Building, is the highest up of all San Francisco restaurants.

The restaurant is run by the Davres Corporation, information that we gleaned from some very small print on a matchbook cover, after paying an exorbitant amount of money for a meal that we thought resembled airport food. Davres is a division of ARA Services, which, among other activities, distributes vending machines to factories. One can only wonder why this corporation branched out from vending packaged cakes to peddling *Médaillons de Veau Forestière*. All we can say is that to us the food at the Carnelian Room tastes like it came out of a vending machine.

During the ear-popping ride up on Bank of America's express elevator, you cannot help but be excited about the prospect of dining in a supposedly luxurious restaurant above the clouds. The appointments and decor of the Carnelian Room support this fantasy—real walnut paneling, antique marble buffets, sprays of roses in designer vases, spectacular floor-to-ceiling windows kept sparkling clean to highlight the most breathtaking view of San

Francisco and the bay. However, after a number of disastrous meals at the Carnelian Room, we suggest that you visit there for drinks only. You get the same panoramic views and romantic setting in the bar area without wasting dollars and calories, and you won't be abused by haughty waiters who somehow don't know they are serving some of the worst food in town. Although you can never hope for much from a tourist restaurant, the Carnelian Room may surpass your worst expectations.

PRICE RANGE: Expensive
HOURS: 6:00–10:15 P.M. nightly
RESERVATIONS RECOMMENDED
FULL BAR
ALL MAJOR CREDIT CARDS

Chez Panisse ★★★

1517 Shattuck Avenue
Berkeley
548–5525

For almost a decade now, Chez Panisse in Berkeley has been turning out a different menu each night. That's in the neighborhood of 3,000 new dishes, and they keep doing it. What is so remarkable is that the food is always exciting, very rarely poor, occasionally merely good, and usually superb. No restaurant in the City comes close to it. You can spend twice the money at Ernie's or L'Etoile and be bored to death after eating at Chez Panisse. Here's an example from just one dinner:

A small *Filet of Sea Bass Wrapped in Parchment*. When the packet was torn open, there arose an ambrosia of fresh thyme, lemon, julienned carrots, and scallions. The fish was barely cooked, but still cooked to perfection, its flesh moist and tender. Gentle steaming in paper with the carefully chosen fresh herbs and vegetables brought out the natural richness of the sea bass. Its flavor was revealed, not masked.

Along came a deep green *Sorrel Soup Garnished with a Swirl of Crème Fraiche*, which is slightly soured fresh cream. This thin puree was the essence of sorrel—bright, sour, and spinachy. No heavy-handed use of stock or cream weighed it down, the late addition of cream adding just the right touch of richness.

The hit dish of the evening, and maybe of the year, was *Spring Lamb* from the Dal Porto ranch in Amador County. The kitchen knew that a quick turn over charcoal to sear in the juices was enough. The meat was subtle, sweet, and tender, and we gnawed at the tiny bones feeling blissfully decadent. A *Turnip Puree*, nicely garlicked and topped with delicious bread crumbs, came with it.

A plate of perfect, large-leafed *Watercress Tossed in Oil with a Trace of Good Vinegar* was strong after the sorrel and lamb, but not so much as to dampen our appetite for the two elegant cheeses offered that evening, a creamy heart-shaped *Neufchatel* and a suave, firmer *Chaumes* from the Loire Valley.

Yet we couldn't pass up a *Pear and Armagnac Ice*, the distillation of the juiciest, fruitiest quality of pears. A curled cookie melted the minute it touched the tongue.

Other nights are very French, like one Saturday's menu dedicated to Raimu, a lovable character actor in Marcel Pagnol's films about the south of France. Dinner began with a little platter of *Cauliflower Napped in Garlic Mayonnaise, Three Snails, and Some Radishes*. There followed a thick slice of *Terrine*, a beautiful mosaic of pork, rabbit, and fresh herbs served with piles of tiny *niçoise* olives.

A *Daube of Beef* arrived in its own crock, a classic provincial beef stew steeped in cloves, orange peel, red wine, and garlic that was more than anyone could eat. Then came a lightly dressed *Salad of Tender Greens*, followed by a generous slice of buttery, *Rosemary-Encrusted Goat Cheese*.

If you picked the dinner apart you might be able to say that the *Daube of Beef* was nothing but a plain beef stew, or that *Snails and Radishes* were not what you expected from a restaurant of Chez Panisse's reputation. But when taken together—the variety of food, the imagination of the combinations, the sequence, the presentation, the whole conception so meticulously and creatively realized—you felt as if you had participated in an event. This was clearly not a dinner for stodgy or small-appetited people, but a true feast for those who love garlic, exuberant cooking, and the tastes of southern France translated by California foods.

To descend from the clouds, we have been served some things we didn't like at Chez Panisse. Once we had some horrible *Vegetables à la Greque*; the other night, a large, soggy *Blini* that suffocated a thimbleful of fine California caviar; another time, a *Pacific Coast Spiny Lobster* that wasn't enough to eat—although a second was immediately offered. However, when Chez Panisse's staff falters, even the "tries" are interesting, and its successes are not mere technique.

Chez Panisse has developed an art form of its own, intensely serious cooking that's whimsical at the same time. The meals are elegant and earthy. Authenticity is ensured by using the best local foods—the spring lamb from Amador County, Pacific rock fishes, oysters and mussels, suckling pigs, rabbits, quail, and pheasant from local farms, herbs and wild mushrooms from the countryside, smoked trout from Big Sur, locally caught and smoked salmon, caviar from West Coast sturgeon, and the finest California fruits and vegetables as they come into season.

Since only a single menu is prepared each night, service is somewhat simplified. However, the waiters and waitresses have a working knowledge of the wine and usually can be relied upon to come up with the right suggestion. They also know a lot about the food.

Each meal is a new experience for the diners as well as for the cooks. There's constant experimentation. The palette of foods is so varied and complex that you usually taste something you have never tasted before—and often it could be from your own back yard. We're lucky to have this restaurant in the Bay Area, constantly scouring the countryside for fresh materials that are magically put together with such panache.

PRICE RANGE: Expensive
HOURS: 6:00–9:15 P.M. Tues.–Sat.
RESERVATIONS NECESSARY
WINE
NO CREDIT CARDS

The Chibchas

Highway 140 in Cathey's Valley
209/966–2940

Driving up Highway 140 from the Central Valley to Yosemite might provide some beautiful mountain scenery, but gastronomically it's a bleak desert. Then, suddenly, in the middle of nowhere, a stucco house appears with a sign identifying it as a Colombian restaurant. What's a Colombian restaurant doing there, of all places?

We stopped to find out. The owners, Eduardo and Elias, came to the United States from Columbia eleven years ago, and one day they set out to see Yosemite. They fell in love with the area, saw a little house for sale, and The Chibchas (the name of an old Indian tribe) was in business.

If the word funky fits anything, Chibchas is it. The tables—in four different small rooms—have clear plastic tablecloths covering *paper* place mats. Crucifixes adorn the walls, a souvenir shop greets you as you walk in, and the men's room has a shower. Everyone is extraordinarily friendly.

The menu offers seven dinners plus a daily special. If you get the *Baked Beef Tongue in a Red Wine Sauce*—Latins seem to have an unusual talent for cooking tongue—you're in for a treat. The *Arroz Atollado*, a sort of Colombian paella with shrimp and chicken, is sometimes overcooked. There's also a hearty *Picadillo*, a stew made with beef, pork, and green beans, and a daily *Vegetarian Dinner*. Be sure to ask for tortillas when you're seated, or you'll get mushy "dinner rolls."

PRICE RANGE: Inexpensive to moderate
HOURS: 4:00–10:00 P.M. Wed.–Sat. and Mon.
       Noon–9:00 P.M. Sun.
NO BEER OR WINE (you can bring your own)
MASTERCARD

China First ★

675 El Camino Real
(near University Avenue)
Palo Alto
326–3900

China First is Palo Alto's first and best restaurant specializing in Hunan and Szechuan dishes. The menu is intriguingly diverse, with the hot and spicy dishes printed in red. And they *are* hot and spicy. China First believes that hot peppers have a therapeutic effect on the body, warding off colds and "vapors," and one of their meals of hot dishes will warm you to the marrow of your bones.

Some of the most interesting taste combinations are the cold appetizers infused with hot spices, like the *Three Delicacy Platter*, a colorful arrangement of chicken, cabbage, and smoked beef. We always order it or the smaller *Relish Plate* of spicy-hot cold vegetables. Don't miss the *Spring Rolls* here, perked up by piquant Chinese pickle, or the *Shrimp Toast*, pieces of toast spread with a rich puree of shrimp, scallions, and eggs, and deep fried until they puff. They melt in your mouth.

For main courses we are particularly fond of Hunan-style *Leg of Lamb*, tender and juicy and redolent of fresh ginger and garlic and scallions. It's hot, as is the *General's Chicken*, boned chicken with snow peas and devastatingly hot whole red peppers. It's best to eat around the peppers; the flavor they impart to the succulent chicken is enough to set your tongue tingling.

For respite from the heat, we like *Dragon and Phoenix*, which comes dramatically garnished with a red lobster shell and sprigs of parsley. Lobster meat (*Dragon*) and chicken (*Phoenix*) are combined with water chestnuts in a clear white sauce that is actually subtle but not flavorless, as so many Chinese white sauces tend to be. Another tamer dish is *Beef with Spicy Tea Sauce*, which is remarkable for its variety of ingredients. Miniature ears of corn, carrots, tiny button mushrooms, and lots of scallions are a few of the items tossed into a sauce seasoned with a mild type of hot pepper seed.

China First also does an exquisite *Peking Duck*, which must be ordered in advance, as well as the readily available *Szechuan Smoked Tea Duck*, which has a wonderfully spicy, crisp skin and creamy flesh. You dip the pieces of duck into black bean sauce and eat them with steamed white buns. You can also get *Fresh Duck Braised with Ginger and Green Pepper*, an unusual preparation that leaves the duck flavorful and chewy.

Finally, the vegetable dishes here, such as *Dry Sautéed Long Beans*, each crisp strand coated with minced garlic and spicy pork, and the fabulous *Hearts of Broccoli* with ginger-studded garlic sauce, should not be passed up.

The menu is so large at China First that it's hard to make up your mind, but we have found that practically every dish is meticulously and robustly prepared. Our only objection to this restaurant is that it uses MSG in its sauces, which causes some susceptible people to get headaches. You can request the kitchen to cook without it. You can also ask the cook to tone down the hot peppers in spicy dishes, but this we don't recommend. After the first shock to your palate, an adjustment takes place that makes it all taste very good.

PRICE RANGE: Inexpensive to moderate
HOURS: 11:30 A.M.–2:00 P.M. Mon.–Sat.
       5:00–9:00 P.M. Sun.–Thurs.
       5:00–10:00 P.M. Fri.–Sat.
RESERVATIONS ACCEPTED FOR LARGE PARTIES
BEER AND WINE
MASTERCARD, VISA

Chin Szchawn ★★

If you closed your eyes and imagined what a nominee for the best small Chinese restaurant in the Bay Area would look like, you'd probably come up with something like this: a bustling place in a Chinese neighborhood, with formica tables and fluorescent lights, jammed with large Chinese families, where heaping plates of food are brought by the armful by a harried staff and thrown down in front of you.

Not quite the reality of Chin Szchawn. Would you believe a small, moderately priced Chinese restaurant that insists on reservations, has tablecloths and candles, bars little kids, and elegantly serves one dish at a time? And that's located in Albany, of all places?

Chin Szchawn definitely has style, not only in the atmosphere, but also in the careful preparation of a long and unusually interesting menu. It's no surprise that owners Richard and Jacqueline Ng (Jacqueline does the cooking), can on occasion be seen dining at Chez Panisse. They really care about food, and over the years, while we've had many fine Chinese meals all around San Francisco, no other Chinese restaurant has maintained the consistently high quality of Chin Szchawn.

The Ngs came from Singapore in 1970, and brought with them a love for a wide variety of Asian food. This is reflected in Chin Szchawn's menu, which is divided into four parts to reflect four different varieties of Chinese cooking: Northern, Cantonese, Shanghai, and Szechuanese. A few times the Ngs have even prepared special Burmese and Malaysian banquets, introducing dishes that can't be gotten anywhere else in the United States.

You don't have to try exotic dishes at Chin Szchawn, though, to eat beautifully. The *Chicken and Cucumber Salad*, cold, shredded strips of chicken and cucumber in a pungent sauce of sesame oil, garlic paste, lemon, honey, soy sauce, and ginger, puts every similar dish at Bay Area Chinese restaurants to shame. The *Mu Shu Pork rolled in Pancakes*, that old workhorse of Chinese menus that is so often an undistinctive mess, is done here with such extraordinary delicacy that you can taste the contrast of textures and flavors. The *Hot-and-Sour Soup* is filled with mushrooms, coriander, and bamboo shoots and perfectly combines the spicy and sweet tastes that give it its name.

Among the more unusual dishes don't miss Szechuan-style

K'ou Jou. In a process that involves braising, refrigerating, then steaming, Chin Szchawn serves sliced tenderloin of pork on a bed of sautéed spinach with a spicy chili and sesame oil sauce, which comes out so tender it literally melts in your mouth. If you like hot food, consider the *Oil-Dripped Chicken*, where steamed, shredded chicken is served with bamboo shoots, carrots, and scallions in a hot, spicy sauce filled with garlic and chili peppers. The vegetable dishes are generally excellent, particularly the hot, spicy *Eggplant*, served in a thick, brown sauce that will leave you tasting garlic and chili pepper for days.

On weekends, Chin Szchawn probably turns away more people than it seats. But the Ngs refuse to expand, fearing that it would compromise the quality of the food. It's that kind of place.

PRICE RANGE: Moderate
HOURS: 5:00–8:30 P.M. Mon.–Sat.
RESERVATIONS NECESSARY
BEER AND WINE
MASTERCARD, VISA

Ciao

230 Jackson
San Francisco
982–9500

Ciao is an ultrastylish, ultramodern restaurant inspired by chic Italian high-tech design, but not by real Italian cooking. The spirit here is Beverly Hills rather than Milan, so Ciao is a good place to dress up, look good, and be seen, but not necessarily to eat. It's a glittering white space, busy and brittle, with lots of shiny polished brass rails and trim, mirrors peeking out from every angle, white swimming-pool latex floors, white metal hanging fixtures, revolving fans on the ceiling, and vespas hung on the walls. There is a classic Italian stand-up bar made of exquisite white marble, where you can get good espresso and a huge variety of imported aperatifs. That's the place to head at Ciao. Bring whomever you meet at nearby MacArthur Park, owned by the same restaurant corporation, to Ciao's bar for a quiet drink.

On the face of it, the menu sounds terrific with its list of simple grilled foods, Italian antipastos, and homemade pastas. The problem is that the food is carelessly prepared and bland. At

Ciao's prices, which are hardly cheap, you often come away disappointed.

The antipastos are not a bad bet here. They change every day and often include marinated mushrooms, eggplant, zucchini and other vegetables, calamari, sardines, anchovies, and Italian sausages. *Carpaccio*, paper-thin slices of raw steak with a good Dijon mustard sauce, is our favorite dish here. The *Salad*, a pile of romaine lettuce with finely chopped salami, imported cheese, tomatoes, and sliced mushrooms in a creamy dressing, is a nice variation on the American chef's salad, and the *Prosciutto and Melon* is usually fresh and appealing.

However, Ciao's specialty, the pasta, is a big letdown. A great show is made by the *pastaio*, the pasta maker, who works at an open counter hanging the pasta on shiny racks and combing it with his fingers like long, golden hair. The pasta itself is excellent, but by the time it's been overcooked, inundated with bland sauces, and kept warm until it's picked up by none-too-swift waiters, the pasta has lost all its charm. The pesto sauce needs more garlic, the bolognese more spirit, the marinara more basil, the creamy sauces more definition and less flour.

Treated as an elegant, uptown cafe, Ciao works well. The wine list is good and reasonably priced, the bar carries all sorts of great liqueurs and aperatifs, and the menu offers a number of good, cold, light items, and stays open late all day. But as a full-scale restaurant, you can do much better elsewhere.

PRICE RANGE: Moderate
HOURS: 11:00 A.M.–midnight Mon.–Sat.
        5:00 P.M.–midnight Sun.
RESERVATIONS ACCEPTED
FULL BAR
AMERICAN EXPRESS, MASTERCARD, VISA

City Hotel ★

Main Street
Columbia
209/532–1479

City Hotel is the centerpiece of Columbia, a restored mining town in the foothills of the Sierra Nevada that is now a living historical museum of the Old West. It's a wonderful place to stay for the weekend, and—remarkably, considering the food in this part of the world—it has a first-rate French restaurant.

The restaurant, run by ex-Ernie's chef Barry Marcillac, serves as a training ground for students from Columbia College. But don't think this is an amateur sort of restaurant with variable food. Every time we've eaten there, the food has been of consistently high quality. And the wine list is reasonable and excellent, chosen by the man who teaches wine courses at the college.

The veal and steaks are consistently good. We've had *Escalope de Veau à la Normande*, whose paper-thin slices of veal almost melt into a lavish preparation of tender-crisp sautéed apples and mushrooms in a light cream sauce. A variety of *Broiled Steaks* is offered, with classic béarnaise sauce and seasoned butters or coated with green peppercorns and flamed in brandy. A succulent, tender *Rabbit* has always been among our favorite dishes here.

If you want to get away for a couple of days, you don't have to leave behind the high culinary standards of the Bay Area if you eat at City Hotel.

PRICE RANGE: Moderate to expensive
HOURS: 11:30 A.M.–2:00 P.M. Tues.–Sat.
    5:30–9:00 P.M. Tues.–Sun.
RESERVATIONS NECESSARY
FULL BAR
MASTERCARD. VISA

Clown Alley

42 Columbus
San Francisco
421–2540

2499 Lombard
San Francisco
931–5890

Clown Alley represents the best of fast-food hamburger stands, because it's (thankfully) not all that fast. Its *Quarter-Pound Hamburgers* are cooked to order over a charcoal grill, leaving them juicy and deliciously charred. It's up to you to garnish them with condiments set out at a refrigerated counter.

Nothing else is very exciting to eat at Clown Alley besides the hamburgers. The shakes are the frozen custard type, with minimal taste and gooey texture. The fries are on the soggy side. However, you can get an imported beer to drink with your burger.

The other advantages of Clown Alley are that they are open all night and there is pleasant outdoor patio seating at the stand on Columbus, in a choice city location.

San Francisco has relatively few fast-food chain restaurants, and we're glad to say that the ones we do have are a cut above the usual. For on-the-run hamburger dining, you can't do better than Clown Alley.

PRICE RANGE: Inexpensive
HOURS: Never closed
BEER AND WINE
NO CREDIT CARDS

Cocolat

3324 Steiner Street
(between Chestnut and Lombard)
San Francisco
567–9957

1481 Shattuck Avenue
Berkeley
843–3265

Five years ago cocoa-dusted marbles of extraordinary chocolate began appearing in a few shops in Berkeley.

"What are these?" we asked.

"Eat one," we were told. We did. And then we ate another and another. These *Chocolate Truffles*, as they are called, were addicting. They are soft, creamy, intensely chocolaty, and just a little bit sweet, so that they are like eating chocolate butter. We couldn't get enough of them. Instead of wine or flowers we brought truffles to dinner parties and kept getting invited back.

Then a flat, shiny, single-layered chocolate cake started showing up around town. It had the same quality as the truffles—

concentrated richness, moistness, and chocolateness, without an overkill of sugar. For 75 cents you got a very small piece, but it was worth every penny. This was the best chocolate cake you could find anywhere.

Pretty soon word got out that a young woman named Alice was turning out these chocolate specialties from her home kitchen. As word spread and her chocolate supplanted exotic drugs as the hottest item around Berkeley, she started creating a Cake of the Week, distributed at only a few places. Finally, at the end of 1976, she opened her own bakery on Shattuck near Vine and aptly called it Cocolat.

Now there is a Cocolat in San Francisco, where you can sit at a table with some good coffee and order a slice of any cake in the house.

The small store is white with polished wood trim, a simple backdrop for the gorgeous-looking cakes. The cake counter reminds us of a jewelry store display. The cakes, truffles, and petit fours look like gems behind the shiny glass. Each is perfectly sculpted and elegantly decorated. What distinguishes these classy looking cakes is that they taste as good as they look.

The reason for this is that only fresh, natural ingredients are used—real sweet butter, obviously tons of it, fresh fruits for the syrups and flavorings, good chocolate, and aromatic liqueurs. No artificial flavorings or commercial bakery mixes are used; everything starts from scratch.

Our favorites are the chocolate cakes, which are made with crumbs of ground nuts instead of flour, and which are glazed in heavy, creamy black chocolate. The *Reine de Saba*, made with almond meal lightly flavored with cognac, the sides encrusted with toasted slivered almonds, is, indeed, the queen of cakes for us. The *Whiskey Cake* has liquor-soaked raisins, and the *Plain Chocolate Cake*, unsurpassed for pure, unadulterated chocolateness, is another favorite. These flourless cakes have a light but densely moist texture, a seeming contradiction, but wait until you taste them.

PRICE RANGE: Moderate
HOURS: San Francisco location:
      10:00 A.M.–6:30 P.M. Mon.–Fri.
      10:30 A.M.–6:00 P.M. Sat.
    Berkeley location: 10:00 A.M.–6:00 P.M. Tues.–Sat.

Cordon Bleu

1574 California Street
San Francisco
673–5637

Outside of the student quarter in Paris, San Francisco has more Vietnamese restaurants than any western city we know. One of our favorites for low-budget dining is the tiny Cordon Bleu, on California between Polk and Hyde. The restaurant feels like a cozy cave, with old, exposed red brick walls, dim lighting from ancient hanging globes, and a shaded front window. You sit at an old wooden counter, behind which all the cooking is done. Or, if you prefer, you can sit at one of two small tables at the back of the restaurant. One of them, however, is usually full of Vietnamese students and friends of the family who runs the Cordon Bleu, all of whom are particularly sweet, friendly people. The whole scene reminds us of Left Bank places where space is at a premium.

For your meal, you get a choice of five different *Combination Plates*, which consist of the same four dishes in varying amounts. All told, these are some of the best blue-plate specials in town.

Our favorite is *No. 1*, which includes a crisp, rice paper-wrapped Imperial roll filled with a spicy mixture of pork and vegetables; a skewer of thinly sliced beef marinated in lemon grass and cooked over charcoal; a pile of shredded lettuce, carrot, and chicken called country chicken salad; and rice covered with a rich, red meat sauce. You also get a little paper cup of clear sauce of slightly vinegary and fishy seasoning that makes everything taste delicious.

Combination Plate No. 5 adds to the above a piece of five-spice roast chicken. The skin has been rubbed with lemon grass and chilis, among other more exotic ingredients, and it's grilled to perfection over charcoal. It's the Vietnamese version of bar-bequed chicken. We like this dry-seasoning method better than the American saucy one.

For dessert have the excellent *Fried Banana*, with creamy ripe interior in a golden, crisp batter.

PRICE RANGE: Inexpensive
HOURS: 11:30 A.M.–2:30 P.M. Tues.–Sat.
      3:00–10:00 P.M. Sun.
      5:00–10:00 P.M. Tues.–Thurs.
      5:00–11:00 P.M. Fri.–Sat.

No Reservations
No Beer or Wine
No Credit Cards

Cuba Restaurant

2886 16th Street
San Francisco
864–9871

Could we ever get ourselves to review a restaurant that (a) is so plain it offers little more than a barrackslike room with linoleum floors and dinette-style tables with plastic tablecloths; (b) features a jukebox that almost constantly blares junky rock music; and (c) has service so bad that one of the diners, normally polite and nonassertive, feels compelled to stand up and shout at the top of his lungs for the waitress, who is across the room?

Cuba Restaurant is (d) all of the above, plus (e) it offers copious quantities of very good food at extremely reasonable prices, which makes the whole thing worthwhile.

This isn't the restaurant to take Aunt Tillie from Teaneck, New Jersey. And it certainly isn't the place to go if you have to be out at a certain time to catch a play or movie. But if you want to have lots of interesting and filling food, washed down by a few beers over the course of a couple of hours, definitely try it.

The Cuba appears to be run by a family that speaks very little English; most of the waitresses aren't terribly proficient at English, either. The service is slow, not because the restaurant is unfriendly or understaffed, but simply because the waitresses don't seem to understand the concept that someone might care how quickly they come to take your order. Soak up the Latin atmosphere and relax!

Like so many restaurants that specialize in one type of Latin cuisine, dishes from other Spanish-speaking countries seem inevitably to creep onto the menu. The Cuba's menu features not only many of the seafood and bean dishes we'd associate with Cuba, but also dishes from the Philippines, Spain, Puerto Rico, and even a *Breaded Steak with Two Eggs on Top* from Bolivia.

Among the appetizers, the *Lumpias* are splendid. These are long, thin sticks of beef, breaded and deep fried, and served with a wedge of lemon to squeeze over them. The beef is tender and the breading crispy, betraying not even a hint of grease. Another appetizer worth trying is the *Octopus Served in Its Own*

Ink, an interesting variation on the more usual *Squid in Its Own Ink*, served in other Latin and Italian restaurants in the City, as well as at the Cuba.

The *Potage de Garbanzo* is more like a hearty peasant stew than a soup. A huge bowl brims over with garbanzo beans, chunks of tender beef, and boiled potatoes, which have been cooked with onions in a tasty, thick brown broth. Cuba Restaurant also offers a *Fish Soup* (*Sopa de los 7 Mares*) that is a Cuban equivalent of bouillabaisse.

There is a whole variety of interesting main courses involving fish, including *Bacalao a la Viscaina*, salty, Cuban-style codfish, baked in a spicy red sauce; *Pescado Entomatado*, sea bass sautéed in fresh tomatoes and white wine; and *Tortilla de Camarones*, described as a shrimp omelette, but more like a casserole of eggs, shrimp, and onions, that's beautifully prepared and seasoned. The fish is perfectly cooked, but the sauces could definitely use fresh vegetables instead of an abundance of what tastes like canned peas.

The *Paella a la Valenciana* is somewhat less successful. Although the fish, shellfish, chicken, and sausage are all excellent and plentiful, the rice comes out too sticky and lacks a saffron aroma.

Many of the main courses—including a superb thinly sliced *Roast Pork* in natural juices served with boiled yucca root—are accompanied by a bowl of rice and a pot of black beans simmered in a thick, dark sauce. If you've never had black beans properly prepared, these alone are worth a trip to the Cuba.

PRICE RANGE: Inexpensive
HOURS: Noon–10:00 P.M. daily
NO RESERVATIONS
BEER AND WINE
MASTERCARD, VISA

Delice de France ★

320 Mason
San Francisco
433–7560

Delice de France is the brasserie branch of La Bourgogne, a bright, modern, clean-lined bistro that specializes in *charcuterie*, all made by the restaurant itself and most of which can be bought

65

to take home. It's the best of the Financial District brasserie-type restaurants, because it offers such a large variety of these excellent French delicatessen items.

One of them is *Choucroute Campagnarde*, a plate of warm, pungent sauerkraut garnished with creamy black-blood sausages, slices of ham and pork, and garlic sausages. Not only is it good, it's the only place in town where it's done right. Also exceptional is the *Chicken Liver Mousse Pâté*, a huge slice of velvety, butter-whipped chicken liver reminiscent of the fresh goose liver pâtés you can find only in France.

A cup of *Lobster Bisque*, however, tasted like doctored-up canned tomato soup, and a *Filet of Smoked, Marinated Trout* had exceptional flavor but rubbery texture.

The pastries are none too delicate, but the *Croissants* are the best in town. Also the *Baguettes*, made by the restaurant, can be crusty and flavorful if you get them on the right day, and the sweet butter served with them is extraordinary. It alone can bring us back to this pleasant, bustling, very French bistro.

PRICE RANGE: Moderate
HOURS: 10:00 A.M.–8:45 P.M. Mon.–Sat.
BEER AND WINE
ALL MAJOR CREDIT CARDS

de Young Museum Cafe

Golden Gate Park
San Francisco

The de Young Museum has recently installed a cafeteria-style restaurant on the ground level that opens out into the sculpture garden. Everything about the operation has been done right, perhaps because the likes of restaurateur Modesto Lanzone, a member of the museum's board, handled the project. The food is so imaginative and fresh, and the surroundings are so clean-lined and brightly decorated, that, like The Swallow in the University of California Art Museum, we recommend it as a lunch spot in its own right. You do have to pay admission to the museum to get to it, but the prices are so reasonable you'll still come out ahead.

For example, the *Calamari Salad*, marinated in a lemony vinaigrette, is as good as any we've had in the best restaurants around town, at half the price. *Chicken* and *Tuna Salads* are crunchy with nuts and crisp vegetables, and get gentle applica-

66

tions of mayonnaise. *Green Salads* look like still lifes. The greens have been carefully picked over and tossed to order. The opulent *Fruit Salad* is made with exclusively fresh seasonal fruits.

There's a selection of good-looking sandwiches, all made to order on whole-grain breads with freshly cut tomatoes, as well as a special that changes each day. On one occasion it was a generous *Filet of Salmon* served with homemade chutney, another time a flaky *Croissant Stuffed with Cheese and Ham* and served with a spinach salad. Imported beer and half-bottles of wine are available for these sophisticated little lunches.

An operation of lesser scale, run by the same creative people, is also in the basement of the Palace of the Legion of Honor.

PRICE RANGE: Inexpensive to moderate
HOURS: 10:00 A.M.–4:00 P.M. Wed.–Sun.
NO RESERVATIONS
BEER AND WINE
NO CREDIT CARDS

Diamond Sutra

737 Diamond Street
San Francisco
285–6988

The Diamond Sutra is a clean, spacious neighborhood restaurant that has been around for years. It specializes in vegetarian casseroles, home-baked breads, and crisp, fresh salads. The soups, made with water instead of stock, lack depth, and the meat dishes, many of which are casseroles, also lack soul. However, the basket of thick, dark slices of *Bread*—moist and nutty tasting and slathered with melting sweet butter—that is served with the meal is worth the price of the dinner. Diamond Sutra's loaf is naturally sweet, unusually light, and irresistible.

The *Salad* is also a winner. The greens are chilled and perfect, the garnish of red cabbage, shredded carrot, appealingly crunchy sunflower seeds, and a garlic-infused vinegar and oil dressing of classic proportions, brings it all together.

Some of the main courses we have liked include an *Italian Mushroom Casserole*, a combination of mushrooms, black and green olives, and eggplant in a clean-tasting tomato sauce, and

Snapper Mi Skordia, fresh pan-fried filets sauced with a puree of almonds, garlic, lemon, and olive oil.

Whatever you do, save room for dessert. The bread makers and pastry chefs here have talent. *Crème de Miel* is a delicate, creamy egg custard with a honey glaze on top. The *Georgia Pecan Pie* is a three-inch wedge of buttery crust and mahogany filling that's loaded with pecan halves and topped with hand-whipped cream—a model of lightness in a typically heavy genre of desserts. The *Chocolate Whiskey Cake*, really a slice of soft, black chocolate moistened with whiskey and raisins, will satisfy the strongest chocolate cravings.

PRICE RANGE: Inexpensive to moderate
HOURS: 5:00–10:00 P.M. Wed.–Sun.
RESERVATIONS ADVISED. ESPECIALLY ON WEEKENDS
BEER AND WINE
MASTERCARD. VISA

Doidge's ★★

2217 Union Street
(at Fillmore)
San Francisco
921–2149

While going out for Sunday brunch can be great fun, sometimes it turns out to be more trouble than it's worth. The restaurants with good food and pleasant atmosphere seem to have endless lines, while most of the others just aren't worth eating at.

Look no further than Doidge's for a solution. The food is spectacular—in our opinion the best Sunday brunch in the Bay Area (or breakfast any day, for that matter). With a skylight, large Oriental rugs on the floor, and quilted tablecloths, the restaurant is bright and cheerful. Finally, Doidge's takes reservations, so you won't have to fight off mobs of people, yet the prices are comparable to other brunch places. It's so popular, though, that you'd do well to reserve a couple of days in advance.

In talking about other restaurants that serve brunch, we can say that certain dishes stand out. At Doidge's, a restaurant reviewer has a big problem: Everything we've tasted there so far has been terrific. You can throw a dart at the menu and not lose.

Consider, for starters, the *French Toast*. Not only is it perfectly prepared, never burned or soggy, but also (1) you can choose from six kinds of bread; (2) you can always get it with walnuts, sliced bananas, and cinnamon on top; and (3) when certain fruits, like strawberries, peaches, or blueberries, are in season, you can have them as the topping, heaped on so thick you can't see the French toast underneath. Doidge's chooses its fresh fruits like a great French restaurant chooses its vegetables.

Even restaurants that have excellent omelettes often have trouble with their poached egg dishes, where every constituent has to be timed just right. Not Doidge's. Take the *Eggs Benedict*. The English muffin is perfectly crisp. The slice of Canadian bacon is tender and properly smoky. The eggs have been taken off at exactly the right moment, so that the yolk runs but isn't watery. And the hollandaise sauce is silky smooth and tangy with just the right amount of lemon.

You can get a wide variety of *Omelettes* at Doidge's, and they're done in the French style, with the outside never brown. Besides four types of cheeses, possible fillings include a special honey-cured, nitrate-free bacon, Spanish sauce, herbs, and mushrooms. Also, we've seen a number of people eating with evident pleasure the *Roast Beef Hash Supreme*, made with fresh mushrooms and sour cream and topped with a poached egg. Each time we vow to order it . . . until we walk by someone's *French Toast*.

PRICE RANGE: Moderate
HOURS: 9:00 A.M.–3:00 P.M. daily
RESERVATIONS NECESSARY ON WEEKENDS
BRING YOUR OWN WINE
MASTERCARD. VISA

Double Rainbow

1653 Polk Street
(near Clay)
San Francisco
775–3220

407 Castro Street
(near Market)
San Francisco
621–2350

The Double Rainbow puts out "gourmet ice cream" at gourmet prices, but we feel that the dense, creamy, intensely flavored ice cream is worth every penny, especially the *Blueberry, Strawberry, Mocha Walnut, Ultra Chocolate,* and *Chocolate Chocolate Chip*. What distinguishes this ice cream is its texture—there's more of it per square inch than any ice cream we've ever eaten. You can almost chew it, and you're glad to have this ice cream stay a little longer in your mouth. The Double Rainbow uses no artificial coloring or flavors. You can taste the big chunks of fresh berries or the high-quality chocolate in each bite.

At the Polk Street store you can also order espresso, cappuccino, and carefully selected pastries from different sources around the City, and take them to little cafe tables to eat.

We think the straight ice cream is so good that it should be eaten on cones, but the milk shakes, real old-fashioned sodas made with seltzer and syrup, and sundaes topped with fresh or frozen fruit compotes, are also excellent.

Expect a line at the counter. We've never seen the Double Rainbow empty.

HOURS: Polk Street location:
11:00 A.M.–midnight Sun.–Thurs.
11:00 A.M.–1:00 A.M. Fri.–Sat.
Castro Street location opens at noon

E'Angelo

2234 Chestnut Street
San Francisco
567–6164

Diners in San Francisco were dismayed to see Eduardo's, one of the Marina District's most beloved little pasta restaurants, change hands. Eduardo, famous for his Charles de Gaulle nose, the profile of which served as the restaurant's logo, ran a taut ship. He alone seated the waiting throngs, took every order himself, and dispersed the checks all at his own deliberate pace.

Eduardo's was crowded, understaffed, and maddeningly slow, but we had never been served an imperfect plate of pasta there. The quality of the noodles themselves was extraordinary, and they were always cooked *al dente*. Eduardo's pasta was so good that he began packaging it and selling it in his restaurant and, more recently, in supermarkets.

Then, suddenly, Eduardo's nose disappeared from the door. The name of the restaurant changed to E'Angelo, but the menu stayed the same. It turns out that E'Angelo is admirably keeping up the standards Eduardo set. The food is not as consistently perfect, but the service is better—quicker and more broadminded. Furthermore, E'Angelo uses Eduardo's pasta. Packages of green and pale yellow fettucine are still displayed like fine china in the armoire at the front of the restaurant.

Some of the pastas have admirably survived the transition. Homemade *Fettucine* offers firm egg noodles with body and character, that stand up to the clean-tasting tomato sauce enlivened by still-tender chicken livers and mushrooms. *Fettucine Carbonara* is wet and creamy. The white noodles come in a pool of egg yolk-thickened cream seasoned with bacon and Parmesan cheese. *Green Lasagne*, however, is heavy on the tomato sauce and light on mozzarella and fontina, masking the taste of the noodles.

Some other excellent dishes include *Eggplant Parmigiana*, a suave melting together of eggplant, fresh-tasting tomato sauce, and cheeses. *Proscuitto with Melon* brings a generous serving of peeled, ripe cantaloupe and slices of Italian ham, a few of which have been a little dry around the edges. Nonetheless, this is the best appetizer on the menu. The pizzas are as well constructed as ever, made with fresh tomatoes and mozzarella on a thin, tender crust.

The small number of nonpasta dishes, including veal and lamb, have never been special at this restaurant. The wine list offers a wide choice of good Italian wines at fair prices. The intelligent wine list is indicative of the sophistication of this little restaurant. The emphasis is on a small number of choice items done well. The portions are right, the price is right. You eat as you do in neighborhood restaurants in Europe, ordering a la carte, sitting right next to each other at crowded-together tables in a bustling atmosphere. It's fun to go there. So a toast to E'Angelo, worthy successor to the great Eduardo's.

PRICE RANGE: Inexpensive to moderate
HOURS: 5:00–11:00 P.M. Tues.–Sun.
NO RESERVATIONS
BEER AND WINE
NO CREDIT CARDS

Edokko

2215 San Pablo Avenue
(near Allston Way)
Berkeley
841–9505

We once took a friend to Edokko who had lived in Japan, and he was wildly enthusiastic before we had even been seated. The reason? A little boy, obviously the son of the owners, was sitting at one of the tables watching color television. "Just like the little family restaurants in Japan," our friend exulted.

Edokko is that sort of place. A tiny, friendly restaurant in the flatlands of Berkeley, it serves first-rate food at some of the lowest prices in the Bay Area. The last time we ate there, for instance, there were nine complete dinners for under $5 and three for just $3.50! And if you order their marvelous *Udon* (thick wheat noodles in a rich broth with various meat, fish, and vegetable toppings), you can eat for around $2.

We've never managed to eat a meal at Edokko without getting the *Nigiri Sushi* as an appetizer. For half of what you'd pay in many San Francisco Japanese restaurants, you get an assorted platter of sliced raw fish on seasoned rice (usually shrimp, octopus, squid, one or two white fishes, and tuna), plus several pieces of *tekka maki* (raw tuna surrounded by seasoned rice, rolled into a long cylinder, wrapped with seaweed, and sliced). The sushi at Edokko might not be exotic, but it's as fresh and tender as can be.

Two beef dishes are favorites of Edokko regulars. The *Edokko Nabe* is very similar to sukiyaki, but much more satisfying, in our view, because you get a rich, tangy dipping sauce for the slices of beef. The *Beef Teriyaki* tastes like unusually high-quality flank steak is used, and the teriyaki sauce is perfect. There's also an outstanding *Yosenabe* for cold nights—a huge bowl of broth and vegetables, heaped with chicken, fish, and shellfish.

PRICE RANGE: Inexpensive
HOURS: 11:30 A.M.–2:00 P.M. Tues.–Sat.
        5:00–9:00 P.M. Tues.–Sun.
NO RESERVATIONS
BEER AND WINE
MASTERCARD, VISA

El Tazumal ★★

3522 20th Street
San Francisco
647–9880

Two acquaintances of ours, Luis and Carlos, hail from Havana and Panama, respectively, and now live in San Francisco. We've had many a discussion in broken Spanish and English about which are the best restaurants in the Mission.

Carlos feels that any restaurant that charges more than $3 for a meal is a den of thieves. "How many tacos did you get with it?" is his standard question.

Luis, on the other hand, feels that most of the restaurants we like are third class. He's a decor and service aficionado, and he likes *beurre blanc* on his fish.

We think we have found the restaurant that would please them both. It's a small place on 20th near Mission called El Tazumal. It doesn't have the rough edges of many of the Mission District eateries, the food is consistently well prepared, and no one could possibly argue about the prices.

It's run by a Salvadoran couple. The loquacious, helpful husband waits on tables and the wife does the cooking. She's good at it.

The first time we went to El Tazumal we tried the Salvadoran dishes. El Salvador, if you aren't sure, is a tiny Central American country on the Pacific Ocean, right below Guatemala, but its cuisine is more varied than its neighbor's.

Tazumal is the name of a Mayan ruin. The Salvadoran specialties served at El Tazumal are characterized by sauces based on sautéed vegetables.

Lengua en Salsa is a particular favorite. It's beef tongue cooked to buttery softness in a sauce of onions, red and green peppers, and fresh tomatoes that have been seasoned with cumin, fresh coriander, and garlic. It's a sauce that would make an old shoe taste good. A hearty portion of this fabulous stew comes with snowy white rice and black, creamy refried beans pleasantly smoky with the taste of bacon fat.

Higado Encebollado, fresh beef liver sautéed with onions, was as tender as could be. It was cooked to perfect pinkness, as we requested. It came smothered in sweet, crisp, lightly browned onions—onions only a sensitive sautée cook could turn out. We've had the identical dish for twice the price at other restaurants and it hasn't lived up to the dish here.

The Mexican dishes exude wholesomeness and abundance. The *Chile Rellenos* look bigger than life on a plate loaded with the excellent beans, rice, and salad garnish. Fresh green chilis are used, stuffed to bursting with Jack cheese, and treated to a cooked-that-day tomato sauce.

Enchiladas Suizas, corn tortillas filled with Jack cheese and green onions, have the tarditional green chili sauce. They come with lots of sour cream. There's no skimping on dairy products in the Mexican dishes. The sauces are bright in color and taste, and each item is carefully constructed. Nice.

Ceviche, served in a cocktail glass, looks festive garnished with slices of ripe avocado slices. Finely diced pieces of firm, white fish, chopped tomatoes, and green onions, all marinated in lemon juice and hot chilis, is similar in style to the *ceviche* we've had in the Yucatan made with sea conch. Eating it at Tazumal brought back tropical memories.

We all have a favorite neighborhood restaurant where you don't have to plan in advance to get a table, or dress, or try to decipher a wine list. El Tazumal is probably like ten other little places in the area that's run by families who spend much of their time there. They eat their daily meals out of the same kitchen that you do and the food has the simplicity and nourishment of family cooking.

El Tazumal is a cheerful place. It's well kept up. The blue and white tablecloths are fresh and clean. The jars of *salsa* on the tables are newly filled, the floors are swept, the juke box is lit, the plate-glass storefront windows are shiny. The plates of food are generous. Bottles of ice-cold imported beers are served in frosty glasses and the tortilla basket gets refilled. In short, it's a place you can relax in after a day of hard work.

74

PRICE RANGE: Inexpensive
HOURS: 10:00 A.M.–10:00 P.M. Sun.–Thurs.
        10:00 A.M.–11:00 P.M. Fri.–Sat.
NO RESERVATIONS
BEER AND WINE
NO CREDIT CARDS

Ernie's ★★★

847 Montgomery Street
San Francisco
397–5969

If we were going to spend a major amount of money on dinner in San Francisco, we would go to Ernie's. After our recent visits there, we have come away feeling just the way we should after dropping such solid sums on fleeting pleasures.

Ernie's, with its well-kept-up bordello decor, opened years ago as a Barbary Coast steakhouse. It fast became the most expensive and "touristed" restaurant in San Francisco. It is our distinct impression that Ernie's went through a period of decline in the midsixties and early seventies as it started to take on continental pretensions. Our memory of this restaurant at that time has focused on an unfortunate *Veal Oscar*, an overdone slab of veal topped by pasty white sauce and canned asparagus. Things have changed. With a new, young French chef, Jacky Robert, Ernie's has taken on a new identity as a truly innovative French restaurant in San Francisco.

It is still possible to order a completely mundane meal at Ernie's. The restaurant continues to specialize in showy presentations and flaming carts and baroque service. However, if you are on the lookout for some new-tasting food, this is the one place in town to go.

One meal we were served there began with elegant *Fans of Raw Shitake Mushrooms in a Simple Salad* designed to show off their meaty texture and fruity, earthy flavor. Spectacular! Then we had fresh *Eastern Scallops* that were barely poached, capped with brilliant green kiwi slices, and surrounded, not immersed, in a scallop-flavored butter sauce. For a main course, four of us shared a small *Rolled Roast of Milky White Provimi Veal*, stuffed with Ernie's fresh goose liver pâté and garnished with tiny turnips and carrots. For dessert there were individual *Orange Soufflés* baked in orange halves, light as a feather, moist and alive with the flavor of fresh orange juice. It was a sophisticated, beautifully presented meal, and we were so impressed we returned the following week to sample more from Ernie's new kitchen.

This time we started with a *Pâté of Fresh Leek*, molded together in abstract impressionist layers and splashed with a puree of fresh tomato. The outcome, stunning and austere in the *nouvelle cuisine* manner, wanted more of the taste of leek. However, our next course could not be faulted: *Shaved Slices of Raw Eastern Scallops on a Bed of Watercress* in a dressing of hot olive oil, mustard, and sherry vinegar. If these scallops were a tour de force, the main course, a *Braised Squab* in a harlequinesque pattern of molded vegetables, was a major culinary achievement. A turban of turnips and carrots encased bright green, butter-simmered cabbage and nuggets of dark, juicy, tender squab. This dish is not to be missed. It's up to the standards of a handful of restaurants in France, where it would cost you the price of the plane fare plus twice the amount that Ernie's charges. By contrast, *Noisettes of Lamb* crowned by fresh foie gras tasted a bit leaden, definitely of the old style. For dessert we had a classic *Tarte Tatin* made with buttery, light puff pastry, tart apples, and caramelized sugar.

The wine list at Ernie's is extensive, yet, curiously enough, most of the imported wines come from a single shipper. Ernie's is the only place in town where you can drink '61 Bordeaux at a semireasonable price, but the relatively recent Burgundy list is not so illustrious. California "boutique" wines from the likes of Chateau St. Jean, Joseph Phelps, and Villa Mt. Eden are priced within reason. Corkage is $15.

There's much to explore at Ernie's: a *nouvelle cuisine Sweetbread Dish*, a *Chicken Preparation that Incorporates Purees of Endive and Pear*, and *Baked Tripe with Tomatoes and Carrots*. The menu is exciting if you read it the right way. Stuck in between the filets of beef and noisettes of lamb are dishes of true creativity, indicating that the kitchen is actively moving forward. This marks a real event for San Francisco dining.

PRICE RANGE: Expensive
HOURS: 6:30–11:00 P.M. nightly
RESERVATIONS NECESSARY
FULL BAR
ALL MAJOR CREDIT CARDS

Fat Albert's

1346 Grove Street
(at Rose)
Berkeley
526–2260

How many hamburger places are there in this world with classical music coming from the speakers? Or whose owner, back in the days of more reasonably priced wine, used to select some of the finest wines as a hobby and sell them to hamburger munchers for a dollar over his cost? Fat Albert's is the place to go to have hamburgers with class.

Once you get in (there's almost always a wait at the crowded entrance hall), you'll find Fat Albert's to be a very pleasant restaurant, decorated with Jack London memorabilia, and offering a far more relaxed atmosphere than most hamburger places. There's not even a counter; all the seating is at tables.

The menu doesn't take long to read. There's a *One-third-Pound Hamburger* on a bun, with cheese, bacon strips, and chile offered as extras, or a *Half-Pound Hamburger Steak Dinner*. We prefer the dinner, since it comes with a choice of soup or salad, a fine baked potato with sour cream, and home-baked whole wheat rolls.

The hamburgers are superb—too good, in fact, for the unexceptional buns. The meat is lean, tasty, and charcoal broiled exactly as you want it done. The cheddar cheese isn't melted, but instead served grated in a huge heap. The *Chile*, which can be ordered separately in a bowl, smacks of cumin, but could use a few more hot spices. Our only quarrel is with the *French Fries*, which taste very bland and ordinary.

Albert's desserts, baked next door in an adjoining bakery, are a marvel. Particularly good is the *Apple Pie*, made with tart green apples and with a light hand on the sugar. You can also usually get *New York-Style Cheesecake* and *Pecan*, *Walnut*, or *Chocolate Pie*.

The food is so good, and the atmosphere is so convivial, that you can eat a hamburger at Fat Albert's and walk out thinking you've just had a fine French dinner.

PRICE RANGE: Inexpensive
HOURS: 6:00 A.M.–midnight daily
NO RESERVATIONS
BEER AND HOUSE WINE
NO CREDIT CARDS

Firehouse Station No. 1 Barbecue

501 Clement Street
(near Sixth Street)
San Francisco
386–5882

Firehouse Station No. 1 has a real brick oven with a blazing wood fire. However, once the ribs are done, they are stored in hot metal drawers. Firehouse compensates by cooking the ribs less, which actually improves their *Beef Ribs*. These long, meaty ribs pick up the smoky flavor from the barbecue, yet remain pink and moist. With a side order of excellent *Cole Slaw*, crunchy, fresh cabbage and carrots lightly dressed, without too much mayonnaise, the *Beef Ribs* rank as our favorite barbecue meal.

The *Barbecued Chicken* is overdone and mushy, and the barbecue sauce bland and artificial tasting.

Orders come with a white bread roll and soupy canned baked beans perked up by bits of raw onion. You can get orders of either *Pork* or *Beef Ribs* or the *Sampler Plate*, big enough for three people.

PRICE RANGE: Moderate
HOURS: 11:00 A.M.–10:00 P.M. Mon.–Thurs.
       11:00 A.M.–midnight Fri.
       Noon–midnight Sat.
       2:00–9:00 P.M. Sun.
NO RESERVATIONS
BEER AND WINE
NO CREDIT CARDS

Fourth Street Grill ★

The Fourth Street Grill must have hit a culinary nerve in Berkeley, because the minute this restaurant opened its doors in 1980, it was full and has stayed that way. Some of its instant popularity had to come from the background of its owners. Both worked at Berkeley's redoubtable Chez Panisse for years, so a dedication to high quality and inventiveness was assumed. Perhaps the Fourth Street Grill's location in an uncongested, semi-industrial section of Berkeley, just down the street from Spenger's, also helped. A quick car ride from the center of town gets you there and parking is no problem.

We think the main reason behind the success is that the Fourth Street Grill institutionalizes the way many people shop and cook for themselves these days. It turns out the kind of food you can eat every day and not tire of, the kind of food you would cook for yourself at home, if you had the time to shop every day and if you were clever enough, at prices that it would be hard to beat if you were doing it yourself.

This restaurant gathers together an array of carefully chosen foods and presents them in the most simple and appealing ways. It is always the essence of the food itself that stands out—cleanly, clearly.

The Fourth Street Grill has the sensibility, though not the style (it's much too eclectic), of a French working person's cafe, where the food is unelaborate, affordable, but always treated respectfully. It's the California version of the good French truck stop.

The grill is fueled by mesquite charcoal, which imbues the meat and fish cooked on it with a delicate, smoky flavor. The *Hamburgers*, served plain or with combinations of melted Swiss or cheddar cheese and green chilis, comes on tender egg rolls. The proportion of meat to roll is just right and it comes off the grill at your specified degree of doneness—no small feat when food is cooked over the varying heats of burning charcoal. *Louisiana Hot Sausages*, made from the family recipe of a woman who works in the Oakland Housewive's Market, are enhanced by the grill and come with Fourth Street's exceptional homemade shoestring potatoes, as does a *Top Sirloin Steak Sandwich* that is distinguished by the tenderness of the rare, charcoal-grilled beef. *Marinated Lamb Chops* and *Pork Chops* are attentively grilled and served with the shoestrings for a very reasonable price. Don't except trimmed morsels of "French-cut" lamb chops, but instead, thick loin chops with bone, fat, and sinew all present.

The dinner menu drops the sandwiches of lunch, but is expanded by a pasta of the day or a fish stew, announced on a blackboard where you enter. The grilled fish of the day is impeccably fresh or simply not served. It is almost invariably of high quality. So are the fish stews. A *Basque Stew* includes fresh mussels, clams, rock fish, eastern angler, and locally made chorizo sausage. A *Bretonne Fish Soup* is seasoned with bacon and freshly chopped thyme, and includes potatoes. The *Provençal* version adds fresh crab, fennel, and orange peel. The stocks are rich and the seafood never overcooked. A small wine list typed on the back of the menu includes good, inexpensively priced wines that go well with the food.

Lines form at the Fourth Street Grill during peak meal hours, so it's best to avoid them by coming either early or late. The service may fall apart, but the kitchen is always under control. The owner-chef has an almost religious respect for food, which is reflected in an ardent professionalism.

PRICE RANGE: Moderate
HOURS: 9:30–11:30 A.M. (coffee and rolls), 11:30 A.M.–2:30
P.M. (lunch) Mon.–Sat.
5:30–9:30 P.M. Sun.–Thurs.
5:30–10:00 P.M. Fri.–Sat.
NO RESERVATIONS
BEER AND WINE
NO CREDIT CARDS

Frank's Extra

1421 Stockton Street
San Francisco
788–9429

Frank's Extra, on Stockton above Broadway, may not appeal to most people, but we like it just because it's so stark, fluorescently bright, dominated by a pool table that attracts most of the fourteen year olds in the neighborhood, and borders on unwholesomeness.

An odd assortment of characters hangs out at Frank's, most of whom speak Italian. Frank's reminds us of identical coffee bars in small Italian towns. We like its authenticity. The television is always on and the juke box is usually blaring. Someone's idly playing the pinball machines at all hours. Plastic roses decorate the formica tables. A few imitation grapes hang from an ersatz pergola attached to the ceiling. There's not one concession to beauty in Frank's. The best that can be said is that it's a clean, well-lighted place, although no one runs to empty the ashtrays.

We like to go there late at night, have a small *Combo Pizza*, which is homemade with fresh ingredients, and a *Cappucino*, which must be made by the smiling young woman who works the late-night shift.

It's a paradox that two different operators working the same machine and using the same coffee can turn out two completely different cups of espresso—but it happens, particularly at Frank's. The young woman's coffee may be some of the best in North Beach. The other espresso makers at Frank's are not as good.

We don't recommend Frank's as a main-meal restaurant, but for snack pizza-eating and just plain hanging out, it's a great place. We feel perfectly comfortable there and we never have to worry about running into someone we know.

PRICE RANGE: Inexpensive
HOURS: 9:00 A.M.–2:00 A.M. daily
BEER AND WINE
NO CREDIT CARDS

Gaylord India Restaurant ★★★

Ghirardelli Square
San Francisco
771–8822

On occasion, an enterprising businessman with a novel idea for a restaurant can be so successful that the restaurant spreads across the country or even around the world. Two examples are Trader Vic's, which started here in San Francisco, and Benihana of Tokyo.

The problem is that to reach this position of mass appeal, the quality of the food almost inevitably suffers. The menu can become so standardized that the various cooks aren't creating food, but merely following instructions like a person who fills in numbers for an oil painting. Also, inherent in the idea of mass

81

appeal is a certain blandness; the idea is not so much to please as not to offend.

Remarkably, Gaylord India Restaurant has avoided these pitfalls, and has soared to culinary heights that make it not only the best Indian restaurant in San Francisco, but also one of the best restaurants in the City, period. Even more amazing is the fact that Gaylord is located in Ghirardelli Square, where a ready supply of tourists could provide every incentive for a restaurant owner to forget about the quality of the food and to concentrate on raking in bucks. Repeated visits have shown us that Gaylord has resisted every temptation to compromise on quality.

The original Gaylord began in New Delhi in 1941. The family that owned it then started branches in some of the world's major cities, beginning with Bombay and spreading to London, Hong Kong, Japan, Chicago, and New York. The San Francisco branch opened in 1976. All the restaurants have similar menus, and the chefs were all trained in New Delhi and sent to the various branches.

But this is no assembly-line Indian food. We've eaten twice at Gaylord in New York and several times at the San Francisco location, and our meals here have been consistently the better of the two. The food sparkles with the delicacy and subtlety of the freshest ingredients combined with the finest Indian spices, administered in the glass-enclosed kitchen with a knowing hand.

The restaurant itself is a delight to the eye, with luxurious and comfortable Indian furnishings and a glass-walled view out to the bay. The couches in the waiting area are so pleasant you might not even mind being shunted there for a drink, or often having to wait up to an hour for your table, despite having made reservations. Once at your table, the service is polite and impeccable, but with a touch of the formality that comes so readily to Indians and can sometimes be a bit disconcerting. For such atmosphere and such fine food, the prices are surprisingly low, about half of what you'd pay at most good French restaurants.

While the food can be ordered a la carte, it's best on your first visit to try one of the three complete dinners, which gives you generous samples of several of the dishes, as well as soup, dessert, the varied Indian breads, and condiments. If you go as a large group, consider the experience to be similar to a Chinese restaurant: Order all three complete dinners and several other appetizers and main courses, and pass everything around. One of the three dinners, incidentally, is vegetarian—and you're guaranteed not to walk away from it hungry.

If our experience is duplicated, the very first thing put on your table will be the only disappointment of the evening: The *Mulligatawny Soup*, an invention generations ago of the British who

82

lived in India, tasted for all the world like Campbell's cream of chicken soup. The *Dal Soup* was also disappointing: The chicken broth was so concentrated that it overwhelmed the lentils and seasoning.

But everything from there on ranged from good to great. The *Tandoori Chicken*, for instance, is a classic of its kind. This exquisite Indian dish consists of chicken marinated in yogurt and enough different spices to start a spice store. The chicken is then hung in a *tandoor*, a clay-lined oven with a blazing wooden or charcoal fire, and baked. *Tandoori Chicken* can end up as dry and tasteless as sawdust, but not at Gaylord. Here it is succulent and juicy, smacking of the spicy marinade.

Another outstanding dish is *Sag Gosht*, chunks of boneless lamb cooked with spiced, creamed spinach. The pureed spinach blends into the spicy sauce, providing a creamy contrast of tastes that any French *nouvelle cuisine* chef would have been proud to have invented. Also, don't miss the *Seekh Kebab*. Instead of the usual chunks of lamb and vegetables as in standard shish kebab, the lamb has been ground, mixed with chopped onions, herbs, and spices, and then roasted on skewers.

On the vegetarian side, the dishes with cheese are unusually tasty. The *Navratan Korma*, vegetables with farmer's cheese and nuts in a cream sauce, and the *Mattar Paneer*, cubed farmer's cheese and green peas in a spiced sauce, demonstrate the unique things Indians can do with their bland farmer's cheese, which would be totally uninteresting if you were to taste it alone. Also, the *Kashmiri Pillau*, saffron-flavored rice with fresh peas and cashews, is not to be missed. The delicate saffron scent and the crunchiness of the cashews combine to make the perfectly cooked rice a delight.

The bread at Gaylord to our minds would alone make the trip there worthwhile. The *Poori* (whole-wheat dough that has been deep fried) displayed not a trace of greasiness, but most impressive is the *Onion Kulcha*. This is a puffy, round bread made with yogurt in the batter that is stuffed with onions and then slapped onto the side of an oven to bake. The crisp, puffy bread combined with the pungency of the onions makes a perfect accompaniment to the rest of the dinner.

Indian desserts may seem cloyingly sweet to some, but after a spicy meal, intense sweetness can hit the spot. You probably won't even have room for dessert after eating your way through the astonishingly good meal that came before.

PRICE RANGE: Moderate to expensive
HOURS: 11:30 A.M.–2:00 P.M., 5:00 –11:00 P.M. daily

RESERVATIONS NECESSARY
FULL BAR
AMERICAN EXPRESS. BANKAMERICARD. CARTE BLANCHE.
  DINER'S CLUB. MASTERCARD

Gelato

201 Parnassus Street
(at Stanyon Street)
San Francisco
566–9696

2211 Filbert Street
(at Fillmore Street)
San Francisco
929–8666

Gelato was the first to bring Italian ice cream to the Bay Area, and we can only say that this cultural exchange didn't take place a moment too soon. Gelato's ice cream, made with special Italian machines, tastes like the thickest imaginable, barely frozen cream, sort of a frozen custard, except five times more dense. It's too soft to eat on a cone, so it's paddled into small paper cups—you get a choice of two flavors per small serving—and eaten with a tiny plastic spoon.

The flavors are subtle and delicate at Gelato. We think Vivoli's in Berkeley does a better job with the fresh fruit ice cream; but the rum and liqueur flavors, often teamed with espresso or chocolate, are more intense at Gelato. Try the *Coppa Mista*.

Although there are probably just as many calories in a tiny portion of Gelato's Italian ice cream as there are in large scoops of regular ice cream, your ice cream cravings are satisfied by less. Don't be alarmed by the seemingly miniscule portions.

HOURS: Parnassus Street location: 3:00–10:00 P.M. daily
Filbert Street location: Noon–11:00 P.M. daily

George's Specialties ★★

Angelina Semenoff, proprietor, chef, and natural talent behind George's Specialties, was born in eastern Siberia, emigrated to Shanghai, and now reigns at Balboa and 35th. Since she happens to be Russian, her cooking voice is expressed in blini, borscht, and shashlik, but she's an instinctively creative cook with a missionary zeal for freshness and carefulness in the kitchen.

She alone prepares every plate of food served in her restaurant, so you must be patient. The dishes come very slowly.

Also, you must pretend that the imitation gilt mirrors and ersatz gold-leaf lamps, the formica wall paneling, and vinyl furniture in the neighborhood storefront are made of the real stuff, because her food really belongs in the Winter Palace.

After one smashing meal there, which took no less than three and a half hours to arrive at the table, dish by dish, a diminutive, gray-haired Angelina arrived at the table herself to tell us her cooking philosophy. "I prepare everything myself," she said, "because only I do it perfectly."

It's worth the twenty-minute wait for *Blini*. None we've ever tasted comes close to her small, oval buckwheat pancakes, crisp and buttery on the outside, creamy and yeastily fermented inside, holding their own against the onslaught of sour cream, red salmon roe caviar, smoked salmon, and scallions.

This woman elevates the mundane to the spectacular. Take, for example, the delicately pink Russian dressing on her impeccable, seagreen *Butter Lettuce Salad* garnished with a red slash of tomato—it's ambrosial. Her *Beet Borscht* is thick, snappily sweet and sour, brilliantly maroon with a snowy dab of sour cream, a work of art.

Her *Stroganoff* is an *émincé* of beef—tender shreds, sautéed momentarily and swathed in richly seasoned cream with firm mushroom slices in equal proportion to the meat.

Timursky Shaslyk, described on the menu as "ancient nomad-style cubes of lean young lamb marinated in extra-hot marinade fit for fearless warrior," turns us into a Mongol horde. Beautifully grilled skewers of lamb are rubbed with a dry mixture of herbs and fiery spices to create the best shish kebab dish we've ever tasted. It's served with *plov*, a moist pilaf of brown and white rice, toasted almonds, raisins, and dried apricots.

Her version of *Podjarka*, a still life of eggplant, apple, and zucchini, each dipped in the sheerest of egg batter and deep fried just till the outsides turn golden brown, would make a Japanese tempura artist proud. The vegetables are arranged around excellent-quality veal, sautéed quickly, and finished off with a light sauce.

As a complete dining experience, George's Specialties has a few problems, but the food is unique and is worth any inconvenience. A chef with her talent and dedication should stay close to the fire, and she does.

PRICE RANGE: Moderate to expensive
HOURS: 6:00–9:00 P.M. Tues–Sat.
RESERVATIONS NECESSARY
BEER AND WINE
BANKAMERICARD. DINER'S CLUB. MASTERCARD. VISA

Giramonti ★

655 Redwood Highway
Mill Valley
383–3000

Giramonti is a family-run restaurant hidden away in a redwood office complex off Highway 101. It's Marin County's best bet for Italian food. The dining room is small and homey. A blackboard of daily specials is a sure sign that the kitchen is alive and changing with the seasons. When the congenial, aproned owner greets you at the door, you immediately get a good feeling about this place. Giramonti is a personal restaurant.

Although the food is mainly old standby Italian veal and pasta dishes, it's done so well and the servings are so generous that it all becomes special again. Each dish is done to order and it always tastes fresh and lively. You can sense the presence of an inspired chef's hand in the works. The chef is the wife of the man who greets you at the door, the portly Adriana, a woman who knows how things should taste, obviously from a good deal of tasting.

Rumor has it that Adriana worked the whole counter of Marin Joe's for years, and when she left to open her own restaurant they had to hire three men to replace her. When she emerges from her kitchen during a lull in the ordering, her admirers call out, "Mama, Mama, come over here," and she loves it. Adriana is the life force of the kitchen.

Freshness is the keynote of *Antipasto Italiana*, a platter of paper-thin slices of prosciutto, smoked ham, imported black olives, and marinated artichoke hearts, one of the best antipasto plates around.

Nine pastas are generally offered, and they are all cooked *al dente*. You can taste the sea in *Linguine with Baby Clams*, delicately seasoned with clam broth, parsley, garlic, and the barest hint of cream, and garnished with juicy steamed clams in their shells. You could not hope for a brighter, cleaner-tasting dish. *Tortellini Adriana* does justice to the woman who created it. Tender rounds of homemade pasta are stuffed with a spicy mixture of veal, ham, and cheese, and served in a light cream sauce brightly flecked with peas and bits of prosciutto.

Another smashing dish is the fresh *Eastern Mussels*, steamed just until they open to release their liquor into a wine, herb, and fresh tomato sauce. *Caciucco*, a hearty fish stew, uses the same broth as a means of gently simmering clams and thick filets of petrale and snapper, always impeccably fresh.

Veal Adriana, fork-tender scallops of white Provimi veal, is slathered with a delicious mixture of mustard and cream. And an equally hugh portion of *Veal Scallopini* gets a trencherman's serving of fresh mushrooms and an understated sauce of wine and tomato. There's no skimping on the capers in *Adriana's Veal Piccata*. It's as good as any we've tasted.

We should add that the service, watched over by Adriana's husband, is attentive, efficient, and better than in many restaurants that are twice as expensive. Giramonti makes you feel like a guest rather than a customer. You get the feeling that the staff gets as much pleasure from the experience as you do. You become part of Adriana's family.

PRICE RANGE: Moderate
HOURS: 5:00–10:00 P.M. Wed.–Sun.
RESERVATIONS RECOMMENDED
BEER AND WINE
MASTERCARD, VISA

Golden Eagle

729 Webster Street
(at 8th Street)
Oakland
465—4866

It's easy to miss Oakland's Chinatown. It's small—only a couple of blocks long and a few blocks wide—and surrounded by the redevelopment area on the southeastern outskirts of downtown Oakland. It hardly seems like a neighborhood, but it offers, on a small scale, the culinary advantages of San Francisco's Chinatown. There you can buy the best fresh ducks, squabs, and chickens at reasonable prices, as well as fresh produce like lichee nuts and water chestnuts, which are hard to find elsewhere. In small, noisy shops you can choose a freshly caught rock fish with clear, shiny eyes and get it fileted to order, or live crabs in season, bay shrimp, smelts, and all sorts of shell fish. That's why I like to eat at Chinatown restaurants. They take advantage of these excellent raw materials and pass on the inexpensive prices to their patrons.

The Golden Eagle is one of several similar-looking establishments on Webster Street that have given me pleasure over the years. The kitchen is particularly skillful with seafood and soups. The deep-fried foods are crisp and not greasy and the Cantonese sauces have character. Because it's frequented by Chinese, the Eagle offers dishes that westerners don't often eat.

There are several things that distinguish the Golden Eagle from our average Bay Area Cantonese restaurant. The cornstarchy blandness that characterizes so many Cantonese sauces here is missing. Some of the dishes—particularly a marvelous *Squid in Black Bean Sauce*—are actually hot. The squid is unusually fresh tasting and tender, the green peppers and onions crisp, and the black bean sauce as spicy and fragrant as you can get it in any northern Chinese restaurant.

Perhaps the Golden Eagle's masterpiece is *Braised Oysters* cooked with fresh ginger and scallions. In most kinds of dishes, Pacific oysters are a dismal second to the varieties that come from the East. But this is different: The thicker, meatier Pacific oysters soak up the sauce, and seem made for the ginger that accompanies it. The Golden Eagle prepares it beautifully, gently braising the oysters so that they come out firm and juicy.

No matter what you think of *Won Ton Soup* at other restaurants, don't miss it at the Golden Eagle. Big, plump, tender won tons stuffed with ground pork put the competition to shame. So does the hearty broth, and the wide variety of meats, vegetables, and fish you can get in the soup. Our favorite is *Beef*: The thin, tender slices of beef are accompanied by oyster sauce and perfectly cooked Chinese greens.

PRICE RANGE: Inexpensive
HOURS: 11:00 A.M.–10:00 P.M. daily
RESERVATIONS RECOMMENDED
BEER AND WINE
BANKAMERICARD, MASTERCARD

Golden Turtle ★

308 Fifth Avenue
(near Clement Street)
San Francisco
221–5285

We bring our meat-and-potato eating friends to the Golden Turtle because this Vietnamese restaurant specializes in grilled meats and huge portions. Yet the prices remain amazingly low.

The Golden Turtle is a typical neighborhood storefront restaurant, but more than usual has been done to make it feel intimate. There's carpeting and soft lighting, and the dining area is broken up by a raised platform surrounded by a railing and covered by a decorative thatched roof—sort of a poor man's Trader Vic's. The difference is that the family who runs the Golden Turtle is friendly and gracious. Coziness and harmony pervade.

Such universally served dishes as *Imperial Rolls* get special treatment here. They're sliced into rounds and arranged on a bed of red leaf lettuce and cold rice noodles and served with a piquant, clear dipping sauce—a hot hors d'oeuvre and salad combined. *Vietnamese Pork Kebabs*, grilled over charcoal, get the same lavish treatment.

The Vietnamese technique of marinating thin slices of meat and cooking them over charcoal works to fine effect on *Beef Seasoned with Lemon Grass, Vinegar, and Hot Peppers*. They, too, are served on fresh lettuce that is meant to be eaten, not just served as a garnish. You increasingly appreciate the combination of cold, leafy vegetables with the hot, rich meats as you dip them together in the clear, spicy sauce served with practically everything. Our favorite grilled item is *Beef Imperial*, rolls of marinated beef stuffed with lardoons of pork fat and garnished with chopped, roasted peanuts.

We also always order the *Saigon Fried Chicken*, thick pieces of boned, white meat pan fried in butter, hot red pepper oil, and delicate fish sauce. The result is a glistening, amber-colored breast with the velvety texture of tender filet of beef.

All the dishes at Golden Turtle are extraordinarily rich. The shells of seasonal *Pan-Fried Crab*, sautéed and then steeped in lobster sauce seasoned with garlic and fresh ginger, become brittle and chewable as they absorb all the cooking liquids. The tomalley, the soft, yellow part of the crab that too often gets discarded, is sautéed separately with chopped scallions and pieces of fresh ginger, and then is replaced under the crab shell. This is one of the best crab preparations we have ever tasted.

The stir-fries, like *Stuffed Chicken in Mushrooms*, really a mixture of black mushrooms, straw mushrooms, and button mushrooms teamed with big chunks of chicken in a clear, satiny sauce, have unusual flavors and unthickened sauces. They are notably clean tasting.

Every dish we have sampled at Golden Turtle has been made with exquisitely fresh ingredients and exotic spices, but we always end up ordering from the list of Vietnamese grilled meats at the front of the menu. The tender, delicate rolls and kebabs make those huge slabs of unseasoned American steak seem pretty boring.

PRICE RANGE: Inexpensive
HOURS: 5:00–10:30 P.M. Tues.–Fri.
       11:00 A.M.–11:00 P.M. Sat.–Sun.
NO RESERVATIONS
BEER AND WINE
MASTERCARD, VISA

Great American
Meat & Potatoes ★

5305 College Avenue
Oakland
655–8780

The Bay Area in recent years has seen a host of new restaurants started up by young people who are intent on creating an honest food experience: nothing frozen, nothing overcooked, breads home baked or the best available sourdough, and all ingredients as fresh as possible. Some of these call themselves French restaurants, but inevitably almost all at least lean toward French cuisine for ideas.

Great American Meat & Potatoes Restaurant has taken this concept of an honest food experience and applied it to something unique: American food. You remember American food, don't you? It's the stuff that brings back dim but pleasant memories of eating at Grandma's house on Sunday night, and more recent but stomach-wrenching memories of being caught on a highway in the Central Valley at dinnertime.

If you take away the Wonder Bread and the canned soups and vegetables and start preparing things from scratch, what is American food like? At Great American Meat & Potatoes, the answer is wonderful. Imagine getting a real *Turkey Dinner* on Sunday nights, with the meat tender and juicy, and the gravy freshly made from giblets and pan drippings, and the dressing from apples and sausages. Imagine sitting down any night and having put in front of you a basket of light and fluffy *Biscuits* scented with rosemary, just out of the oven. Imagine real *Tomato Soup*, with huge chunks of fresh tomatoes in a thick, spicy broth, or desserts like *Apple Brown Betty*. These are the sorts of things that put Great American Meat & Potatoes leagues above any other American restaurant in the Bay Area.

Several of the nightly dinners are first rate. The *Lamb Chops* are tender and juicy, and done just as ordered (now if only they'd replace that sugary mint jelly with a made-from-scratch, fresh mint sauce . . .). The *Ham Steak* grilled in butter with "red-eye" gravy is a thick, moist, tender piece of meat beautifully smoked (although the pineapple slices on top taste canned). The catch of the day is a *Fish Filet* pan fried in butter and not the least overcooked. The *Fresh Spinach Salad* with a tangy vinaigrette dressing is perfect for those who think that otherwise American food would be too leaden to survive the evening. Our only quarrel is with the *Fried Chicken*, which clearly is on the greasy side.

Besides the regular menu, every night there are specials, including *Chicken 'n' Dumplings* on Wednesday, *Corned Beef and Cabbage* on Friday, and the classic *Turkey Dinner* on Sunday. Everything is moderately priced and served by friendly, young waiters and waitresses in an extremely pleasant setting.

PRICE RANGE: Moderate
HOURS: 5:00–10:00 P.M. daily
RESERVATIONS FOR FIVE OR MORE
BEER AND WINE
MASTERCARD, VISA

Greens at Fort Mason ★★

Building A of Fort Mason
(nearest the Marina)
San Francisco
771–6222

For eleven summers now the Tassajara Zen Mountain Center has been running a unique spa in an isolated corner of the Carmel Valley. For a moderate fee, guests are treated to natural hot springs, rustic open-air cabins, and three delightful vegetarian meals a day. The beautiful natural setting, relaxing baths, simple, aesthetic accommodations, and gentle and efficient staff are all part of the appeal, but everyone raves about the food. Most of it is grown in lovingly cared-for gardens in composted soil around the compound, augmented by exceptional breads, pastries, tofu, and dairy products.

The breads gained such a following that the Tassajara Bread Bakery, 1000 Cole at Parnassus, was opened four years ago and now sells hundreds of loaves a day. This same community opened a store on Page and Laguna that sells fresh produce grown at the Green Gulch Farm in Marin.

So, it was no surprise that a local restaurant would develop out of all this food activity. It could use the breads and pastries from the bakery, the fresh produce from the Zen farm, and draw on the talent and experience of the Tassajara Mountain Center dining room. Yet, when we walked into Greens at Fort Mason, we were flabbergasted. The Zen community's new restaurant is breathtaking.

The restaurant is located in a high-ceilinged warehouse. It has exposed steel beams and a bank of floor-to-ceiling windows that look out onto the Marina, the bay, and the Golden Gate Bridge. The room is painted white and brightened by the oil paintings of New York artist Edward Avedisian.

The food boasts the same combination of simplicity and style that distinguishes the decor. For lunch, you order a la carte from a menu that features many of Tassajara's specialties. For dinner, while you get no choice, but order a price-fixed meal, the dinner menus are constantly changing.

Many people envision vegetarian food as a bunch of sliced vegetables thrown into a wok with some oil and soy sauce, and served with brown rice. This is about as far from Greens as you can imagine. Greens, whose chefs have been heavily influenced by Berkeley's Chez Panisse, couples innovation with extensive research into French country cooking to produce a cuisine so unique you won't believe what you're eating. Combine this food and the magnificent setting with some of the best breads and pastries in town—and a beautifully chosen, low-priced wine list—and you'll understand why Greens is jammed day after day.

Here's a typical lunch at Greens: On one occasion we sampled a cup of fresh-tasting *Sorrel and New Potato Soup*; a *Tostada*, immersed in creamy, spicy black beans, guacamole, melted cheese, lettuce, and tomatoes; a plate of superb homemade *Egg Noodles*, lightly tossed in freshly grated Parmesan cheese and a little cream; a sandwich called *Pan Bagnat*, a coarse dice of cucumbers, feta cheese, tomatoes, and peppers tossed in olive oil and herbs on a grilled egg roll; and *Brochettes of Marinated Tofu, Mushrooms, Tomatoes, and Peppers* skewered and cooked over mesquite charcoal and served with chewy, short-grained brown rice seasoned with herb butter.

The notion of cooking vegetables and tofu over charcoal represents a breakthrough in vegetarian cooking that is just beginning to be explored at Greens. The hot, aromatic fire cooks food quickly, sears in the juices, and adds a distinctive flavor of its own. Practically any vegetable is enhanced by this method of cooking.

The salads at Greens, needless to say, are superb. *Spinach Salad* is tossed in hot olive oil and sherry vinegar, with Greek olives, red onion, feta cheese, and croutons made from homemade baguettes. Even the *Dinner Salad*, often featuring bitter lettuces and lightly tossed with a nut oil and vinegar, are a revelation. The pastries are elegant, and improving all the time. The chefs are learning the secret of baking with a light hand on the sugar, one thing that distinguishes pastries in France from the overly sweet concoctions found in much of the United States.

Whether you go for lunch, or for the beautifully served five-course dinner, you'll find dining at Greens unique and satisfying. There isn't another restaurant in San Francisco that serves such fresh, innovative food at reasonable prices in so striking an atmosphere.

PRICE RANGE: Moderate
HOURS: 11:30 A.M.–2:30 P.M. (lunch), 2:30–4:30 P.M. (drinks and pastries) Tues.–Sat.
       Dinner seatings 6:30, 7:00, and 7:30 P.M. Fri.–Sat.
RESERVATIONS RECOMMENDED FOR LUNCH, REQUIRED FOR DINNER
WINE
MASTERCARD, VISA

Hahn's Hibachi

2121 Clement Street
San Francisco
221–4246

Korean restaurants, which proliferate in Los Angeles, have always been a rarity in San Francisco. Their absence hasn't generally been mourned: Korean food, at least in these parts, can be pretty bland and uninteresting.

A section of the menu at Hahn's Hibachi devoted to *Korean-Style Stew* definitively overcomes this problem. The three stews— *Fish*, *Beef with Bean Cake*, and *Pork with Kimchee* (Korean pickled cabbage)—are done in a broth zinging with hot chili oil. Spicy hot soups can often pose a problem, because the chili oil overwhelms the other tastes. At Hahn's the proportion of seasonings is just right, and the meat and crispy vegetables retain their flavors.

Hahn's menu also features several other interesting Korean dishes, including *Squid* and two different preparations of *Octopus*, but stay away from the so-called *Korean Bar-B-Q Dinners*. On your table is not a charcoal hibachi at all, but a gas burner. The *"Barbecued" Chicken* we had turned out to be marinated chicken sautéed with vegetables—and cooking it at the table couldn't salvage a basically uninteresting dish.

94

PRICE RANGE: Moderate
HOURS: Noon–10:00 P.M. daily
RESERVATIONS NOT NEEDED
BEER AND WINE
AMERICAN EXPRESS, MASTERCARD, VISA

Hamburger Mary's Organic Grill

1582 Folsom Street
San Francisco
626–5767

A fifteen-year-old cousin flew up from Orange County for the weekend, and we could see he was going into culture shock after spending two days dogging our tracks. So as a finale to his initiation, we took him to Hamburger Mary's.

We were starving after tennis on a Sunday afternoon. We couldn't muster any enthusiasm for a Chinese tea lunch or a Mongolian hot pot—the poor cousin had eaten so many exotic meals in his short stay that what he really wanted was a plain old hamburger. We drove over to Folsom Street, signed onto Hamburger Mary's waiting list, and proceeded to the bar area, where a punk, leather-attired bartender, dressed for Sunday in his chains, was turning out festive-looking Mexican resort drinks. Pounding disco music nearly rocked the glasses off the tables. The place was hopping.

My cousin could barely keep his eyes in his head. A "presence" in a flowing, floor-length dress, long curly hair, and a mustache was chatting with a man in tight blue jeans. A couple of nine- and ten-year-olds were eating the pineapple off their dad's *piña colada* and playing the pin ball machines while he was reading the paper. Seven mean-looking guys, some in black leather pants, others in black leather jackets, were discussing the opera. Two girls with green and pink hair were joined by a guy with green and pink hair, and there we were in tennis shorts.

"I don't think we belong here," said the cousin.

"Don't be silly," we said. "You don't *have* to dress to eat here." We gave him some fresh-squeezed orange juice to sip while we waited. What he really wanted was the delicious, coconut-milky *Piña Colada* we were drinking.

"I've never seen anything like it," he said, looking around at the mismatched tables and chairs, the crazy artifacts haphazardly attached to the walls and ceiling, and the mélange of customers.

95

"You're kidding," we said, forgetting that he had lived his fifteen years in Huntington Beach, while we had lived our years in Berkeley and San Francisco.

The food at Hamburger Mary's fits nicely into the ambience, a curious mixture of hamburgers and bean sprouts, chile, and vegetarian sandwiches.

Our waiter, who did not write down our order, did fairly well in bringing us the right food. The cousin wanted a hamburger without anything on it., i.e., the *Plain Mary Burger*. When he pulled out the lettuce and tomato and scraped off the whole-wheat toast it came on, he had pretty much what he had requested. The *Grilled Onions* we asked for with the *Meaty Mushroom Burger* came much later. Despite the raw milk cheddar cheese and the mushrooms and onions, the sandwich was bland, perhaps because the hamburger itself was so small. We felt the same way about the *Maryburger with Cheese*. Potato chips, black olives, alfalfa sprouts, and pickled peppers come with all the sandwiches.

A side order of *Home Fries* was limp, cold, and tasteless, despite the onions and spices with which they were supposedly fried. Mary's homemade *Zippy Beef Chile* was actually mildly seasoned but perked up by raw chopped onions and grated cheese sprinkled on top. Heavy on the beans, it's the best dish we've had at Mary's.

Hamburger Mary's also serves reasonably priced breakfasts all day and night and a variety of sandwiches, such as *Tuna Salad*, *Grilled Cheese and Mushrooms*, and *Ham and Cheese*, for around $3.50.

The food is not bad here, just indifferent. We like the zany atmosphere and it's always open, though it may not appeal to uninitiated fifteen year olds or anyone else, for that matter, from out of town.

PRICE RANGE: Inexpensive to moderate
HOURS: 10:00 A.M.–1:45 A.M. daily
NO RESERVATIONS
FULL BAR
MASTERCARD, VISA

Hana ★★

408 Irving Street
(between 5th and 6th Avenues)
San Francisco
665–3952

Hana, a little neighborhood restaurant near the University of California Medical Center, serves the best informal, inexpensive Japanese food in the city. This may seem like a crazy claim in a city that must support at least fifty similar Japanese restaurants, but there's something special about the way food tastes at Hana. Hana's versions of the most often served Japanese dishes are more succulent, substantial, and flavorful than any we've tasted.

Take, for example, *Fried Oysters*, so often soggy or tough, or mealy or overbattered. The oysters at Hana are always meltingly tender, barely grazed with a crumbly batter, and deep fried in very hot oil until they're just firm. The portion is huge for the small price, which includes a bowl of miso broth, a tiny pile of pickled cabbage, and a western salad transformed by the addition of cold glass noodles and a delicate sweet-and-sour miso dressing.

Chicken Teriyaki brings a whole chicken breast with wing attached, basted in the lightest of teriyaki sauces, sprinkled with toasted sesame seeds, and as tender and juicy as any chicken can be. The *Tempura* is done with the same delicacy. The batter is thinly applied and the frying done in the cleanest of oils at high temperatures, so the shrimp and vegetables stay crisp but are thoroughly heated. *Gyoza*, Japanese-style potstickers, in which a crinkly noodle is folded around a spicy pork filling, have the same combination of textural lightness but intense flavor.

Even *Sashimi*, served here at half the price charged at most other restaurants, has never been the slightest bit off. Similarly, impeccably fresh seafood is the highlight of Hana's *Yosenabe,* a perfectly timed stew of clams, shrimp, oysters, chicken, and vegetables in a ginger and miso broth. Every dish we've eaten at Hana reflects the kitchen's care and integrity. In a restaurant that charges rock-bottom prices, this is a small miracle.

Here's the rub. The restaurant is tiny. The tables are packed together. The kitchen is only separated from the dining area by a flimsy screen. There's not much ventilation, it's very noisy, and you almost always have to wait to get in, most of the time outside on the street. To match the heroic performance of the kitchen, two patient, efficient Japanese women who wait on the tables do twenty things at one time and keep the tables turning over. Because of them you never have to wait too long for a table, and once you have one you are never rushed. Hana is that rare restaurant that has succeeded because it's so good, yet refuses to raise prices, and consistently maintains the unsurpassed quality of its food.

PRICE RANGE: Inexpensive
HOURS: 11:30 A.M.–2:00 P.M. Mon.–Fri.
       5:00–9:00 P.M. Mon.–Sat.
NO RESERVATIONS
BEER AND WINE
NO CREDIT CARDS

Happy 6 Chinese Mandarin Restaurant

104 Maze Road
(Route 132 near Freeway 99)
Modesto
209/524–9029

A good Chinese restaurant in the Central Valley? Good even by San Francisco standards? What have we been drinking? Nothing but Tsing-tao beer, thank you.

Those of you passing through the Central Valley on the way to the mountains or Los Angeles will find Happy 6 an oasis of good eating amidst a sea of greasy hamburger joints. How did it happen? It seems that one branch of a large Chinese family got jobs in Modesto and moved there from New York. The rest of the family, who were running a New York Chinese restaurant, decided to follow. They found what looks for all the world like an abandoned Denny's (the old salad bar is still there, complete with the plastic "sneeze guard" over it), and Happy 6 was born.

The menu goes on for seven pages, and what a menu it is. There are twenty-one chicken and seven duck dishes alone, plus four different preparations of bean curd. Many of the dishes are so unusual they appear to have been invented by Happy 6. Take, for instance, the *Fung Wong Chicken*. Pieces of boned and skinned chicken breast are rolled around slices of smoky ham and then deep fried, and served with a host of crispy Chinese vegetables in a tangy, light sauce. The frying is perfect—the food stays crisp and greaseless on the outside and tender and juicy on the inside. Even more remarkable is the sauce. Happy 6 appears to use little or no cornstarch—an ingredient that bedevils otherwise good dishes at all too many Chinese restaurants—and as a result the sauces come out light and delicate.

When you see things on the menu like a host of extraordinary barbequed lamb dishes, *Fried Duck with Mandarin Orange Sauce*, and some unusual Szechuanese noodle preparations, you'll wish you had come with a large group. Being able to look forward to a great meal in the Central Valley during a long drive can be a real treat.

PRICE RANGE: Inexpensive
HOURS: 11:00 A.M.–9:00 P.M. Sun.–Thurs.
       11:00 A.M.–10:00 P.M. Fri.–Sat.
NO RESERVATIONS
BEER AND WINE
MASTERCARD, VISA

Hayes Street Grill ★★

324 Hayes Street
(near Franklin)
San Francisco
863–5545

In retrospect, it seems like such an obvious idea: Instead of the Fisherman's Wharf-type restaurants, where much of the fish is often frozen and served overcooked, start a San Francisco fish restaurant that offers *only* fresh fish properly prepared, whose menu changes depending on the catch of the day. Yet, until Hayes Street Grill opened in April 1979, it was strictly "let the eater beware" at San Francisco fish houses. Would the fish truly be fresh? Would the sauces ruin it? Would it come to the table overcooked or dried out? At Hayes Street Grill, you know the answers before you walk in. The fish is always fresh, supplied by the best fish purveyor in the Bay Area. (The other side of the coin, of course, is that on some days, particularly in winter, there might only be a couple of kinds of fish on the menu.) The sauces are served on the side, so you don't have to eat them if you don't like them. Finally, the fish, at least in my experience, has never once been the least bit overcooked.

For main courses, Hayes Street Grill is a formula restaurant, but the formula works. Cook everything on charcoal, but not ordinary charcoal; instead, the fuel is mesquite, which burns hotter and cleaner. Offer grilled steak, hamburger, chicken, and homemade sausage for those who don't want fish, but make sure the meats are of the highest quality, too. Serve *French Fries* done in the real French style—blanched in oil first, then cooled, then cooked rapidly in very hot oil so they emerge crisp and greaseless.

There is no formula for appetizers and desserts, just good cooking, and to my mind these often overshadow the main course. If the *Cold Calamari Salad* is offered, don't miss it. I maintain that squid is the real test of a restaurant, and Hayes Street passes with flying colors, producing the tenderest, most beautifully seasoned calamari imaginable. The daily *Composed Salad* is also excellent, with the marinated vegetables smacking of expertly applied herbs and spices. The desserts come from a Berkeley pastry chef and are uniformly good, with the rum-soaked cakes heading the pack.

My only quarrel with Hayes Street involves some of the sauces, which are too routine and too heavy for the superb, delicate fish—fish that needs nothing more on it than a little lemon juice to make a marvelous meal. You get your choice of herb-shallot butter, tartar sauce, *beurre blanc*, or béarnaise sauce, and I've found the herb-shallot butter to be the most satisfying. There are also special sauces. On one visit *Scallops Brochette* were ordered with a simple and delicate sauce containing garlic and fresh basil, offered when fresh basil is in season.

Mercifully, Hayes Street takes reservations, so you don't have to put up with long lines, like at many other popular fish houses. But you must reserve several days in advance, particularly for opera or symphony nights at the nearby Civic Center. The wine list is unusually good, with lots of attention obviously being paid to coming up with low-priced wines of high quality. This alone, contrasted to the Almaden/Paul Masson-type lists of many other fish restaurants, makes a visit to Hayes Street worthwhile. The restaurant has been carefully decorated in an old San Francisco style, and the service is generally relaxed and attentive.

PRICE RANGE: Moderate
HOURS: 11:30 A.M.–10:00 P.M. Mon.–Fri.
　　　　6:00–10:00 P.M. Sat.
RESERVATIONS NECESSARY
BEER AND WINE
MASTERCARD, VISA

Hoffman's Grill

619 Market Street
San Francisco
421–1467

Hoffman's Grill is literally a San Francisco landmark. This bustling no-nonsense restaurant completely fills its own compact ninety-year-old building. There was some talk about tearing Hoffman's down to make way for an office building, but the Financial District rallied behind one of its favorite watering holes and lunch spots, and the Grill received historical landmark status.

If only the food were as wonderful as the original interior, constructed of old, dark wood; black and white ceramic tiles; mirrors; wainscoting; and high, pressed ceilings. But it's always fun to eat lunch there on the blue-and-white-checked tablecloths amidst the bustle of business lunch.

The menu is printed every day, but only five or six daily specials at the top of the menu change. On Tuesday, it's the traditional *Braised Short Ribs*. On Thursday, *Corned Beef and Cabbage* and maybe a spicy German-style *Rabbit Stew* if you're lucky, Hoffman's best dish. Other good bets are *Yankee Pot Roast*, *Roast Stuffed Filet of Pork*, and a tasty *London Broil* at very cheap prices. Hamburgers and steaks are broiled over real charcoal. We like to order from the sausage section—*Club Sausages* or *Polish Sausages*, accompanied by sweet-and-sour cabbage and boiled potatoes. The bread is always fresh, crusty, San Francisco sourdough served with lots of chilled butter. Salads are made with head lettuce, but the blue cheese dressing is surprisingly good. The vegetables always taste canned. Skip the gooey *Cheesecake* for dessert, and have Hoffman's aromatic coffee instead.

The advantage of old-style Financial District restaurants like Hoffman's is that you can get a hearty, honest meal for a reasonable price in a downright festive atmosphere. Hoffman's is one of the handful of restaurants that carry on San Francisco's original style and spirit.

PRICE RANGE: Moderate
HOURS: 11:00 A.M.–8:00 P.M. Mon.–Fri.
RESERVATIONS FOR GROUPS OF FOUR OR MORE
FULL BAR
MASTERCARD. VISA

Hog Heaven

770 Stanyan Street
San Francisco
668–2038

The new Hog Heaven is the Maxim's of rib places. It's a spacious, professionally decorated restaurant full of pig posters and a big stuffed pig that greets you at the door. No expense has been spared—no vinyl and formica here. Hog Heaven is sheer luxury when it comes to rib places. Calvin Trillin would hate it.

The food is inspired by Memphis-style barbecue and the oven is almost a room-sized red brick structure fueled by hickory wood and mesquite charcoal. The meats are slowly smoked for up to ten hours on cast-iron shelves, but then they are put into metal heating units until they are served, which can be much later.

The *Taster Plate* includes long-cooked *Barbecued Pork Shoulder* that has fallen into juicy shreds, a comparatively lean and mild *Link Sausage*, a moist *Chicken Breast*, and a small slab of *Pork Ribs*. The meats have an aromatic hickory-smoke flavor unmuffled by an intentionally light barbecue sauce. There's nothing distinctive about the sauce, but it doesn't taste artificial, either—no liquid smoke.

We especially like a square of crumbly, warm *Corn Bread*, served with butter and a crock of molasses; also, darkened *Baked Beans* made from scratch and put to simmer in the barbecue oven. The *Cole Slaw*, however, is dry. Raw cabbage needs more than a few drops of lemon. The *Pecan Pie* is mostly jelly with a few pecans on the top, and the *Lemonade* tastes like a mix.

For in-house barbecue eating, Hog Heaven is the place to go. The food and decor represent the lighter side of barbecue.

PRICE RANGE: Moderate
HOURS: 11:00 A.M.–10:00 P.M. daily
NO RESERVATIONS
BEER AND WINE
MASTERCARD, VISA

Hunan

924 Sansome Street
San Francisco
956–7727

853 Kearny Street
San Francisco
397–8718

A few years back, the *New Yorker* magazine's "Talk of the Town" section called the Hunan "the best Chinese restaurant in the world." A couple of days later, Herb Caen, in his *San Francisco Chronicle* column, quoted a Chinese-American journalist here as saying that not only was the Hunan not the best Chinese restaurant in the world, it wasn't even the best Chinese restaurant in its block!

Since then, a new Hunan has opened; it's the *only* Chinese restaurant in its block. But the controversy continues, affecting even the authors of this book. While we almost always readily agree on the quality of a meal we've eaten, we're hopelessly split on this one. One thing we can agree on: If you love arguing about a dinner, you're going to love eating at the Hunan.

The old Hunan on Kearny Street is a typical, hole-in-the-wall Chinese restaurant that accommodates what seems to be an insatiable demand for its chili-pepper-laced dishes. The new Hunan on Sansome is a huge, warehouselike room, featuring a red banner hung from the ceiling announcing that the restaurant uses no MSG in its food.

To summarize succinctly on the negative side, the Hunan offers to my taste buds a truly bad Chinese meal. The absence of any sort of finesse in the cooking is disguised by dosing every dish with ground-up red chili peppers. With your eyes closed, you can't tell which meat or vegetables you're eating; you're simply overwhelmed with the heat of the chili peppers. Khan Toke and Chin Szchawn, two Asian restaurants I like very much, also cook stingingly hot food, but a bouquet of other tastes comes through besides the chili peppers. At the Hunan, there are no other tastes. During the last meal I had there, with six people, no one was able to detect even a hint of garlic or ginger, two staples of Hunanese cooking.

Four of the dishes we ordered—*Smoked Ham*, *Smoked Chicken*, *Hot-and-Sour Beef*, and *Braised Fish Balls*—came with exactly the same three vegetables: green peppers, bamboo shoots, and carrots. The *Beef* also included onions, but they were almost raw. The sauces on all four tasted identical, too. The *Ham* and *Chicken* were so overwhelmed by an acrid smoke taste that you couldn't tell the two meats apart. Finally, the *Fish Balls* tasted heavily floured.

The *Dumplings* came off no better: The filling was tasteless, the wrapping too thick, and the sauce overwhelmed by chili peppers. The *Shredded Chicken with Cucumber Strips* was passable, but not done with nearly the delicacy as at Chin Szchawn. Only the crispy, deep-fried *Green Onion Cake* proved first rate, hardly enough compensation for the rest of the meal.

Remember, though, judging from the crowds here, I'm in the distinct minority.

PRICE RANGE: Inexpensive to moderate
HOURS: Sansome Street location: 11:30 A.M.–9:30 P.M.
       Mon.–Fri.
       Kearny Street location: 11:30 A.M.–9:30 P.M. Tues.–Sat.
RESERVATIONS NECESSARY
FULL BAR
AMERCIAN EXPRESS, MASTERCARD, VISA

Ichigo

3232 Scott Street
(between Lombard and Chestnut)
San Francisco
441–8155

Some restaurants—Ichigo being a prime example—have menus so dull it's hard to get yourself to walk in. Sukiyaki, tempura, sashimi, teriyaki—the chop suey and chow mein of Japanese restaurants. In this case, forget the menu and try it anyway. The cooking turns out to be so innovative that the most ordinary-sounding dishes spark interest when you take the first bite.

You know you're in an unusual place as soon as the first course, the *Miso Soup*, comes to the table. What you get is not the usual soy-bean-paste broth, but a rich, thick soup filled with carrots, onions, and radish leaves—a sort of Japanese minestrone. The food is dotted with surprises like this. The *Yakitori*, the

Japanese version of shish kebab, which is usually chicken and beef, this time is chicken and chicken livers, a much more logical combination. Many of the sauces smack of sake (Japanese rice wine). The *Tempura* tastes almost like it was pan fried in butter (we prefer it crispier). And the usual ice cream for dessert this time is *Fried Ice Cream*, actually dipped in tempura batter and deep fried! Somehow, it still manages to stay cold in the center.

If you order anything that is barbecued, you'll do well at Ichigo, where the chef has a deft hand at charcoal grilling. The *Salmon*, for instance, remains rare and juicy in the center. Particularly appealing is the *Rib Steak Misoyaki*, a steak marinated in soybean paste and sake, then grilled to medium-rare perfection, and served with a rich, black soybean-based sauce. You can also get *Chicken*, *Salmon*, and *Mahi-Mahi* done misoyaki style.

Ichigo not long ago moved to the Marina from its former location near the Cannery. The restaurant is tastefully decorated in Japanese style, with lots of light wood, several small rooms with low tables, and an illuminated pond and rock garden out back.

PRICE RANGE: Inexpensive to moderate
HOURS: 5:00 P.M.–midnight daily
RESERVATIONS ACCEPTED
BEER AND WINE
MASTERCARD, VISA

Il Pirata

2007 16th Street
(near Potrero)
San Francisco
626–1845

Good main courses at a family-style southern Italian restaurant? It seems almost a contradicton in terms, as anyone who has tried some of these restaurants in North Beach knows. But Il Pirata— where you can get an astonishingly large dinner of soup, salad, antipasto, pasta, entree with vegetable, dessert, and coffee for around $10—offers several main courses of surprisingly high quality.

The small menu features mainly chicken and veal dishes. The veal is quite decent, white and tender, though hardly as delicate as you'd expect at a much fancier (and considerably more expensive) French or northern Italian restaurant. Our favorite is the *Chicken Mattone*—chicken that has been seared in olive oil under a very high heat to get the skin crackling crisp, then baked in a garlic and wine sauce. The garlic permeates both the meat and the sauce, and the sauce itself is light and flavorful, making you want to reach immediately for the good sourdough bread.

The rest of the dinner (the main course alone can be ordered for $2 less) doesn't live up to the entree, although the soup, served in a big tureen, can be quite good. But at prices like this, you'll hardly feel taken. Il Pirata can also be a lot of fun. When it's someone's birthday, out go the lights in the whole restaurant, on goes the music, and in comes a candle—sticking in a scoop of ice cream.

PRICE RANGE: Inexpensive to moderate
HOURS: 11:30 A.M.–2:00 P.M. Tues.–Fri.
       5:30–10:00 P.M. Wed.–Fri.
       4:30–10:00 P.M. Sat.–Sun.
RESERVATIONS ACCEPTED
FULL BAR
MASTERCARD, VISA

Ino Sushi

1620 Webster Street
San Francisco
922–3121

Ino Sushi, near the Japantown complex, is small and peaceful. The eight-seat sushi bar, a few tables, and the chairs are made of clean blond wood. The walls are white with a few carefully placed Japanese decorative items. The sushi chef and hostess are in traditional Japanese garb. You are struck by the simplicity and elegance of the decor. The sushi and sashimi we've eaten there have been notably fresh and appealing.

At Ino, we eat *Ikura Sushi*, seaweed-wrapped rice rolls topped with sparkling orange salmon roe, and *Uni Sushi*, capped with creamy yellow sea urchin roe with a marvelous nutty flavor. *Mirugai Sushi*, with a chewy slice of horseneck clam, tastes like a piece of the sea, briny and primal. *Ika*, a slice from large squid, dissolves into milkiness as you chew it.

There is a minimum charge per person if you sit at the sushi bar, and a lesser minimum if you sit at the table, which is not nearly as much fun. This often brings you more sushi than you want.

We take home our remaining sushi in beautifully wrapped foil boxes complete with chop sticks and soy sauce. But sushi must be eaten a second after it's made to be at its best. It's a cuisine of the moment.

PRICE RANGE: Moderate to expensive
HOURS: 5:00 P.M.–midnight Mon.–Sat.
NO RESERVATIONS
BEER AND WINE
NO CREDIT CARDS

Jack's ★

615 Sacramento Street
San Francisco
986–9854

Jack's, a 110-year-old establishment in the Financial District, is as "San Francisco" as you can get.

The atmosphere is old San Francisco men's club. If you're not Herb Caen, Joe Alioto, or one of the other regulars, don't expect much attention. Just be thankful someone comes to take your order.

Jack's has changed very little over the years. A long, detailed menu is still printed every day with separate listings for steaks and chops, roasts and grills, entrees and specialties. The same tuxedoed waiters play the aisles; the dining room still smells faintly of thousands of after-dinner cigars, and gentlemen are still required to wear ties.

The antique building that houses Jack's was originally a bordello. You can still get a private room upstairs, but only for eating. The long, narrow dining room is closely packed with white-linened tables. Brass coathooks are fixed to the molding for topcoats.

You can always get something good at Jack's if you're careful. All the grilled steaks and chops are of high quality, cut very thick and expertly cooked. Couple any of the grilled meats with, say, a *Romaine Salad* sprinkled with imported blue cheese and strong vinaigrette dressing, and you've got a meal that makes you want to join Jack's club for life.

Chicken Sauté Jerusalem, a dish for which Jack's is famous, is

107

another winner. The chicken is browned and served with a rich sour cream sauce with sliced mushrooms and artichoke hearts. The sauce is so delicious you'll want to clean the plate with bread crusts. We also enjoy the *Broiled Calves Liver with Bacon and Onions*, two buttery slices of sweet liver cooked medium rare, with a thick slice of crisp bacon and lots of beautifully carmelized onions.

On the fish side of the menu, you can sometimes be stuck with something less than fresh, and with unappetizing sauces. We were once told by our waiter that "of course" the crab in the crab salad was fresh, because it was crab season. After one bite we called the maître d' over. Yes, the crab was fresh, he told us, because it had never been frozen—but it did come from a can.

Jack's is the prototype of several popular new grill-type restaurants that have taken up the idea of high-quality seasonal foods that are prepared in an uncomplicated manner. It doesn't maintain its success by dint of tradition; with very few exceptions, it has kept its kitchen up to snuff.

PRICE RANGE: Moderate to expensive
HOURS: 11:30 A.M.–2:00 P.M. Mon.–Sat.
        5:00–9:30 P.M. daily
RESERVATIONS RECOMMENDED
FULL BAR
NO CREDIT CARDS

Java Restaurant

417 Clement Street
San Francisco
752–1541

Indonesia is a country made up of many romantic-sounding islands—Java, Bali, Sumatra, Borneo—to name a few, in a part of the world where the Indian Ocean, the South China Sea, and the Pacific Ocean meet. Its cuisine likewise reflects Polynesian, Indian, and Chinese influences. The aromas of these influences—garlic, peanuts, curry, and pungent spices—entice you into the small Javanese restaurant, where you can gaze at a wall-sized poster of a paradisiacal Balinese white-sand beach while you eat your food. Otherwise, the decor of this popular storefront restaurant fits into the bare-bones category.

No matter. You can either order the Dutch-influenced *Rijsttafel*, or *Rice Table*, which brings you practically every dish in the house, or individual combination plates that can actually be more satisfying for half the price.

Nasi Rames Special includes portions of slowly simmered beef and carrots with perfumy nutmeg, chicken in a mild coconut and curry sauce, another chicken in a hot and spicy green pepper puree, a skewer of grilled beef with peanut sauce, Indonesian-style cole slaw, and airy shrimp chips. You can choose either rice or noodles to go with it. What you are getting is a miniature *Rijsttafel*, half a world of flavors on one plate.

If you prefer to order a la carte, try the Javanese-style *Fried Chicken*, with crisp, spicy skin and tender flesh, or *Pork in Anise-Spiced Soy Sauce*, or the searing-hot *Green Pepper Beef*. A plate of soft, fat linguine-type *Noodles* is particularly appealing, with the Java's copious dousing of hot, peppery meat sauce. *Gado-Gado*, a salad of raw shredded vegetables in a sweet-and-sour vinegar dressing, is refreshingly cool in contrast to all the spices.

PRICE RANGE: Inexpensive
HOURS: 11:30 A.M.–11:30 P.M. Wed.–Mon.
RESERVATIONS ACCEPTED
BEER AND WINE
MASTERCARD, VISA

Joe's

5351 Geary Boulevard
(at 18th Street)
San Francisco
751–1950

The sign says "45 Flavors," but forget them all. Joe's is the place to go for the best It's It in town—only here it's called an *It*. This concoction, for those who have never tried it, consists of vanilla ice cream sandwiched between two oatmeal cookies, with the whole thing dipped in chocolate. It's It can really be awful. But what happens if you use the best ingredients, transforming it from a gooey, sweet mess to a really refreshing dessert? At Joe's, *It* becomes a hit.

PRICE RANGE: Inexpensive
HOURS: 11:00 A.M.–11:00 P.M. Sun.–Fri.
11:00 A.M.–11:30 P.M. Sat.

KC Bar B-Q ★

2613 San Pablo Avenue
Berkeley
548–1140

KC Bar B-Q is our favorite ribs place. KC cooks its *Ribs* in slow-burning brick ovens and leaves them there in cooler spots until ordered. This means that the meat remains smoky, moist, and tender, without being too fatty. The lean ribs are carefully trimmed, and we also like the sauce, which comes in varying degrees of hotness. It's bright red and tangy, with a definitive sweet-and-sour seasoning. You can order the choice *Short-end Slab* or the *Long End*.

Slices of commercial white foam bread and gooey yellow potato salad are the accompaniments.

The people behind the counter are some of the nicest rib-slingers in the business.

PRICE RANGE: Moderate
HOURS: 11:00 A.M.–9:00 P.M. Tues.–Thurs.
       Noon–2:00 A.M. Fri.–Sat.
NO RESERVATIONS
NO BAR
NO CREDIT CARDS

Khan Toke Thai House ★★★

5937 Geary Boulevard
San Francisco
668–6654

Eating out is often something of a compromise. The food can be good, but the surroundings hectic and uncomfortable. Or if the food and atmosphere are both enjoyable, you might be paying dearly for it.

There are no compromises at Khan Toke Thai House. Prices are as moderate as at any neighborhood Thai restaurant. You sit on the floor at low tables in a peaceful, candle-lit room that is exquisitely decorated with Thai ornaments, and there is low Thai music in the background. Most important, the food is as good as

110

any Thai food we've ever tasted. In fact, on one of our visits we brought a guest who had just returned from a month in Thailand, and she said she hadn't had a single meal there as good as at Khan Toke's.

The striking accomplishment at Khan Toke is the preparation of dishes with the widest variety of spices, flavors, and textures imaginable—but with each cooked superbly. Eating there feels like taking a gastronomic tour of every facet of Thai cuisine. Some of the dishes—like the *Squid with Onion, Hot Chili, Lemon Juice, and Lemon Grass*—will set you on fire. Here, the squid is sautéed so delicately it almost melts in your mouth, and, despite the fiery chili oil, the taste of a bouquet of spices still manages to come through.

Other dishes will set your taste buds tingling with the sensation of beautifully prepared curries accompanied by coconut milk, one of the staples of Thai cooking. The *Beef with Red Curry, Onion, Peanuts, and Coconut Milk*, as well as the *Chicken with Spicy Green Curry, Peas, and Coconut Milk*, are not to be missed. If you've only tasted curries that are made from commercial curry powder, you won't believe what a subtle blend of exotic spices a great curry can be.

Then there are the mild dishes to serve as an interlude. The *Thai Omelette Stuffed with Ground Pork and Vegetables* will probably be unlike any omelette you've ever eaten, since the egg acts as a thin, delicate wrapping for a thick, juicy filling. The crispy *Egg Noodles Fried with Shrimp, Pork, Chicken, and Vegetables* boasts the lightest of sweet-and-sour sauces, made tangy by fresh lime juice.

Be sure to start your dinner with an appetizer of *Pork Balls with Oriental Fine Herbs.* You'll get a platter of deep-fried meat balls, along with diced ginger, garlic, hot green peppers, and peanuts. You put each ingredient in a wrapping that resembles a won ton skin, add a fruity tamarind sauce, and pop the whole thing into your mouth. It's a bite that encompasses the whole range of Thai cooking.

All this can be accompanied by *Singha Beer*, the delightful and strong Thai brew, and by a unique *Tea* that has vanilla ground into the tea leaves.

PRICE RANGE: Moderate
HOURS: 11:00 A.M.–3:00 P.M. Mon.–Sat.
   5:00–11:00 P.M. nightly
RESERVATIONS ACCEPTED
BEER AND WINE
AMERICAN EXPRESS, MASTERCARD, VISA

Kichihei

2084 Chestnut Street
San Francisco
929–1670

The Marina district has a few good restaurants and a surplus of mediocre ones, but whatever the quality of the food, there's a certain sameness about the atmosphere. It seems that almost everywhere lots of people are making lots of noise and downing lots of booze; in many places the food itself seems secondary.

Kichihei, a traditional Japanese restaurant that makes no concession to its location, is a welcome exception. A very pleasant room with an illuminated Japanese garden out back, it divides itself equally into a sushi bar, a row of western-style tables, and a row of low Japanese tables.

This is a marvelous place to come for "iron-pot" dishes—those bubbling creations that usually involve fish, meat, and vegetables in a light broth, generally served with a soy-sauce-based dipping sauce. You eat it right out of the iron pot, and it proves both warm and satisfying without being as filling as an American or European stew. You get five choices, one vegetarian, one beef, and the others a mixture of seafood and chicken. We particularly like *Udonsuki*, a mixture of shellfish, chunks of juicy, fresh fish, chicken, and vegetables served in a broth over tender, thick wheat noodles. Start out your meal with a marvelously greasless *Eggplant Appetizer*, which has been spread with a sweetened soybean paste and then put under the broiler.

Unfortunately, the other main courses we've tried aren't nearly as good as the iron-pot dishes. The batter on the *Tempura* is too thick, and it tastes heavy and greasy. The *Sukiyaki* is uninspired, and the *Tuna Sashimi*, while tender and fresh, is served in chunks instead of thin slices.

PRICE RANGE: Moderate
HOURS: 5:00–10:00 P.M. Thurs.–Tues.
RESERVATIONS ACCEPTED
BEER AND WINE
AMERICAN EXPRESS, MASTERCARD, VISA

Kinokawa ★★

347 Grant Avenue
San Francisco
956–6085

Kinokawa is considered by knowledgeable chef friends to be the best sushi bar in town. This urbane-feeling sushi bar is part of a complex that includes a Japanese piano bar and a Japanese restaurant. It stays open until 3:00 in the morning and has a good number of seats around the counter, almost always full of Japanese businessmen. Because of its popularity and long hours, the fish turns over quickly and is usually the freshest in town.

Freshness is the key to great sushi and sashimi. In Japan, tuna are actually auctioned off one by one like rare artifacts to professional tuna buyers, who judge them by a nub of flesh taken from their tails. The fish are never more than twelve hours out of the water and always kept refrigerated from boat to sushi counter. The chef rarely handles the fish with his hands. He uses the knife to cut and pick up the pieces so that the heat from his fingers won't warm the fish. The sign of a good sushi chef is lightning quickness. The faster the preparation, the fresher the sushi.

At Kinokawa we eat *Toro*, a tuna sashimi—four thick pieces of light yellowtail tuna of incomparable quality cut from the fattier belly area. We dip these buttery pieces into soy sauce mixed with hot, green horseradish paste and eat them with shreds of daikon radish. When we finish, we eat shavings of pink, preserved ginger to clean our palates for the sushi to follow.

We particularly like the *Unagi Sushi*, made with cooked freshwater eel that's reheated over a small broiler and placed on ovals of rice with a strip of seaweed. It has a delicate perfume and sweetness. *Maguro Sashimi* consists of dark red slices of tuna with a meaty flavor, and *Toro Nori Maki*, rice and seaweed rolls with rectangles of light tuna in the center. You dip one side of these into soy sauce.

Use the sushi charts on the bar to order. The fish is never questionable at Kinokawa and the rice is never sticky. Its seasoning of vinegar, sugar, and *mirin*, Japanese sherry, is always in harmony with the fish and seaweed accompaniments. Kinokawa is an excellent place to begin your career as a sushi eater. You can trust what you eat there.

PRICE RANGE: Moderate to expensive
HOURS: 11:30 A.M.–3:00 A.M. Mon.–Sat.
RESERVATIONS ACCEPTED
FULL BAR
ALL MAJOR CREDIT CARDS

Kum Moon ★

2109 Clement Street
San Francisco
221–5656

Many devotees of Chinese food avoid Cantonese restaurants, because, they complain, the food so often turns out to be bland and tasteless. If you put yourself in that category, try a meal at Kum Moon and you'll be in for a big surprise.

The menu here is staggering—ten pages long and filled, not only with Cantonese, but also with northern and Szechuanese dishes. Stick to the Cantonese; the chef is from Canton, and the same dishes that taste so ordinary in other Cantonese restaurants sparkle here.

The *Seaweed Soup with Bean Cake Pork* is an extraordinary way to start the meal. The base is plain old egg-drop soup—but added to it are pieces of bean curd, pork, shrimp, peas, and lots of seaweed, in a chicken broth that is rich and well seasoned. Then go on to some of the fish dishes, a specialty of Cantonese cooking. The steamed *Whole Rock Cod in Ginger and Onions* is as fresh and delicate a steamed fish as you can get in a San Francisco Chinese restaurant. Sautéeing large local *Clams in Their Shells* in a pungent black bean sauce is the perfect way to disguise the sometimes flavorless Pacific species. The clams here are tender and sweet.

Two other dishes not to be missed: the *Chinese Broccoli in Oyster Sauce*, which is an old sawhorse of Cantonese menus, but never have we seen it come out as bright green and crispy yet tender as it does here; and the *Kum Moon Lettuce Blossom*, a stir-fry of minced pork with mushrooms, onions, water chestnuts, and bamboo shoots, all to be rolled up at the table in lettuce leaves with plum sauce—an unusual and satisfying variation on the more common minced squab in lettuce leaves.

You'll be eating your meal in a noisy room jammed with diners, a room that is spartan even by Clement Street Chinese restaurant standards, but the food at Kum Moon puts many of its nearby competitors to shame.

PRICE RANGE: Inexpensive
HOURS: 11:00 A.M.–9:30 P.M. daily
NO RESERVATIONS
BEER AND WINE
MASTERCARD, VISA

La Bourgogne ★★

330 Mason
San Francisco
362–7352

San Francisco has made its name as a restaurant town from the hundreds of moderate and inexpensive restaurants that are small and chef owned, and serve ethnic cuisine. If the City were to be judged on its so-called best restaurants—expensive French—it would lose to New York, Chicago, and Los Angeles. While we have three or four entries in this category, none of them is innovative, strikingly decorated, or particularly ambitious in its menu offerings. However, La Bourgogne, one of the best, is highly professional and consistently solid when it comes to the cooking. You can make an occasion out of dining there and not be disappointed. You'll be treated well and your meal will be carefully presented and prepared.

The dining room of La Bourgogne is like hundreds of others in French continental restaurants scattered throughout the United States: snowy linen, comfortable banquettes that are romantic for two and convivial for larger groups, acoustic ceilings, carpeted floors, hokey light fixtures turned down low, fresh red roses, and waiters in tuxedos. The decks have been cleared for serving.

The menu covers all the traditional French-American bases, with a few added specials your waiter will tell you about. On one occasion we tried two of them, a half-dozen *Eastern Mussels* on the half shell in a cream sauce flavored with shallots and mushrooms, and a poached *Filet of Salmon* in a similar sauce, this time with fresh tarragon. The same basic sauce reappeared on *Croute de Homard Brillat-Savarin*, a harlequinesque dish of gently poached fresh lobster in a puff pastry shell with a yellow curry sauce as well as a pink lobster sauce. All the sauces were opulent and velvety, if repetitive. They were based on a good fish stock that had not been overreduced. The salmon had poached a little too long, but the mussels were still juicy.

Another time we ordered three different appetizers, each of which was split for us in the kitchen at our waiter's suggestion. Nice. *Toasts à la Moelle* are simply baguette toasts with rounds of bone marrow and chopped chives that have been put under the broiler. *Oysters Rockefeller*, six fresh eastern blue points whisked under the broiler on a bed of Pernod-flavored creamed spinach, were correctly handled. Thin slices of Bayonne ham, moist and fresh, came with lemon wedges and ground black pepper.

Double-cut Lamb Chops arrived medium rare, not rare, with deep-fried swirls of bland, mashed potato. *Squab à la Diable* should have been aged, because it was tough. It didn't have the creamy, livery quality that small, red-fleshed birds should have. However, it was not inundated with sauce and the thumbnail-sized turned potatoes that came with it were tender, buttery, and hot.

Soufflé Grand Marnier for two rose four inches over their dishes. They were light, eggy, and not too sweet, with a lovely thin Grand Marnier-tainted *crème anglaise* spooned first onto the plate.

Strict, traditional French standards of formality, presentation, and cooking techniques are at work here. What you are eating is not as perfect as it is in the best restaurants in France, nor is it as interesting. There's not one dish on the menu that sparks the imagination, but everything is competently done, and when it's off, it isn't off by much. You don't need to turn down any invitations to eat at this restaurant. This is one expensive French restaurant where you get a fair shake.

PRICE RANGE: Expensive
HOURS: 5:30–11:45 P.M. Mon.–Sat.
RESERVATIONS RECOMMENDED
FULL BAR
ALL MAJOR CREDIT CARDS

La Chaumiere ★

337 San Anselmo Avenue
San Anselmo
454–6790

La Chaumiere in San Anselmo is not a discovery for people who follow restaurants in the Bay Area. As a matter of fact, it has been glowingly reviewed by a number of knowledgeable critics. Yet this relatively small restaurant never fills to capacity on week nights. Everyone knows how important location is in the restaurant business, how a well-placed restaurant can serve undistinguished food and be wildly successful; but one hopes that a special restaurant can draw patrons to its door, no matter how far away. We are convinced that this is a restaurant worth seeking out.

The suburban location is actually fitting, because the dining experience there is provincial in the best sense. The restaurant is run solely by a French family. The chef-father, René Hechinger, who started cooking when he was fifteen, was the executive chef at Alexis for eight years and previously the executive chef at Bardelli's. He has his son François work as maître d' and another adolescent son and daughter help prepare food and wash dishes. His wife expertly waits on tables and keeps the books. When you walk into the cozy, canopied dining room and put yourself in the hands of this very professional restaurant family, you feel that you might not only be in a different country but in a different era as well.

La Chaumiere is old fashioned; neither its menu nor its decor is *au courant*. Perhaps that's one source of its popular neglect. There's no French food faddism here, no *nouvelle cuisine*, but rather an archetypical French menu of items that Hechinger thinks Americans expect. It might be considered plodding if it weren't for his talent and dedication. Hechinger is a superb saucier and a perfectionist. He's been working on the same dishes for years, developing them to their highest potential.

Take, for example, his classic *Quenelles Façon Chaumiere*, an appetizer of the most delicate fish dumplings we've tasted anywhere. He has discovered through constant experimentation that Pacific petrale sole comes closest to the pike used in France, and his *quenelles* melt in your mouth. Their sauce is an appropriately light, cream-enriched fish *fumet*.

Croustade de Clams Josephine, an amusing appetizer of two little clam tarts on a buttery crust with a fresh clam-and-mushroom

117

filling, can be shared, since dinner comes with excellent soup and salad.

The list of entrees runs long for a restaurant of this size, perhaps too long, but one of the best is *Le Poulet Imagination*, a chicken breast cooked to perfection and served in a deep brown, piquant sauce with an unusual addition of red wine vinegar.

Scallops, Salmon, and *Petrale Sole* are all offered as fish of the day. The *Sole* is stuffed with finely minced mushrooms *duxelles*, and served in a hollandaise sauce lightened by rich fish *fumet*.

Scallops of Veal in Mustard Sauce is prepared in numerous French and northern Italian restaurants, but René's mustard sauce sets the standard. Cream, Dijon mustard, white wine, and veal stock are in exquisite balance over fork-tender pieces of veal.

The French wine list offers a good selection of wines from Beaujolais and Alsace. There are some real finds on the wine card.

La Chaumiere does not break any new culinary ground; it is a purposefully conservative restaurant, a bastion of classical taste that's charming because it's done with such personal conviction. You can taste the hours of work and the lifetime of tradition behind each bite.

PRICE RANGE: Moderate to expensive
HOURS: 6:00–9:30 P.M. Tues.–Fri.
         6:00–10:00 P.M. Sat.
RESERVATIONS REQUIRED ON WEEKENDS. RECOMMENDED AT
  OTHER TIMES
WINE
MASTERCARD, VISA

La Cumbre ★

515 Valencia Street
(at 16th Street)
San Francisco
863–8205

La Cumbre has white adobe arches and Spanish grillwork outside and colorful ethnic decor inside. There are big, bright Mexican murals on the walls, carved wooden chairs and tables, and tiled floors. It's actually the only burrito place we enjoy staying in to eat.

There are two ordering stations on the cooking line, one for grilled "steak" burritos and another for barbecued pork, chicken, tongue, and pork tripe, which are all cooked ahead of time and kept warm.

The *salsa* is chopped onion and green chilis without tomato, and the hot sauce is a thin, red, potent liquid that can definitely be felt the next day. We prefer the raw *salsa* to the hot sauce.

The *Carne Asada Burrito with Melted Jack Cheese* is La Cumbre's most popular burrito—and rightfully so. The thin slices of beef are grilled to order over charcoal, and absolutely delicious with the simple bean and *salsa* accompaniments. It does have a tendency to stick to the roof of your mouth. *Cheese Burritos with Green Chili* have also captured the hearts of many.

Besides the usual soda and Mexican beers at very reasonable prices, La Cumbre carries Boing fruit drinks from Mexico. One in particular, the *Strawberry Boing*, must have been invented to go with burritos.

PRICE RANGE: Inexpensive
HOURS: 11:00 A.M.–9:00 P.M. Mon.–Sat.
       Noon–8:00 P.M. Sun.
NO RESERVATIONS
BEER
NO CREDIT CARDS

La Fiesta Market

2737 20th Street
(at York)
San Francisco
826–5050

You might think La Fiesta Market is just a neighborhood grocery store, but it is much more. It makes *Burritos* behind the checkout counter—the kind that have fillings that are precooked and kept warm. These include *Beef*, *Pork*, and *Chicken*, and also a *Cold Crab Burrito*.

La Fiesta has a loyal following; this is definitely a word-of-mouth place.

The burritos are well balanced; the meats and beans have been seasoned with a sure hand. The fresh tomato *salsa* is excellent and the finished item is fat and juicy. The drawback is that La Fiesta has a limited choice of fillings and no grill. Also, the hot relish of carrots and green chilis can make you breathe fire. La Fiesta's burritos seems very authentic.

PRICE RANGE: Inexpensive
HOURS: 9:00 A.M.–7:00 P.M. Mon.–Fri.
9:00 A.M.–6:00 P.M. Sat.–Sun.

La Mirabelle ★★

1326 Powell Street
(near Broadway)
San Francisco
421–3374

In recent years a number of new, innovative French restaurants have sprung up in the Bay Area, eclipsing, at least in publicity, the well-known, long-established, expensive San Francisco French restaurants. For many French food lovers, this trend has been a blessing. Too often, the traditional San Francisco French establishments have featured overly high prices; tired, unchanging menus; and—from the taste of the food—tired chefs.

In our view, one outstanding exception to this pattern has always been La Mirabelle. True, the food is expensive—although not nearly so much as some others in this class. True, some of the same items have remained on the menu for years. True, many of the offerings, like *Rack of Lamb*, *Pepper Steak*, *Vichyssoise*, and *Snails*, don't generate much interest. However, there's a big BUT: The quality of cooking at Mirabelle has always been superb, and a recent visit there produced a meal that was one of the best we've ever eaten in San Francisco.

Mirabelle is a relatively small and pleasantly attractive restaurant, but attractive in the sort of way (pink tablecloths, plush draperies, and wallpaper) that could give premonitions of snooty service. No worry on this account. The service is uniformly friendly and helpful, with the waiters displaying obvious interest in the food when they make recommendations. (In one instance, our waiter steered us away from a lemon cake he said had gone a little stale.)

The wine list is surprisingly reasonable. It offers a number of modestly priced California wines and, if you bring your own wine, corkage is only $5 a bottle. (Where are the names of the shippers of the French red Burgundies? Without this information, you have no way of knowing what you're getting.)

While the menu has a number of those standard, dull dishes that can be termed "fancy" French, there is still lots of interest to choose from. The hot hors d'oeuvres in particular stand out; you're tempted to go through the list ordering one of everything. The *Quenelles Normande* (mousse of white fish in a lobster sauce) are light and airy, yet have real fish character. The *Barquette de Fruits de Mer* (fresh seafood in puff pastry) is an old favorite; a light, flaky pastry shell is filled with scallops and shrimp and served with a creamy white sauce of which you'll want to mop up every drop. The *Cervelle au Beurre Noir* (calve's brains sautéed in butter and capers) are an unusual treat. Don't let the name scare you away; they melt in your mouth, and soak up the rich brown butter sauce.

Among the main courses we've always particularly enjoyed the fish. A visit during salmon season produced fresh *Poached Salmon* served in a sauce of shallots, sweet butter, white wine, and cream. Never had we tasted a piece of salmon fresher and more perfectly cooked, and the sauce was light and tangy enough to enhance the fish rather than compete with it. During our most recent visit, the waiter suggested fresh *Scampi*, and he claimed the scampi were in fact baby lobster tails instead of the usual shrimp. We were skeptical, but the skepticism vanished with the first luscious bite.

If you yearn for genuine, milk-fed white veal, a rarity in San Francisco, try the *Medallions of Veal with Fresh Artichoke Hearts*. They are simply sautéed in a lemon butter sauce—another indication that Mirabelle stays away from heavy sauces that can ruin delicate veal or fish.

Desserts have never been La Mirabelle's strong point, but the *Chocolate Mousse* is appropriately dark and velvety. When we had *Cheesecake with Fresh Raspberries*, the kitchen had the sense to leave the raspberries unglazed, so that they didn't compete with the rich cheesecake filling. You can also get a competent *Soufflé Grand Marnier* for two if you order it at the beginning of the meal.

La Mirabelle may have been around for a long time, but the food remains inspired. Some of the chefs at the newer French restaurants in San Francisco could learn a great deal by eating there.

PRICE RANGE: Expensive
HOURS: 5:30–10:30 P.M. Tues.–Sat.
RESERVATIONS NECESSARY
FULL BAR
ALL MAJOR CREDIT CARDS

La Pergola

2060 Chestnut Street
San Francisco
563–4500

Getting a table at La Pergola, a small Marina District Italian restaurant with a big reputation, is not easy. You must call days in advance, and, even then, very well may have to arrive at an hour assigned to you. When you finally get to the entryway of La Pergola and are perused by the maître d', you may have to add or subtract certain articles of clothing. Don't come late, even if you reserve, or your table may be given away.

On the weekends, particularly, be prepared to be rushed in and out. This tiny restaurant is run by the numbers, and when you are spending an average of $20 a person for food and an additional 15 percent on service, you must carefully weigh whether it's worth it.

For us, it is not, because we found most of the food we tried to be a lackluster cross between northern Italian and French cooking. The preparations lacked definition, sparkle, and character, though there is no doubt that everything was meticulously prepared and that excellent ingredients were used. It's the bland, creamy, soft-edged style of food we don't care for. La Pergola serves food that puts taste buds to sleep.

Dish after dish at La Pergola lacked the kind of distinct, fresh taste we expect from good Italian cooking. *Chicken Vecchia Usanza*, a sauté of chicken with crisp skin, was smothered in a thickened cream and white wine sauce that blotted out rather than enhanced the skillfully cooked chicken's best qualities. *Scallopine di Vitello alla Pergola* had the same muted quality—cream sauce, mushrooms, good-quality veal, all smudged together and canceling each other out.

Pepper Steak al Cognac, a small, thin cut of beef coated with crushed peppercorns and splashed with a shot of burned-off brandy, did not capture anyone's imagination.

We did, however, like La Pergola's *Veal Piccata* with capers and artichoke hearts. You can distinctly taste the tart, fresh lemon and the sharp capers whisked into the butter sauce, beautifully framing velvety pieces of veal.

As for the pastas, the noodles in *Fettucine Alfredo* were silky and eggy, the rightful stars of the dish. A copious cream sauce tasting of flour, however, did not have enough butter and cheese.

The sauce on *Linguine alla Vongole* had more spunk. We even tasted some garlic in the rich tomato sauce that nicely adhered to the long strands of pasta. The chopped clams incorporated into the sauce were uncommonly tender and mild.

La Pergola is named for the latticework trellises built on Italian vineyards to elevate the grapes, one of which decorates La Pergola's ceiling. The wine motif is further carried out by walls lined with wooden wine racks. All this would suggest a fine Italian wine list, but few noteworthy bottles are offered. And the California list is mundane.

PRICE RANGE: Moderate to expensive
HOURS: 5:00–10:30 P.M. Tues.–Sun.
RESERVATIONS IMPERATIVE
BEER AND WINE
AMERICAN EXPRESS, MASTERCARD, VISA

La Rondalla ★

901 Valencia Street
(at 21st Street)
San Francisco
647–7474

La Rondalla is a Mission District institution. It has a counter, a bar, is open from noon until 3:30 in the morning, and it's busy the whole time. You can see the cooks at work when you sit at the counter. They never stop for a minute, turning out top-notch *Mexican Grilled Steaks*, smothered in sautéed onions, tomatoes, and pepper, and accompanied by creamy refried beans and rice and a chopped lettuce salad. It's one of the most satisfying plates of food in town.

The restaurant also has lots of funky atmosphere. Someone forgot to take down the Christmas decorations; the four labyrinthine rooms of assorted booths and tables are decorated with tinsel streamers, blinking Christmas tree lights, crazy ornaments, and knickknacks. Fitting right into the mélange are waitresses in bright red sweater-girl tops and short black skirts. There's even a costumed mariachi band that plays at various times in the bar.

The best dishes are cooked on the grill, like La Rondalla's house special, *Asado*, a thin slice of beef smothered with fresh tomatoes, onions, and julienned potatoes, a remarkably tasty combination. Another of our grill favorites is *Adobada*, an equally thin slice of pork that has been marinated in chilis, garlic, lemon, and Mexican spices. It's topped with a light red vinegary sauce and that fabulous grilled vegetable combination. The pork is cooked on a piece of tin foil on the grill, drizzled with sauce, and then finished off for a few minutes directly on the grill, keeping it moist and tasty. *Lomo Saltado*, done in a sauté pan, gets diced, chewy beef, peppers, onions, and potatoes, and a bath of spicy tomato sauce.

La Rondalla's *Chile Verde* is one of the best we've sampled. The chopped pork picks up the flavors of a piquant green chili sauce in which it's simmered. If you like the stronger flavor of mutton, try *Birria de Chivo*, a hearty stew of goat meat in an earth-colored, spice-rich sauce.

La Rondalla also turns out the more commonly prepared Mexican dishes like *Chile Rellenos*, which are stuffed with good Jack cheese, lightly battered but oversauced. Most of the chicken items lack body, because the chicken is merely boiled and tastes a bit like straw, but the meat fillings are excellent. The beef and pork are separately stewed in well-seasoned sauces, which makes *Beef Enchiladas* unusually moist and tasty, and gives a succulent foundation to the *Beef Tacos*.

For late-night supper, have a bowl of *Albondigas*, a soothing meatball soup into which you dip hot buttered corn tortillas. Or have the generous portion of *Guacamole*, finely turned with lemon and chili peppers. At 3:00 in the morning you may feel more like eating breakfast, so La Rondalla offers such dishes as *Chorizo and Eggs* served with rice and beans and *Huevos Rancheros*, correctly runny fried eggs on tortillas with the restaurant's good tomato sauce.

Wash it down with one of ten imported beers, real Mexican *Fruit Soda*, or one of La Rondalla's well-mixed *Margaritas*. After you eat there you'll understand why La Rondalla is always so busy.

PRICE RANGE: Inexpensive
HOURS: Noon–3:30 A.M. daily
NO RESERVATIONS
FULL BAR
NO CREDIT CARDS

La Taqueria

2889 Mission Street
(at 25th Street)
San Francisco
285–7117

La Taqueria House of Tacos is the MacDonald's of burrito establishments. It has its own arches—Mexican adobe with Spanish iron grill work, along with wooden picnic tables and a tiled floor inside, which looks as if it gets hosed down each night. You order at the cash register, pay in advance, and get a numbered receipt. When your order is ready, your number is called out in Spanish, so listen carefully.

La Taqueria has a production kitchen cleanly lined with shiny stainless steel. The meats are grilled over gas, have an excellent fresh *salsa*, and put out a good small *Burrito*. There are advantages and disadvantages to the small size. It's neatly and easily eaten while driving. Because there's less filling, the flavor of the grilled meat stands out. However, the texture of the *Burrito*, due to whole beans instead of saucy beans, is rather dry and starchy, and sometimes the meat can be gristly here. Although the whole-bean treatment is traditional with grilled beef, we still prefer Panchito's wet bean (see the review of Panchito's Tiajuana Village).

The *Pork and Green Chili Burrito*, juicier and alive with Mexican spices, is a good bet here.

PRICE RANGE: Inexpensive
HOURS: 11:00 A.M.–8:00 P.M. daily

La Traviata ★★

2854 Mission Street
(between 24th and 25th Streets)
San Francisco
282–0500

In San Francisco, lots of Italian restaurants are long on atmosphere but short on food. You can have a good time in a bustling, friendly setting, but too often the bottom line is that the entrees taste like they came out of a supermarket frozen food case.

La Traviata is one of the friendliest of them all. Incongruously located amidst the Latin restaurants of the Mission District, it features a long, narrow room whose walls are lined with signed pictures of opera stars. Although the candles, tablecloths, and fancy plate settings would ordinarily lend an air of formality, this is quickly punctured by the delightful waiters bustling about to the tune of opera music playing in the background.

Now for the good news. The food is excellent. Most important, La Traviata does a superb job preparing veal and calamari, which in most San Francisco Italian restaurants leave you longing for a meal in New York City's Little Italy.

Take veal, for instance. How many times do you get a thick, gray slab of anonymous meat bathed in a goopy, heavily floured sauce? Not at La Traviata, where the veal is usually thinly sliced, white, and tender. (We were going to say "always" but at our latest meal there, one person's veal turned out tough, the first time we've seen this happen in about twenty visits.) Our favorite preparation is the *Veal Traviata*, where the veal is topped with the thinnest, most delicate layers of prosciutto and melted Parmesan cheese, and served in a light and tangy butter and sherry sauce.

As for calamari, too often squid in an Italian restaurant turns out to taste like it was sliced from a rubber tire. Calamari is one of the loveliest, most delicate of seafoods, but it simply won't put up with improper cooking. If you want to test the quality of a restaurant, order the squid and you'll know quickly. At La Traviata, we'd rate the *Calamari*, which is sautéed with mushrooms and capers in a tomato and butter sauce, as one of the two best in the City. The other is the sensational squid at Vanessi's, which unfortunately is only served on Fridays for lunch.

Most Traviata dinners come with an appetizer of *Tortellini in Cream Sauce*, which gives you a chance to taste this restaurant's excellent *al dente* pasta without feeling overloaded. If you feel like pasta alone, you can order one of eight different preparations of *mostaccioli*, a long, tubular spinach noodle. If veal or calamari doesn't turn you on, try the *Chicken Beverly Sills*, where a boned breast of chicken is stuffed with prosciutto and Parmesan cheese and sautéed in a butter and wine sauce. The *Eggplant Parmigiana* is also excellent, in keeping with La Traviata's tradition of doing main courses with cheese with extreme delicacy, instead of glopping everything together in a casserole dish.

PRICE RANGE: Moderate
HOURS: 4:00–10:30 P.M. daily

126

RESERVATIONS NECESSARY
BEER AND WINE
ALL MAJOR CREDIT CARDS

Le Candide ★

301 Kearny Street
San Francisco
981–2213

Le Central ★

453 Bush Street
San Francisco
391–2233

Le Candide and, across the street, Le Central, are brasseries frequented by stylish Financial District business people, politicos, and fashion mavens, particularly at lunch.

The decor at Le Candide is not carried off with as much panache as it is at Le Central, where, after a few glasses of Ricard, you feel as if you're on the Boulevard St. Michel, but much has been done to recreate a similar bistro atmosphere at the newer restaurant. There are white tile floors, a mirrored bar, brass rails, and cafe windows set in darkly stained wood partitions that cozily section off tables in the high-ceilinged room. These clever partitions probably keep the sound level manageable in this busy, hard-surfaced restaurant.

The menus at both restaurants, however, could not be more to the point, with eight or so first courses and entrees, a daily special or two, and a few desserts, all respectable examples of simple brasserie cooking.

The nice thing about French short-order cooking is that it's the best of its kind, and both Le Central and Le Candide offer unpretentious, uncomplicated food in this tradition. You get just what you order with no frills or froufrou.

Some recent first courses are *Pâté de Campagne* and *Pâté de Canard* from the City's main supplier of *charcuterie*, Marcel and Henri. The large slices of finely textured pâté are always well balanced and well seasoned, although as commercial products, preservatives are used in them.

127

For a meat first course, we would choose the excellent *Cold Beef Tongue Ravigotte*, three cleanly trimmed slices of meat with a pickly vinaigrette sauce that nicely sets off the richness of the tongue.

What could be better than a succulent *Roasted Quarter Chicken*, skin crisp and aromatic with thyme, tarragon, and garlic, the flesh firm and juicy? With a pile of slender, french-fried potatoes, hot, fresh, and cooked to order, it makes the ideal lunch for a reasonable price. The same wonderful chicken with a rasher of thick-sliced bacon and a small grilled garlic sausage alongside the haystack of potatoes becomes *Manhattan Mixed Grill*. A thin *Steak with Béarnaise Sauce* is also satisfying, and if you like the unctuous texture of *Blood Sausage*, this is one of the few places around here where you can get it.

Daily specials are posted on a blackboard by the bar. One day we greatly enjoyed two grilled *Garlic Sausages* from Marcel and Henri, attractively presented on a bed of creamy, old-fashioned mashed potatoes. On another occasion, the *Roast Pork Loin* special was gone by the time we were seated.

For dessert, have *Bosc Pears*, poached whole and served with their syrupy red-wine cooking liquid, or *Vanilla Pots de Crème*, a firm egg custard that would elicit praise from a French grandmother. The tarts come from the Court of Two Sisters on Union Street and should be avoided.

Le Candide and Le Central run like clockwork. Service is efficient, flexible, and cheerful. You never feel as if you've been forgotten in these busy restaurants.

Both Le Central and Le Candide, presided over by the two Cappelle brothers, are highly professional operations that maintain a personal flavor. Their idea of expanding by opening a second medium-sized restaurant with its own kitchen, instead of enlarging the existing one, turned out to be the best way for the Cappelle brothers to cultivate their garden.

Le Candide:
PRICE RANGE: Moderate
HOURS: 11:30 A.M.–2:30 P.M., 5:30–10:30 P.M. Mon.–Fri.
RESERVATIONS ACCEPTED
FULL BAR
MASTERCARD, VISA

Le Central:
PRICE RANGE: Moderate
HOURS: 11:45 A.M.–10:15 P.M. Mon.–Sat.
RESERVATIONS ACCEPTED
FULL BAR
MASTERCARD, VISA

Le Chalet

River Road
Guerneville
707/869–9908

The Russian River might be a pleasant place to spend a weekend, but it's never been synonymous with good food. It was, therefore, with trepidation that we walked into Le Chalet, which bills itself as a French country restaurant. We were even more dubious when we looked around; the place has all the atmosphere of a college beer hall, everything but a pool table in the corner. Moreover, our visit being on a Saturday night, the restaurant was jammed, and we were left for about fifteen minutes to cool our heels at the entrance before anyone even came up to take our name.

The doubts vanished, however, when the food started coming. The chef, Gerard Moser, who grew up in Bordeaux and was trained in Switzerland, is clearly talented. And the prices make Le Chalet one of the best bargains around; for between $6.95 and $11, depending on the entree, you get a dinner with soup, salad, home-baked French bread, and fresh vegetables with hollandaise sauce.

Every one of these items was sensational. A *Cream of Spinach Soup*, instead of the usual blender-manufactured amalgam, was packed with thin strips of spinach, and tasted beautifully of nutmeg and pepper. The *Salad* had a perfect mustard and vinaigrette dressing, and, like the soup, it was served family style in a big bowl. The vegetables were crispy, and the hollandaise sauce on them was nice and tangy, and clearly freshly made.

We asked the waitress if the veal was milk white, and she replied, "It's the best available in the United States." She wasn't far off. Le Chalet offers *Veal, Cordon Bleu Style*, with ham, cheese, and mushrooms, and sautéed with white wine and vegetables. Don't pass it up. The *Rack of Lamb*, in a garlicky, red wine sauce, was also a big winner. The lamb was wonderfully tender, and done exactly as we had ordered it.

Our only real quarrel with Le Chalet is the wine list. Not only was it sparse to start with, but they were out of many of the wines listed. Corkage is $5 a bottle, far too much unless they're willing to stock a decent wine cellar.

PRICE RANGE: Moderate
HOURS: 6:00–10:00 P.M. Tues.–Sat.
    Closed Dec.–Jan.

RESERVATIONS FOR LARGE GROUPS
BEER AND WINE
MASTERCARD, VISA

Leon's Bar-BQ

1913 Fillmore Street
San Francisco
922–2436

2800 Sloat Boulevard
(at 46th Avenue)
San Francisco
681–3071

Of all the ribs places, Leon's is the most soulful. Leon's serves heavy-duty, mainline barbecue. Leon's at the zoo is better than Leon's on Fillmore, because the meats are more carefully cooked and presented, but the two are spiritually united by the way customers are treated in a kind of urban, bored, deadpan manner.

The *Sampler Plate* can feed four, although the menu suggests two. Heaps of ribs, a half chicken, barbecued beef, and a hot link sausage are piled on top of each other and submerged in Leon's dusky-tasting sauce.

The meats are partially cooked in a regular oven and finished off in the barbecue oven. The *Ribs* are meaty, sometimes fatty, the *Chicken* not overdone, and the *Links* too hot for us. *Barbeued Beef* is cooked till it falls apart.

With regular orders, you get a choice of tasty, firm baked beans, mushy potato salad, or spaghetti, as well as chewy corn muffins. Homemade *Chile* is made with minced beef, no beans, and a Texas-style sauce.

Leon's is a no-nonsense barbecue joint. You get lots of food in appropriately grim surroundings, and most of it is pretty good.

PRICE RANGE: Moderate
HOURS: Fillmore Street location:
        11:00 A.M.–10:00 P.M. Mon.–Thurs.
        11:00 A.M.–midnight Fri.–Sat.

(HOURS:) Sloat Boulevard location:
    11:00 A.M.–10:00 P.M. daily
NO RESERVATIONS
BEER AND WINE
NO CREDIT CARDS

Little Italy

4109 24th Street
(near Castro)
San Francisco
821–1515

The fact that Noe Valley has long needed a serious restaurant is attested to by the crowds waiting to get into Little Italy, an attractive newcomer on 24th near Castro. Reminiscent of those old storefront restaurants on Mott Street in New York's Little Italy, the San Francisco version offers a large, ambitious menu, sardine-packed seating with no waiting area, and an unhelpful maître d'. Uncharacteristic of New York restaurants of this type, there are no authentic Italian mothers in the kitchen and the service waxes pleasant but low key—very San Francisco.

The service will undoubtedly tone up with time. The kitchen presents a more serious problem. The menu is too long and complicated for the physical facilities and for the two overworked cooks who have to prepare the majority of the menu to order. The result is rushed, soul-less food in a restaurant that is conceived around Italian soul-food cooking.

The *Chicken Cacciatore* provides an example. It is hacked into difficult-to-eat, unanatomical pieces, sautéed to dryness with green peppers, and splashed with a little desultory tomato sauce, which also appeared on a plate of *Spaghetti with Meatball*, a bland, lifeless bowl of pasta with a giant, bready, unseasoned meatball plunked on top. The veal tends to be chewy. *Sea Bass, Little Italy Style*, however, is more successful, with the fish immersed in lemon, butter, and white wine, and only slightly overcooked.

Some of the appetizers are significantly better than the entrees. The *Stuffed Baked Clams* are redolent of garlic and herbs, with the delicate bread stuffing basted with olive oil. *Fried Mozzarella Marinara* is a thick slice of breaded cheese deep fried to a creamy consistency with a pungent tomato sauce. The *Linguini with Clam Sauce* is worth coming back for; the correctly cooked

131

pasta is studded with fresh clams in festive, open shells bathed in herbs, garlic, juice from the clams, and butter.

Prices are reasonable here. We weren't expecting subtlety, rare ingredients, or fussy preparations, but something along the line of Little Joe's in North Beach: big, broad, hearty, honest food. Instead, except for some very good appetizers, the cooking lacked character, and the execution was too slapdash. The food pooped out.

PRICE RANGE: Moderate
HOURS: Noon–11:00 P.M. daily
RESERVATIONS NECESSARY
BEER AND WINE
MASTERCARD, VISA

Little Joe's ★

325 Columbus
San Francisco
982–7639

Some fanatical home cooks we know are always apologizing for their kitchens. "If I had to do it over," they complain, "I'd get an eight-burner Wolf range with a salamander. This six-burner is just impossible." Then they walk dejectedly through their sleek designer kitchens filled with a fortune in gleaming copper pots and chrome-bright machines, pointing out what they consider woeful inadequacies. This is brought to mind by a recently expanded North Beach restaurant that feeds literally hundreds of people from a kitchen my food-fanatic friends would consider a nightmare.

At 4:45 Saturday evening, as we were plastered against the wall of Little Joe's, along with twenty-five others waiting for a seat, we watched with fascination as two expert sauté chefs turned out plate after plate of simple, aromatic, good-looking food. Not a motion was wasted. The fires were turned up full blast, olive oil was splashed into hot pans with abandon, a few basic sauces were set up for easy ladling—and *voilà*! A hearty fish soup, a trencherman's serving of *Veal Parmigiana*, platters of cooked-to-order pasta and sautéed vegetables, and giant slabs of *Ground Beef Slathered with Melted Cheese*. Our mouths were watering by the time we finally got seated at a table in the relative luxury of adjacent Baby Joe's.

Little Joe's has been cranking out its delicious Italian soul food behind a fourteen-seat counter for years. When the lease of the storefront next door became available, Little Joe's doubled its seating capacity, but not its kitchen. We were concerned that the quality of the food might have declined. Not so. The chefs just weren't working to capacity.

Beware that Little Joe's is often overcrowded to the point of being claustrophobic. The best time to go is at lunch or in the early afternoon. Getting on towards 5:00, Little Joe's becomes impossible.

Veal Parmigiana is the most expensive item on the menu. It fills an oval dinner plate with pounded, breaded veal cooked just to tenderness, awash in tangy tomato sauce enriched by melted cheese. With it comes enough sautéed Italian green beans, cauliflower, carrots, and chard for three people.

On Friday and Saturday, the special is *Caciucco*, a stew of prawns, snapper, petrale sole, and clams simmered to order in wine, tomato sauce, and fish stock. It's a fish stew that tastes almost like a beef stew, with its thick, rich broth and substantial chunks of meaty, fresh rock fish.

Roast Beef consists of two thick slabs of surprisingly tender beef cooked well past medium doneness. We opted for *Spaghetti* with this dinner, and the pasta was firm and covered with a meaty, workmanlike tomato sauce.

We astonished each other by finishing most of the huge portions. Little Joe's may not put out haute cuisine from its déclassé kitchen, but it serves some of the best inexpensive food in the City.

PRICE RANGE: Inexpensive
HOURS: 11:00 A.M.–8:00 P.M. Mon.–Sat.
NO RESERVATIONS
BEER AND WINE
NO CREDIT CARDS

Lois the Pie Queen

851 60th Street
Oakland
547–9977

The name is ''Lois the Pie Queen,'' but the specialty is breakfast, not pies. The big sign in front says ''lunches, dinners,'' but it closes in the early afternoon. People come from miles around for the breakfasts, but it's not open on Sunday morning, the most popular breakfast day of the week.

Forget the contradictions, and think for a minute about the food. Imagine waking up famished one morning and being able to order the following breakfast: juice, two pork chops, two eggs, potatoes, grits, homemade biscuits, and coffee. Yes, such a breakfast exists at Lois's, named the *Reggie Jackson Special* in honor of one of their favorite customers. The last time we ate there, the price tag on this little snack was all of $4.25—less than many places charge for a cheese omelette alone.

The decor at Lois's is formica and fluorescent, but the food is what has soul. The grits and homemade biscuits beat any other restaurant's soggy home fries and Orowheat toast. The little sausages are done to a turn, served absolutely greaseless. The eggs taste fresh, and are cooked exactly as you want them. But nothing fancy here; a cheese omelette will be made with American cheese, and will definitely not taste like the fluffy French version.

Lois presides over all this from her perch in the open kitchen, and will often come out to greet new customers. Judging from how much at home everyone seems in the place, there couldn't be too many of those.

PRICE RANGE: Inexpensive
HOURS: 7:00 A.M.–1:30 P.M. Tues.–Sat.
NO RESERVATIONS
NO CREDIT CARDS

L'Olivier

465 Davis Court
San Francisco
981–7824

L'Olivier reminds us of restaurants on main streets in small French cities, where both the cities and the restaurants exist to accommodate local commerce. The restaurants are always in new buildings, although their decor tries to hide this fact. They serve the refined basics of French cuisine—proper, traditional food that is rarely innovative though usually good value for money spent. L'Olivier, tucked away in the Golden Gateway project, does most of its business in serving lunch to Financial District businesspeople. The restaurant is best avoided at these crowded times when every shortcut is taken by the kitchen to get the food out fast. Dinner at L'Olivier is another story.

In the evening, the large, comfortable room is mostly empty of customers, quiet and inviting. The hanging globe lamps are dimmed. Such touches as floral French provincial wallpaper and matching floor-length table skirts, pink linen, and huge vases of cymbidium all work to soften the modern Golden Gateway-style room. Christian, the maître d', who looks like a Dior suit model, is on the floor, charming you with his French accent and genuine concern for your pleasure. Now is the time to order that vintage *Perrier-Jouet Champagne* or a good Bordeaux, all reasonably priced.

In this relaxed dinner atmosphere, the very French menu takes on new appeal. For appetizers order the elegant *Mousseline de Coquille St. Jacques*, robed in a buttery pink lobster sauce, or *Baked Pacific Oysters* sprinkled with buttery bread crumbs, bacon, and grated Gruyère. Such simple dishes as *Fresh Asparagus Vinaigrette* are perfectly executed, and the pâtés are fresh and tasty, if not spectacular.

Meats are the best main course offerings. A small *Steak with Green Peppercorns* is meticulously trimmed and meltingly tender, as is L'Olivier's *Rack of Lamb* broiled with fresh herbs. Accompanying vegetables like French-cut green beans are always fresh and crisp.

The more complicated dishes have their highs and lows. *Sweetbreads* served in a casserole topped by a golden brown turban of puff pastry gets an A for the Madeira sauce and flaky pastry, but demerits for being overcooked. *Duckling Stuffed with Mousse of Veal*, a house specialty, sacrifices the proper cooking of the duck in order to get the stuffing done.

The lavish dessert cart is straight out of a French provincial restaurant **and** equally good. The fruit on crisp tart shells is mercifully naked, not coated down with gooey glazes. Airy *Charlottes* with satiny *crème anglaise*, floating islands of crisp *Meringue*, and *Chocolate Mousse* dished out of a bowl and served with the excellent *English Custard* bring back memories of meals in France.

You get all the amenities, at night, of a true French restaurant. Port or cognac after dessert with *café filtre*, good wines, rich, well-prepared food, attentive service, and an atmosphere conducive to dining—no distracting decor or music. L'Olivier is pleasantly professional in the traditional French sense.

PRICE RANGE: Moderate

HOURS: 11:30 A.M.–2:00 P.M. Mon.–Fri.
6:00–10:00 P.M. Mon.–Sat.
RESERVATIONS RECOMMENDED FOR LUNCH
FULL BAR
AMERICAN EXPRESS, MASTERCARD, VISA

Louie's of Grant Avenue

1014 Grant Avenue
San Francisco
982–5762

We were taken to Louie's of Grant Avenue in the heart of San Francisco's Chinatown for tea lunch by a busy lawyer who can't stand to wait for a table, but who ends up spending two hours over generous repasts. He had wandered into the huge, upstairs *deem sum* room of Louie's because he liked the name, and stayed because he was seated immediately. Chinese tea lunch appeals to people who love appetizers. At Louie's you can legitimately eat a whole meal of assorted, savory tidbits rolled to your table on carts.

Some of the tastiest *deem sum* include *Pork Bow*, a white bread bun stuffed with a sweet mixture of pork and bean paste; *Braised Duck's Feet*, which taste like pig's feet, fatty and succulent; *Molded Shrimp Rice on Triangles of Green Pepper*; a huge green *Tea Leaf Wrapped Around Sweet Rice with a Chicken, Bacon, and Pork Stuffing* that took on the leaf's smoky flavor as it was steamed; tulips of *Noodles Stuffed with Spicy Ground Pork*; *Noodle Dumplings Stuffed with Delicate Shrimp and Egg*; tender *Meatballs on a Bed of Swiss Chard*; spongy *Bean Cake Stuffed with Chinese Parsley and Pork*; paper-thin leaves of *Soy Bean Filament Wrapped Around Garlicked Chicken*; and for dessert, *Coconut Snowballs* with a gummy exterior and toasted coconut centers.

Not one cart driver could speak enough English to describe her load, and then we noticed that the carts with the most exotic-looking items seemed to pass us by. The duck foot lady was amazed when we flagged her down. She said they were "Chinese food."

One problem with Louie's was that most of the *deem sum* had cooled down considerably by the time they reached us. Also, the room is so large that if you get a table at the end of the

136

traffic pattern, you may be doomed to a picked-over assortment.

PRICE RANGE: Inexpensive
HOURS: 9:30 A.M.–2:30 P.M. daily
NO RESERVATIONS
FULL BAR
NO CREDIT CARDS

MacArthur Park

607 Front Street
San Francisco
398–5700

MacArthur Park is a trendy, popular Financial District watering hole that goes through periodic menu and decor overhauls to keep up to the stylish minute. The results are always the same—an ever-expanding drinking area that is packed every afternoon at 5:00, and a menu that sounds terrific—very California in its emphasis on fresh, local products and straightforward preparation.

The problem is in the execution. Some of the food that gets to your table is topnotch. Some is carelessly prepared, not well thought out, or downright inferior. This inconsistency in the kitchen has plagued MacArthur Park since it opened many menus ago. It becomes all the more frustrating because the trappings of an innovative restaurant are there.

Lack of focus may be the key. Is MacArthur Park mainly a bar or a restaurant? Pop music always plays nonstop, adding to the already high noise level, and it's always very smoky—atmospheric conditions more suitable for a bar than a restaurant.

There is, however, immaculate pink linen on the tables, correct wine service, and one of the best California wine lists in town. MacArthur Park also specializes in meats cooked in an oak-fueled smoker, such as the delicious *Stacked Ham Sandwich*, made with many thinly sliced pieces of succulent meat; slabs of *Baby-back Ribs*; and *Whole Chicken* superbly smoked and tender, with just the right amount of barbeque sauce baked into it to create a crisp skin.

Alas, the rest of the plate is loaded with soft, tepid french fries and cole slaw that is tangy at some meals and bland at others. Such a simple thing as a *Green Salad* is carelessly thrown together with knife-chopped greens and an uninspired, unseasoned vinaigrette dressing. However, *Onion Rings Harry's Bar*, a tangle of battered, deep-fried onion threads, are a real treat, and a *Salad of Romaine Lettuce with Chunks of Roquefort and Walnut Halves* isn't bad.

If you order the *Ribs* or *Chicken* and a good bottle of wine, you can be well fed at MacArthur Park for a reasonable price. But anything the kitchen has to cook to order will be hit-or-miss. The restaurant is huge, and by the time most people sit down to eat, they probably don't care what the food tastes like anyway.

PRICE RANGE: Moderate
HOURS: 11:30 A.M.–2:30 P.M. Mon.–Sat.
       5:30–10:30 P.M. Mon.–Thurs.
       5:30–11:30 P.M. Fri.–Sat.
       5:00–10:00 P.M. Sun.
RESERVATIONS RECOMMENDED
FULL BAR
AMERICAN EXPRESS, MASTERCARD, VISA

Maggie Gin's

1234 Main Street
St. Helena
707/963–9764

Maggie Gin's in St. Helena is a new-wave Chinese restaurant that is no discovery to locals who pack in for lunch and dinner daily. It looks like a low-budget cafeteria with a steam-table serving area in the center, wooden folding chairs, and high, barren walls and ceilings. The only decoration is a green and white Chinese-motif paint job and some handsome fresh fruit behind the counter.

Menu items are listed on the walls on placards, and the similarly displayed beer and wine list is far longer than the menu. Basically, a cold *Chinese Salad* and a hot *Lunch Plate* are offered. The food is dished out of the hot table, and our first thought was that it would be overcooked.

This was far from the case. Instead, the food we ate was crunchy, nearly raw, and extraordinarily fresh and clean tasting. You could taste each vegetable distinctly and their colors were bright. Furthermore, there was very little sauce or oil or cornstarch or sugar on the food. Maggie Gin, the chef-owner, describes her food as "pure and fresh Chinese cooking," and it is just that.

Don't be put off by the cafeteria atmosphere, the small menu, or the precooked food. You're bound to taste something new here.

PRICE RANGE: Inexpensive
HOURS: 11:30 A.M.–2:30 P.M. Tues.–Sat.
5:00–8:30 P.M. Tues.–Fri. and 5:00–9:00 P.M. Sat.
NO RESERVATIONS
BEER AND WINE
MASTERCARD, VISA

Mai Viet-Nam ★

316 Clement Street
San Francisco
221–3046

Mai's specializes in a light, delicate style of Vietnamese cooking that is almost Japanese in character. It serves a simple, mildly spicy, lean type of cooking that's still fun to eat.

We always order the soups, which are notable for their vivid flavor and clarity. No thickeners are used here. *Hanoi-Style Soup* has a thin, exotically seasoned broth loaded with rice noodles and with bits of beef and scallions strewn over them. *Hot-and-Sour Soup with Fish* picks up the flavors of gently poached rock cod, an excellent addition to the delicately balanced play of lemon and hot chilis. An order of soup paired with Mai's famous *Imperial Rolls* makes for a fine meal. The rolls are noted for their crispness. They're whisked out of the kitchen to your table and they practically melt in your mouth. Similar rolls stuffed with cabbage and spicy pork but served cold, their rice-pepper wrappers white and chewy, are called *Vietnamese Rolls*.

The *Chicken* and *Beef Salads* are bright and crunchy, with the shredded cucumber, celery, and carrots looking and tasting as if they had been grated just that minute. No sitting around the kitchen all afternoon for these vegetables. The salads are dressed with the traditional clear, hot Vietnamese fish sauce.

Some dishes on the extensive menu are more exotic, like *Shrimp Balls*, where you eat only the outside wrapping. The sugar-cane core is used only for structure and flavor. You peel off the crisp shrimp batter and make your own roll with

139

membranelike sheets of rice paper, lettuce, and carrots, and spicy dipping sauce.

Whatever you do, don't miss the *La Lot Beef*. Ground beef is wrapped in what's called "la lot" leaves, which are grown in Hawaii and resemble grape leaves. The beef is flavored with a number of exotic spices, and the whole thing is charcoal broiled and served with the ubiquitous Vietnamese fish sauce. This is a variation on stuffed grape leaves you won't believe, and it will be hard to order ordinary grape leaves ever again at a Greek restaurant.

There are lots of other interesting dishes on the menu, including a succulent and inexpensive *Clay-pot Chicken; Barbequed Pork Balls* served with rice paper, lettuce, and bean sauce; *Lemon-grass Chicken*, and *Sautéed Beef in a Coconut-Curry Sauce*. The prices are extremely reasonable, and the portions generous.

Drink the freshly made real *Lemonade* with dinner, and afterwards have *Vietnamese Coffee*, an espresso-strength brew mixed with sweetened condensed milk. It's the best dessert.

PRICE RANGE: Inexpensive
HOURS: 11:00 A.M.–10:00 P.M. Tues.–Fri.
      10:00 A.M.–10:00 P.M. Sat.–Sun.
RESERVATIONS FOR LARGE PARTIES
BEER AND WINE
AMERICAN EXPRESS, MASTERCARD, VISA

Mama's ★

1701 Stockton Street
(at Washington Square)
San Francisco
391–3790

Once upon a time, there really was a Mama (Frances Sanchez), a papa, and all their kids, who personally ran this pleasant and quaint very San Francisco restaurant in North Beach. Today, alas, Mama's is all over the place, including Macy's basement, Nob Hill, and the suburbs. (The phone book even lists an "Executive Office.") But Mama's at North Beach still goes on as usual, serving some of the best breakfasts and lunches in the Bay Area.

It used to be that if you wanted a first-rate omelette in San

Francisco, you'd have but one choice—going to Mama's, and, if it was a weekend, standing in a long line to place your order at the counter. Now there are lots of places with first-rate omelettes, but the long lines at Mama's haven't diminished. The people who work there are nice; the people who eat there are nice; and the view of Washington Square Park is still delightful. If the food today might be matched elsewhere, it's still carefully prepared from the best and freshest ingredients.

Our favorite omelette is called *Mama's Children's Favorite*; it contains mushrooms, green onions, melted Jack cheese, and tomatoes. All the vegetables are fresh and not the least bit overcooked, and the omelette itself is lightly done and fluffy. If you're in the mood for *French Toast*, try it with Swedish cinnamon bread and fresh fruit salad on top. The *Fruit Salad*—which at Mama's is a marvel of virtually everything in season—can also be gotten on the pancakes.

There are several interesting sandwiches for lunch. The *Slim Joe*, a big hamburger with grilled onions and melted Jack on a crispy baguette, beats anything on a mushy bun, and you can add other ingredients, like chili peppers. Also try *Charlie's Aunt*, with crab meat, tomatoes, and Jack, broiled on an English muffin.

When you place your order, you'll see in front of you a collection of desserts that will make you want to forget everything else. Some good news: They taste as good as they look. The cakes are perhaps the best in the city, and the homemade *Blueberry* and *Bran Muffins* are unbeatable.

PRICE RANGE: Moderate
HOURS: 8:00 A.M.–8:00 P.M. daily
NO RESERVATIONS
NO BEER OR WINE
NO CREDIT CARDS

Mama's Royal Cafe ★

4012 Broadway
Oakland
547–9561

811 San Pablo Avenue
Albany
525–6066

There are decent omelettes in the Bay Area, but discovering them requires a search almost as diligent as finding a good pizza. The taste of a perfectly prepared omelette can be worth the search, however, and you won't find a better one than at Mama's Royal Cafe.

Mama's Royal Cafe in Oakland (no relation to Mama's in San Francisco, another spot for good omelettes) is the sort of brunch place where you'll feel so pleasantly at home you'll want to stay for a couple of hours, sipping coffee and reading a newspaper. Much of the clientele seems to fit the general description of Ph.D. dropout and no one appears to be in a hurry to leave (although the service is efficient). The more recently opened Albany branch, in a big, high-ceilinged store that imparts too much of a barnlike setting, is decidedly less pleasant.

As for the Royal Cafe's *Omelettes*, there is simply no compromise. Repeated visits to both branches have produced omelettes that would be remarked on favorably even in a Paris sidewalk cafe. The omelette is light and fluffy, but still manages to have some substance and taste. Moreover, the fillings are matched perfectly to the eggs, with enough seasonings to stand out, but not the big, gloppy portions that can overwhelm the rest of the omelette.

The Royal Cafe offers twenty-eight different combinations of fillings, with the most frequent ingredients including Monterey Jack cheese, guacamole, avocados, bacon, chicken, mushrooms, and chili peppers. We challenge anyone to try the *Spanish and Jack Omelette*, and then move on next time to something else. None of the usual bland, pulpy Spanish sauce here. Instead, the tomatoes, onions, and chili peppers are freshly diced and delicately cooked together to produce a sauce whose spiciness blends perfectly with the bland melted Jack cheese. The guacamole is excellent, also. Each *Omelette* comes with delicious home-fried potatoes, cooked with onions and with the skin left on the potatoes, and served with a dollop of sour cream. Only the toast—a choice of raisin, wheat berry, rye, or white, and tasting like it came from a supermarket shelf—leaves something to be desired.

The Royal Cafe also serves dinners at both locations, with continental-style entrees written on a blackboard and changing frequently. One night's entrees included *Chicken Deborah*, *Pepper Steak*, *Scallops Provençal*, and *Poached Red Snapper with Béarnaise Sauce*, all modestly priced, and all including a choice of soup or salad, marinated mushrooms or ratatouille, rice pilaf, and sourdough bread. The dinner food is hearty and decently prepared, although not exceptional. For the price, however, it represents an extraordinary bargain.

PRICE RANGE: Inexpensive
HOURS: 8:00 A.M.–3:00 P.M. daily
       Albany location:
       5:30–9:00 P.M., Wed.–Thurs.
       5:30–10:00 P.M., Fri.–Sat.
NO RESERVATIONS
BEER AND WINE
NO CREDIT CARDS

Mandarin

Ghirardelli Square
San Francisco
673–8812

For us, the Mandarin has always been a puzzle. With its exquisite decor and its bayside location in Ghirardelli Square, it offers one of the most pleasant settings in San Francisco to have dinner, far surpassing any other Chinese restaurant. Its owner, Cecilia Chiang, has a nationwide reputation as a restaurant entrepreneur. Some of the dishes are absolutely superb. Yet every time we've gone there, about half the meal has been disappointing, sometimes to the extent that the dish in question simply can't be eaten.

In compiling reviews for this book, we decided to put the Mandarin to a major test. We got together fourteen people for a banquet, picked a Monday night when the kitchen wouldn't be jammed with orders, and arranged everything in advance. We included a couple of dishes not on the menu, and one, *Beggar's Chicken*, that has to be ordered a day ahead.

Walking into the Mandarin alone almost makes the evening worthwhile. The beamed ceilings, the decorative wooden latticework and emerald green tiled floors, the Oriental carpets and rare Chinese artifacts set against natural brick walls, and the view out to the bay combine to make eating here a real celebration. The tables are thoughtfully far apart, with pink tablecloths and elegant candles. The service is superb, with clean, heated plates and hot towels brought after messy courses. The dishes come out of the kitchen one at a time; you'll never feel rushed at the Mandarin.

The dinner started on a mixed note with the Mandarin's famous *Minced Squab Wrapped in Lettuce Leaves*. It's a perfectly decent dish, despite the unfortunate choice of iceberg lettuce as the wrapping. But the overall effect was bland, and we've had at least the equal at some neighborhood Chinese restaurants.

For the next two dishes there was no quarrel. The *Pot Stickers* have got to be the best ever created, with the crispiest wrapping imaginable, lots of tasty ground pork filling, and not a speck of grease when you bite into them. The *Smoked Tea Duck* left everyone gasping. The skin was perfectly crisp, the flesh wonderfully tender, not a bit of fat, and the whole thing deeply perfumed by the aromatic tea leaves used in the smoking oven. Even the bones, which were crisp enough to be eaten, gave off this delicate, perfumed aroma and taste.

Beggar's Chicken, which is stuffed with mushrooms, bamboo shoots, and water chestnuts, then enclosed in clay and baked, followed. Everyone who had been transported to outer space by the *Tea Duck* was at least brought back to the stratosphere by the *Chicken*. It simply wasn't very interesting, particularly in view of the $24 price tag for a single chicken. The fact that the sauce was bland, and the bamboo shoots and water chestnuts tasted canned, didn't help.

Then the rocket fell to earth. The *Szechwan Eggplant* was so bad that fourteen people couldn't even finish half the platter, despite the presence of several confirmed Chinese eggplant addicts. It came out horribly gummy, with a surprisingly bland sauce just loaded with cornstarch. Too much cornstarch was again the villain in the sauce with the *Whole Szechwan Fish*, a rock cod that didn't impress anyone as tasting overly fresh. The *Fried Rice* was something that should have been relegated to a high school cafeteria, and the *Scallop Soup* tasted of vinegar, cornstarch, and chicken; whatever scallops had been put in were completely overwhelmed. *Chinese Long Beans Sautéed with Pork* and *Oysters Stir Fried with Ginger and Green Onions* were much better, but not outstanding.

The combination of the pleasant setting and several excellent or decent dishes left most people satisfied. But at the Mandarin's prices, we think there should be more—that the freshest ingredients be used for everything, and that every course demonstrate that it has been prepared with care. When your check can easily surpass $20 a person, dishes like the eggplant aren't forgivable.

So if you try the Mandarin, do so with care. Two people splitting an order of *Pot Stickers*, *Smoked Tea Duck*, and a fresh, sautéed green vegetable dish would be eating very well.

PRICE RANGE: Expensive
HOURS: Noon–11:00 P.M. Mon.–Fri.
        12:30–11:00 P.M. Sat.–Sun.
RESERVATIONS NECESSARY
FULL BAR
ALL MAJOR CREDIT CARDS

Mary's

211 23rd Avenue
(near California)
San Francisco
752–2233

Mary's, "a kitchen that serves cakes and coffee," is the place to go for lovingly made, homey pastry, the kind you could make in your own kitchen with butter, eggs, nuts, and apples, if you had the time.

The tiny store is mostly a kitchen that has a counter and four tables covered with blue-and-white checked tablecloths. Sun streams in the Victorian windows and the smells of baking fill the room. All is cheery, warm, country-kitchenish. When the shop is full, you can sit outside on white-painted Italian benches amid flower boxes and spindly city trees.

Mary's makes a large assortment of classic American desserts, such as *Apricot Almond Bars, Blueberry Muffins, Butterscotch Brownies, Pies, Shortbread*, and *Upside Down Cake*. On Sunday morning you can eat fresh *Strawberry and Apple Coffeecake*, still warm from the oven. The apples are crisp, the strawberries soft and juicy, and the brown-sugar topping adds just the right degree of sweetness.

Mary's *Frittatas*, hot from the oven, are also wonderful. A square at least four inches high of fresh spinach, cheese, and eggs, topped with tomatoes and crusty baked cheese—it's a meal in itself.

Blended drip coffee from Capricorn Coffees is strong and aromatic, the perfect accompaniment for all the baked goods.

Mary's epitomizes the small, personal, home-grown, neighborhood business that we like to patronize.

PRICE RANGE: Inexpensive
HOURS: 10:00 A.M.–7:00 P.M. Tues.–Thurs.
       10:00 A.M.–10:30 P.M. Fri.–Sat.
       10:00 A.M.–3:00 P.M. Sun.
NO RESERVATIONS
NO CREDIT CARDS

Maurice et Charles Bistrot ★★★

901 Lincoln Avenue
San Rafael
456–2010

If giving fine service in a restaurant is an old-world art—one, we
might add, you don't often find in Europe today—efficiency is
the hallmark of most American restaurants, including American
French restaurants. When we get service with much flourish, we
become uneasy, as if we are being conned into paying for it
instead of the food. However, Maurice Amzallag, proprietor and
host of Maurice et Charles Bistrot in San Rafael, has made us
appreciate what an artist in the dining room can do.

Ah, elegant Maurice, with his silver, swept-back mane, exquisitely tailored and groomed as only the French can be. His sweet,
hospitable smile, his charming accent, his soft voice greeting you
at the door, taking your coat, bringing you into his veritable
living room, genuinely honored that you could make it that
evening.

He shows you to your white-linened table. A perfect rose in a
crystal vase. Sparkling glassware. Huge napkins.

"Is it too drafty here? No? Fine. Let me bring you a champagne cocktail, and then we will discuss the menu."

He returns with slender flutes. We learn about the menu. Each
item is described—the technique, the ingredients, their origin.
You must choose.

"Let me bring you half a petit *Plat d'Arcachon* and then you
can have *Quenelles*, too, as a first course. You are also interested
in the *Endive Salad*? I will bring that afterwards and split it for
you." Maurice solves all problems.

The meal is considered, arranged, created. We discuss the
wines.

"I have some wines that are not on the list. Shall I bring them
to you so you can see them?" We discuss their origins, their
nature, from whom they were bought.

Maurice goes off to discuss your wishes with his waiters and his cook, who is his new partner. Charles, his original partner, moved to Truckee to open an all-garlic restaurant. He puts garlic in every dish he serves. Marcel Cathala, the new cooking partner, apprenticed under the chef at Le Pere Bise in Talloires, a three-star bastion of haute cuisine.

The *Oysters* arrive—large, fresh West Coast oysters from Washington, served warm on a bed of braised lettuce and masked in a velvety sauce based on the oysters' poaching liquid, tinged with a blush of sauce Nantua.

The silken Nantua sauce reappears on the *Quenelles*, which are dumplings of ground fish with the texture of clouds. They evaporate in your mouth. They're ethereal.

Thin slices of *Duck Liver Pâté*, jeweled with green and red bits of beans and tomatoes and stunningly garnished with tiny aspic flowers, are served in a misplaced buttermilk and sour cream sauce. A cold *Pâté of Scallops and Salmon* is also very handsome, a mosaic of shiny white scallops and pink steelhead salmon held together by a fish mousse. Somehow, these fish tureens seem characterless to us, but a mayonnaise with horseradish brings focus to the dish.

A *Salad of Belgian Endive*, white, fruity, slightly bitter, is served with an anchovy sauce, thereby offering two of our favorite foods in one dish. Garnished with a fan of paper-thin avocado slices, the salad is a Japanese still life in pastel greens. Our only desire at this moment in the meal is for more anchovies in the vinaigrette dressing.

After a civilized interval—coordination between the kitchen and the front never fails here—the main courses arrive. As shiny silver covers are lifted from the plates to reveal textbook culinary composition, you let out a little gasp. This is indeed a meticulous kitchen.

Marcassin de Mendocino is wild domestic boar, a seeming contradiction explained by the fact that the boar are allowed to run around a large Mendocino ranch. The meat is dark and less fatty than pork, but has porcine succulence. You get meat from all parts of the animal—tiny chops from the rib, slices from the leg, all cooked separately to just the right doneness. A sable brown sauce made from the braising liquid does not overpower the delicate meat.

The *Pheasant* served here are raised on a farm and taste domestic, like plump, juicy chickens. Their preparation cannot be faulted, but don't expect game. Juniper berries enliven its creamy sauce. Both the *Boar* and the *Pheasant* are served with the restaurant's signature, chestnut puree made, alas, from a mixture of canned and dried chestnuts, but still the best puree you could hope for without starting with fresh chestnuts.

Médaillon de Veau is thick slices of tender, white, milk-fed veal, richly sauced with brandy and cream. The veal is accompanied by a *nouvelle cuisine* turnip, thinly sliced and reassembled, seasonally sweet and tender, and a two-layered *barquette* of carrot and spinach puree. What an accomplished plate!

The *Duckling* comes frozen from Long Island, yet is quite extraordinary. The plump, medium-rare breast has the satiny texture of sweetbreads, and the legs, braised separately, have the flavor and firmness of a wild bird. I have not eaten a better-prepared duck either here or in France.

For dessert, there are cheeses served at room temperature and slices of apple that have been peeled for you. We always have the homemade *Ices* and *Ice Creams*, a changing medley that might include fresh *Tangerine*, *Walnut*, *Hazelnut*, or *Avocado*.

No espresso, but demitasses of strong *Jamaican Coffee* end your meal.

And so, you are ready to leave. You are a little sad about this, but oh, so satisfied. You've had just the right amount of food and wine—Maurice has seen to that. He helps you on with your coat. He sees you to the door. He puts a rose in your hand. You've been treated so elegantly in every way that the evening has been magic. You plan your return to *domaine* Maurice on the deserted late-evening San Rafael streets.

PRICE RANGE: Expensive
HOURS: 6:30–10:30 P.M. Mon.–Sat.
RESERVATIONS REQUIRED
WINE
AMERICAN EXPRESS, MASTERCARD, VISA

McCallum's

1825 Solano Avenue
Berkeley
525–3510

San Franciscans who argue with Berkeleyites about the merits of Bud's and Double Rainbow don't get paid much attention. Many people in the East Bay consider McCallum's to have the finest ice cream in the Bay Area.

If you want to join the debate, start off with any of McCallum's nut ice creams, particularly *Butter Pecan* or *Banana Walnut*. What you get is not a sprinkling of a few flecks of nuts, but large, unbroken nuts scattered throughout the ice cream in profusion. Then go on to a scoop of any fudge flavor (*Mint Fudge* is our favorite, or *Orange Fudge* in the fall). This is real fudge, the thick, gooey, delicious variety, that tastes like it was made on some grandmother's stove.

There's a sit-down section next door, where you can order sundaes, sodas, and other concoctions. Or, you can just get two scoops of plain ice cream in a bowl, the best thing to do when you're presented with the chance to have such superb ingredients.

HOURS: 7:00 A.M.–11:00 P.M. Sun.–Thurs.
7:00 A.M.–midnight Fri.–Sat.

Mifune

1737 Post Street
San Francisco
922–0337

The Japanese Cultural Center, a monolithic white structure that stretches for three blocks east and west from Fillmore to Laguna and north and south from Post to Geary, looks cold and forbidding from the outside. Once inside (the best way in is from Post Street), you have to ply the corridors and bridges for the real gems inside—the restaurants—if you're not in the market for Japanese electronics or children's wiggle pictures.

Mifune is part of a noodle shop chain in Japan. Noodle shops are the Japanese version of fast-food restaurants. But what great fast-food restaurants they are! At Mifune, you get a choice of thirty-one different noodle and rice dishes, all presented in different bowls and containers and lacquer trays with special condiments.

You can order two types of noodles: *udon*, which are thick and made of white flour; or *soba*, which are thin and made of brown buckwheat flour. You can get either of these noodles in a variety of preparations. For years, we ordered the same dish, *Soba Beef*, a huge bowl of miso soup and noodles with grilled beef and scallions on top.

After a steaming bowl of Mifune's noodles and soup, we always feel satisfied and restored. No oil or fat here, but plenty of flavor and real food satisfaction.

Lately, we have discovered the appeal of the cold noodle

dishes. The *Mifune Special* comes on a lacquer board with a cargo of white and brown noodles on deck, sprinkled with seaweed. Hot shrimp and vegetable tempura is arranged on the prow. You also get a bowl of cold dipping sauce, into which you stir chopped scallions, hot *wasabe* (green horseradish paste), and bits of grated daikon radish. Then you dip the noodles and tempura into your custom-made sauce.

You do a similar self-mixing operation with *Kama Age Udon* or *Soba*. This time, hot noodles come in a covered lacquer jar with a warm, smoky-tasting dipping sauce on the side. You throw in a raw egg and add the requisite amounts of *wasabe*.

Another favorite, *Tempura with Udon* or *Soba*, brings the usual bowl of hot soup and noodles, this time with battered, deep-fried shrimp and vegetables right on top. Somehow they don't get soggy. The deep frying is done so well that the tempura tastes as light and clean as the rest of the food. The same good tempura, held together with an egg in a soft, creamy omelette, comes on top of rice as well in *Tempura Donburi with Egg*.

Each noodle or rice combination is designed to give you protein even if there is no meat, in the form of seaweed, egg, or miso, making this a good restaurant for vegetarians. It's also a good restaurant to take kids, who always seem to like soup and noodles and don't like to wait for their food. You're in and out in less than half an hour, but you are never rushed. You can sit and sip tea all afternoon if you'd rather. Mifune is a little haven of noodly comfort in the Central City.

PRICE RANGE: Inexpensive
HOURS: 11:00 A.M.–9:00 P.M. daily
BEER AND SAKE
MASTERCARD, VISA

Mike's Chinese Cuisine ★

5145 Geary Boulevard
(at 15th Avenue)
San Francisco
752–0120

You can have two kinds of Cantonese eating experiences in San Francisco—one that is authentic and often exotic, and another that has been adapted to American tastes. If you yearn for the latter or you're in a take-the-visiting-relatives-to-a-restaurant-they-will-like situation, Mike's Chinese Cuisine is the place to go. Mike's has long been popular with both Chinese and non-Chinese San Franciscans. The menu is a compendium of such favorites as *Sweet-and-Sour Pork*, *Egg Rolls*, *Won Ton Soup*, and *Chicken with Cashews*. The difference is that these dishes are carefully done at Mike's, incorporating generous portions of meats and good-looking young vegetables in simple, uncluttered preparations without fillers. The restaurant also does *Steamed Whole Fish* and *Smoked Tea Duck* and *Crispy Whole Chicken*, which are not on the menu but often seen on the tables occupied by large Chinese families. For most of its customers, Mike's means *Asparagus Beef* and *Fried Won Ton* at its best.

The *Fried Won Ton* are so light and crisp they practically float off the plate. The *Egg Rolls*, first wrapped in cabbage leaves and then dipped in batter, are plump with bean sprouts and pork. Tender, high-grade beef is used in *Asparagus* or *Broccoli Beef*, depending on the season, and musky oyster sauce is always sparingly applied. *Sweet-and-Sour Pork Deluxe*, Mike's invention, combines nuggets of buttery deep-fried pork with preserved melon rind, lichees, and gingered fruits in a shiny red sauce of silken texture.

Soups are always a test of a Chinese kitchen, and the *Won Ton Soup with Barbequed Pork* at Mike's is a sure sign of skill and integrity. The stock is clear and sparkling and full of flavor. The won tons are fat with well-seasoned pork and ginger, and the lean slices of smoky ham and crisp, bright mustard greens make the soup look like a Chinese painting.

For the slightly more adventurous, we highly recommend *Barbequed Chicken Salad*, a cold dish of shredded head lettuce and chicken tossed with sprigs of coriander, mustard, and sesame seeds. *Crystal Shrimp*, meant to be eaten shell and all, are much juicier than deshelled shrimp. The *Crispy Chicken*, first steamed and then deep fried, may be the most succulent poultry in town.

Expect a wait when you go to Mike's. It's only open for dinner and doesn't take reservations. But this is one Chinese restaurant that serves food worth waiting for.

PRICE RANGE: Inexpensive to moderate
HOURS: 4:30–10:00 P.M. Wed.–Mon.
NO RESERVATIONS
FULL BAR
MASTERCARD, VISA

Milano Pizza and Italian Restaurant

1330 Ninth Avenue
San Francisco
665–3773

For a New Yorker living in San Francisco, finding a pizza like they have them back East can be almost a full-time occupation. Everyone seems to have one recommendation or another, ranging from fancy Italian restaurants to little take-out places in shopping centers in distant suburbs. The only requirement is a bottle of Alka-Seltzer and you're officially in the pizza-chasing business.

Medical science hasn't yet pinned down what exactly in a pizza is so addictive, but we're both hopeless pizza addicts. We're also turned off by the standard pizza found in so many San Francisco Italian restaurants, the kind that tastes like it could have come from a frozen-food case or from a fast-food franchise.

There are many ways to do a good pizza. One of the best, to our mind, is the style featured in some of the best eastern pizzerias. The crust underneath should be crisp and never soggy, and around the edges it should balloon out, being crunchy on the outside and hollow in the center. There must be plenty of tomato sauce, and so much cheese that it drips all over the place in puddles and long strings when you try to put a slice onto your plate. And it must be spicy; you want to walk away with the lingering taste of what you have been eating. Finally, needless to say, the various toppings must be fresh and liberally applied. No canned mushrooms on our pizzas.

The *Pizza* at Milano Pizza and Italian Restaurant might not be the answer to everyone's dreams, but (assuming you cheat a little, and ask for "extra cheese and extra tomato sauce") it comes remarkably close. The crust is perfect, enough to bring a New Yorker to tears. The staff really does listen if you ask for extra cheese and tomato sauce, and the cheese subsequently drips just like it should. The spices aren't quite there yet, but they're certainly not bland. The toppings are excellent, particularly the fresh and beautifully cooked vegetables. The price is right, too, and if two people order an extra large, you'd better be hungry.

Milano's also has other items on its menu, some of which are surprisingly decent. The homemade *Minestrone Soup* is among the best that can be found anywhere. The broth is thick and spicy, and it's filled with big chunks of fresh, crunchy vegetables.

While the *Salad* is plain old iceberg lettuce with tomatoes and cucumbers, the oil and vinegar dressing, laced with garlic, adds interest.

The *Lasagne* with melted mozzarella cheese on the top wouldn't win any culinary awards, but it's tasty and filling. The same is true of *Veal Parmigiana*, a tender, pink slab of breaded veal that is topped with cheese and a spicy tomato sauce. The *Spaghetti with Mushrooms* is your average mediocre spaghetti, but the thick tomato and meat sauce is filled with delicious huge chunks of savory mushrooms. All these dishes are at extraordinarily low prices.

Milano's isn't exactly candlelight dining. At our first visit, in fact, a color television blared from a ledge in the back. But the people who run it are warm and friendly, and the pizza is a genuine treat.

PRICE RANGE: Inexpensive
HOURS: 3:00 P.M.–midnight Sun.–Thurs.
       3:00 P.M.–1:00 A.M. Fri.–Sat.
NO RESERVATIONS
BEER AND WINE
NO CREDIT CARDS

Millard's on Fillmore ★

2197 Fillmore Street
(at Clay)
San Francisco
567–0945

Millard's on Fillmore, a tiny little counter restaurant right next door to the Clay theater, serves the best crêpes in town. They also have an espresso machine. This means that you can dine lightly, have an eye-opening *Cappuccino* and be set for a sitting at theater or opera. We find Millard's to be an ideal place to go before such events.

The whole restaurant is the size of a Pacific Heights closet. A counter with eight stools takes up the narrow front, and a few tiny tables fill the back. A miniature table for two is perched in the front window, and that's the choice place to sit to watch the movie crowd.

The menu offers five different types of crêpes, each one

delicious. The pancakes are delicate and the fillings and sauces are appropriately light. We like the *Gruyère and Mushroom Crêpe* topped with buttered bread crumbs, and the *Chicken Crêpe Italienne*, filled with finely chopped chicken livers, spinach, and mushrooms. A delightful *Fresh Fruit Crêpe* hovers between being dessert and dinner, with whole walnuts, sautéed apple, fresh fruits in season, and sour cream.

The pretty salads shown off in clear glass bowls are carefully composed, and the changing soup of the day is usually a puree of fresh vegetables.

Whenever we're in the neighborhood we stop by Millard's for a coffee or an aperitif. It's so cheerful and pleasant inside that we prefer it to the more urban North Beach coffee houses.

PRICE RANGE: Inexpensive to moderate
HOURS: 11:30 A.M.–2:30 P.M. Tues.–Sat.
       5:30–10:00 P.M. Tues.–Sun.
NO RESERVATIONS
BEER AND WINE
NO CREDIT CARDS

Miramonte ★★★

1327 Railroad Avenue
St. Helena
707/963–3970

Eating at the Miramonte Restaurant in St. Helena reminds us of meals we have had outdoors in the vineyards of Burgundy—not so much because the food is the same, but because being so close to the vines that produce the wines you are drinking at tables makes you feel heady. It's not the 12 percent alcohol that does it, but the air, the landscape, and the heightened awareness that the accomplishments of the most refined chefs and skilled winemakers start in the earth.

Serious eaters have long awaited the opening of a restaurant in the Napa Valley of the stature of the Miramonte. The culinary pedigree of the chef, Udo Nechutny, is blue ribbon. He attended hotel and restaurant schools in Switzerland, apprenticed with Paul Bocuse, and taught in Japan. More recently, he was the first chef at Domaine Chandon's new winery restaurant in the Napa Valley and an instructor at the California Culinary Academy in

San Francisco. He opened the Miramonte with Swiss partner Edouard Platel, formerly executive chef of the Del Monte Lodge.

The partner refurbished the old stone Miramonte Hotel with an eye to simplicity. It's light and airy with pristine white walls framed by polished blonde woods. The bar area is decorated with autographed photographs of local winemakers, and an outdoor patio shaded by a fig tree provides the setting for delightful lunches.

The dinner menu offers two prix fixe meals only, and is a reflection of Chef Nechutny's personal ideas about food. His trademarks are the juxtaposition of raw and cooked foods, unexpected combinations of ingredients, a Japanese sensitivity toward color and arrangement, a French dedication to the best local raw materials, and an ability to put together a rich, five-course meal that is never ponderous. He cuts away every superfluous enrichment, thickener, and seasoning to get the essence of the food he serves.

Since the menu changes seasonally, we can only give you an idea of what to expect. On our most recent visit we were served a crystal-clear, chilled *Chicken Consommé* dotted with bits of green scallions and fresh tomatoes. The presentation in a covered white tureen made the shimmering jelly look like a bowl of jewels. The next course brought four barely cooked *Scallops* in a perfumed *buerre blanc*. The main course was a rare, butter-tender oval of *Beef Tenderloin* covered with raw chopped shallots, beef marrow, and the merest glaze of demiglace. On the same plate there was a Japanese arrangement of dark green spinach, charcoal-colored tree ears in cream, light green baby zucchini, and paper-thin slices of crisp potatoes. A plate of perfect *Butter Lettuce* in a mild, milky vinaigrette dressing followed. Dessert was like a flower arrangement—*Fresh Fruit Sauced with Berry Purees, Homemade Ice Creams, and Sprigs of Fresh Mint* carefully laid out on a big, white plate.

Other dishes in Nechutny's repertoire are tiny *Quail* stuffed with delicate chicken liver forcemeat and presented with peeled green grapes; plump *Chicken Breasts Smothered in Cellophane*; and perhaps his best, *Steak de Canard aux Poivre Vert*, slices from the breast of duck cooked to split-second precision that have the creamy texture of rare beef and the wild flavor of game.

The exclusively California wine list reads like a catalogue from the valley's best vineyards; the prices are not much above what you would pay in a wine store if you could find the selection.

Service is informal and directed by the two gracious wives of the owners. The Miramonte has only one sitting, so you must reserve well in advance.

PRICE RANGE: Expensive
HOURS: 6:15–9:00 P.M. Wed.–Sun.
        11:30 A.M.–2:30 P.M. Sun. (lunch)
RESERVATIONS NECESSARY
BEER AND WINE
MASTERCARD, VISA

Misono

1737 Post Street
San Francisco
992–2728

Misono is a restaurant that specializes in *wappa*—rice, meats, and vegetables steamed together and served in bamboo cooking baskets. The restaurant itself exemplifies the simplicity and sense of proportion of fine Japanese interior design. There are elegant rice paper and wood light fixtures, beautifully handcrafted wooden booths with blue and white Japanese cotton pillows, a low counter with reed-bottomed chairs, tile floors, brown cotton banners, small colorful pictures, and tiny windows that look out to the indoor garden of the Kintetsu Building.

The *wappa* comes on a lacquered tray with miso soup and tiny plates of shredded daikon, carrots, and pickled cabbage. The *Beef Wappa* is the most flavorful, with sweet, brown soy sauce steamed into thin slices of beef, glassy rice noodles, and onion. The steamed rice underneath is almost creamy. The *Chicken Wappa* features tender pieces of breast with bright green scallions. You can get a cup of *Hot Egg Custard* full of scallops, crab, and vegetables to eat with your *wappa*—very light and clean tasting.

Misono also offers *Sashimi* made with delicate, pink tuna cut into thin slices that melt in your mouth. *Sashimi* combined with *wappa* makes a wonderful Japanese meal.

A limited number of sushi are also done at Misono, the best of which is *Salmon Sushi*, which looks like a pink birthday cake cut up into bite-sized squares. Each tiny cake has layers of lightly salted smoked salmon, rice, and green seaweed.

The food at Misono is not extraordinary, but what it does, it does well. Each dish—modest though it may be—gets its own special bowl, arrangement, and treatment. The harmonious style and setting of Misono gives it its appeal.

PRICE RANGE: Inexpensive
HOURS: 11:00 A.M.–2:30 P.M., 5:00–9:00 P.M. Mon.–Fri.
   11:00 A.M.–9:00 P.M. Sat.
   11:00 A.M.–8:30 P.M. Sun.
NO RESERVATIONS
BEER AND SAKE
MASTERCARD, VISA

Modesto Lanzone's ★★

900 Northpoint
San Francisco
771–2880

Restaurants at Ghirardelli Square are big, impersonal places that are only interested in extracting money from tourists, right?

That might be people's impression, but consider this incident. A friend recently told us about taking his difficult mother from Cleveland to Modesto Lanzone's. The waiter suggested that she order the *Canneloni*, Modesto's own mother's special recipe. The Cleveland mother tried it, and when Modesto asked her how she liked it, she said she had tasted better in Florence. Modesto whisked her plate away, dashed into the kitchen, and prepared the dish himself. Result: a canneloni not too different from the original—but one that thoroughly gratified Mother.

This restaurant totally reflects the personality of owner Modesto Lanzone, a ubiquitous figure who greets you at the door, wends his way from table to table to chat and to make suggestions about dishes and wine, checks out the carts of food streaming from the kitchen, and keeps the impeccable service flowing.

The man is a born restaurateur, with a superb kitchen tailored to his own special needs and preferences as a cook. He also appreciates contemporary art and has decorated his restaurant with an impressive collection of works by Sam Francis, Nathan Olivera, Luke Gibney, Joan Brown, and Robert Arneson. But once the meal starts, your attention will quickly turn from the art to the food. In a city whose reputation for Italian food far exceeds the quality of the food itself, Modesto's is one place where you can get a superb northern Italian dinner. Not everything on the menu is equally good, but the best dishes are outstanding by any yardstick.

Several of the pastas are well worth ordering. *Guanciali al Funghi*, a relatively new addition to the interesting pasta list, are

157

large, rectangular raviolis stuffed with ricotta and another cheese, topped with *al dente* mushroom slices, onions, tomatoes, and green peppers. This dish is not only unique, but also the combination of flavors and textures are superb. There is also an excellent *Ravioli Genovese*, pillows of noodles stuffed with meat and tossed in a tomato and meat sauce. The downfall of most ravioli are the edges, which are usually tough and doughy. These, by contrast, are seamless wonders. Finally, we always enjoy the *Agnolotti alla Crema*, round discs of pasta stuffed with chicken, cheese, and prosciutto, and splashed with cream.

One of our favorite pastas here is the simplest: *Linguine Marinara*, long strings of pasta that span the size gap between spaghetti and fettucine in a meatless tomato sauce that reminds us of vine-ripened beefsteak tomatoes at the height of summer. We used to wolf down whole orders of *Linguine Marinara* until we discovered a second favorite dish at Modesto Lanzone's, *Fegato alla Veniziana*. Strips of beef liver are sautéed to just the right doneness, moist but firm, and smothered in a full-bodied sauce of sweet-cooked onions, red wine, and vinegar. Liver haters would be won over.

Veal dishes are typical of the best ones served around town. Excellent-quality meat is sautéed to fork-tender consistency. Abundent capers grace the *Piccata*; lots of paper-thin mushrooms and a dark, rich wine sauce come on the *Scallopini*; but the *Cotoletta Parmigiana*, that hackneyed veal dish served in every Italian restaurant, is an example of what a smart kitchen can do. A thin slice of bread-crumb-brushed veal with good imported cheese melted over it is served with an incomparable marinara sauce on the side; delicate is the best description for it.

Nocciola di Abbacchio alla Romana, lamb roasted Roman style, is a hunk of boned loin that has been marinated in oil and herbs for three days, broiled to sear in the juices, and then roasted to order, arriving at the table a perfect pink. Somehow, despite all this, we found that it was nothing special. *Scampi Pescatora*, baby lobster tails that are tenderer than the full-sized ones, are sauced in shallots, butter, and wine. *Chicken Cacciatora* for two is a succulent sauté of chicken breast and leg, with those thinly sliced mushrooms, a hint of green pepper, shallots, tomatoes, paprika, herbs, and red wine. It's a masterpiece.

Most of the small selection of desserts is not made on the premises. *Sacripantina* from Stella Pastry in North Beach is a yellow cake layered with frozen zabaglione, but why be bothered with the cake? Order a whole goblet of *Zabaglione* for two, a cumulous cloud of egg yolks, sherry, and sugar beaten over heat. The cream-caramel burnt sugar surrounding a tender molded

Custard is also excellent. You can finish off your meal with *Espresso*, made in an antique copper machine.

The wine list goes on for pages and represents a dizzying selection of Italian wines from places we have yet to locate on the map.

PRICE RANGE: Moderate to expensive
HOURS: Noon–11:00 P.M. Tues.–Fri.
         4:00 P.M.–midnight Sat.–Sun.
RESERVATIONS STRONGLY RECOMMENDED
FULL BAR
ALL MAJOR CREDIT CARDS

Moti Mahal

2650 Bridgeway
Sausalito
332–6444

Moti Mahal is a well-known Indian restaurant that spent many years on Dwight Way near Telegraph Avenue in Berkeley and that several years ago, rather improbably, moved to Sausalito. What used to be the cheapest meal in town and one of the best is now three times the price, but the vegetarian dishes on the menu are still very reasonable and they're just as good. There's more emphasis now on full-scale Indian dining with fancier service, but we have found that by sticking to our long-time favorites, which are mostly vegetarian dishes, Moti Mahal still has soul.

The new building looks like part of a warehouse. It's been hung with curtains and low-flying batik canopies to make it more intimate. Red linen is used on the tables and the staff wears colorful saris. If you're not too lucky, you will be serenaded at dinner by two students from the Ali Akbar Khan Institute.

Always start with Moti Mahal's three appetizers. *Pakora*, the best Indian dish ever invented, are little deep-fried, highly seasoned puffs made of garbanzo bean butter and spiced onions, potatoes, carrots, and peas. The same vegetables go into *Samosas*, flaky deep-fried turnovers. Also, a deep-fried, battered tomato called *Bhaji* is wonderful. You dip these into a chutney of yogurt, buttermilk, cilantro, and hot chilis.

For main courses, we like the vegetable curries, such as a stew of soft, spicy eggplant called *Baingan*, or a *Potato and Pea Curry* that tastes just like the *pakora* filling. The spiciest is *Eri*

159

Cheri, which originates from the tropical southern district of Kerala, made with hard, green, unpeeled bananas. You scoop these curries up with grilled *Parathas*, a flat, whole-wheat bread with a chewy texture.

With the entrees you get a bright array of homemade condiments, such as fresh spiced apple, a very hot onion chutney, grated coconut, the searing-hot *aachar*, lime and mango pickles, and a cooling yogurt called *daahi*. They're alternately sweet, hot, or vinegary, so you can season each bite.

We also recommend that you order all the Indian breads. *Papadum* are crisp rice wafers that are so light they melt the minute they touch a moist tongue, releasing all sorts of spices—a cracker that tastes like a meal. *Pooris* are puffs of light, white bread that puff up as they cook. As you break them they let out a breath of warm, wheaty air.

The chef at Moti Mahal is a Tamil from a heavily populated Hindu area noted for spicy vegetarian food. He does not have a feel for meats of any kind, but by sticking to his specialties you can get an explosively delicious meal.

PRICE RANGE: Moderate
HOURS: 6:00–10:30 P.M. Tues.–Sun.
RESERVATIONS ACCEPTED
BEER AND WINE
MASTERCARD, VISA

Murillo's ★★

633 Merchant Street
Vacaville
707/448–3395

A friend of ours, Armando Menocal, when he's not climbing mountains or practicing public-interest law, pursues his favorite hobby: locating great hole-in-the-wall Mexican restaurants in small towns in Northern California. His theory is that this is where the best Mexican food is to be found, not in the big cities. Murillo's proves him right—it serves the best Mexican food we've ever had in California.

Since we've discovered Murillo's, we can never make it to Sacramento or to the mountains on Interstate 80 without stopping there. Forget the Nut Tree—this is the real find, and it's just a minute from the freeway. Take the Vacaville prison exit, turn north (left, if you're coming from San Francisco), then turn right at the first light. Murillo's is in the second shopping center on the right, close to Foster's Freeze.

Don't expect anything fancy, but also don't expect to pay anything more than a few dollars for a huge dinner. Murillo's is all formica and fluorescent, and no matter when you arrive it's sure to be jammed, although the line moves fast. If you're wearing blue jeans and come in a pick-up truck, you'll feel right at home.

You'll know there's something unusual going on here the moment you sit down. A basket of *hot* corn chips is put on your table; just out of the deep fryer, they're usually so hot that you can't even touch them. The accompanying hot sauce is also splendid, containing little bits of cut-up onions, peppers, and tomatoes.

Whatever your test for a Mexican restaurant, Murillo's is sure to pass. The beef in the *Tacos* and *Enchiladas* is shredded, not ground. While at many Mexican restaurants the sauce for the *Enchiladas* tastes like it came from a can, at Murillo's it's pungent with chili powder, and has liberal melted cheese. The *Quesadilla*, the Mexican "toasted cheese sandwich" made between two tortillas, is so unbelievably superior you'll never be able to order one in another restaurant. The last time we ate there it cost all of 75 cents. The *Chile Relleno* is a marvel, with a beautifully spicy sauce and a generous use of melted Jack cheese.

Many people who eat at Murillo's consider the *Chicken and Avocado Tostada* their great dish. A huge dinner plate comes to the table brimming over with a giant taco, stuffed with beans, shredded lettuce, shredded chicken, and what must be an entire sliced avocado on top. This costs all of $1.85. We admit it's delicious, but if you fill up completely on this, and don't have room for an *Enchilada*, *Chile Relleno*, and *Quesadilla*, you'll really be missing something.

Incidentally, once you become a Murillo's regular, you can depart from the "Tex-Mex" food and try some of the other dishes on the menu. Particularly good is the *Pork Chile Verde*, a plate of tender, fat-free chunks of pork cooked in a peppery brown sauce.

PRICE RANGE: Inexpensive
HOURS: 11:00 A.M.–9:30 P.M. Mon.–Thurs.
        11:00 A.M.–10:30 P.M. Fri.
        10:00 A.M.–10:30 P.M. Sat.
        2:00–9:00 P.M. Sun.
NO RESERVATIONS
BEER AND WINE
NO CREDIT CARDS

Nadine Restaurant

2400 San Pablo Avenue
Berkeley
549–2807

Restaurant Nadine is the type of restaurant that you want to be good. It's run by two cordial, dedicated men of Czech origin who met in Sweden. Over a year ago, they landed in Berkeley at the old Pot Luck building on San Pablo, a solitary wood frame structure that had fallen into disrepair.

The new owners performed miracles on the building, giving it the flavor of an elegant country inn, with skylights, large expanses of white wall broken up by antique sideboards, original paintings by Czech artists, and manicured plants. But the food has turned out to be an odd potpourri of dishes that haven't added up to a satisfying meal. It is simply not special enough for the money.

Some items, like the *Stuffed Mushrooms Florentine*, are excellent. The *Goulash*, which tastes authentically Hungarian, is so good it made us wish the restaurant had an Eastern European rather than a French accent. But other courses are totally unacceptable. The *Fried Cheese*, a slab of breaded Swiss cheese fried until not quite melted and served with a dollop of tartar sauce, has the effect of Mrs. Paul's frozen fish filets. The *Pheasant Soufflé*, with a texture and shape not unlike that of a rubber ball, is a disaster. The desserts, made by the Swedish wife of the owner, are the best part of the meal.

At Nadine's prices, you simply shouldn't have to flounder around the menu to find some successful dishes. It's too bad, because all the basics are here for a fine restaurant.

PRICE RANGE: Moderate to expensive
HOURS: 5:30–10:00 P.M. Tues.–Sat.
       5:00–9:00 P.M. Sun.
RESERVATIONS ACCEPTED
BEER AND WINE
MASTERCARD, VISA

Napoli

2435 Clement Street
San Francisco
752–3003

Napoli is an unpretentious little pasta restaurant that puts out a first-rate plate of spaghetti for a very reasonable price. The pasta is always cooked *al dente* to order and you get a choice of six different sauces to put on it. The basic tomato sauce, a marinara, has been quickly cooked so that it retains its fresh tomato flavor, totally unlike those acidic, back-burner affairs typical of so many Italian restaurants. With the addition of chopped beef to the marinara, you get *Pasta Napoletana*. With the addition of *pancetta*, smoky Italian bacon, the marinara becomes *Matriciana*, and the marinara with chopped clams turns into a fine seafood sauce as well.

Napoli is one of the few restaurants in the City that makes a rich, perfectly balanced carbonara sauce, with just the right amounts of egg yolk, cream, cheese, and *pancetta*.

Have your pasta with a *Romaine Lettuce and Tomato Salad* in a tart vinegar and oil dressing, and you have a casual meal for a very casual price.

We do not recommend the more expensive veal dishes. They're made with baby beef and the pink meat, though tasty, is often tough.

The restaurant is owned and solely run by an Italian chef and a personable Yugoslavian waiter. They will accommodate your requests for sauces not on the menu when it's not too busy.

PRICE RANGE: Inexpensive to moderate
HOURS: 4:00–11:00 P.M. Thurs.–Tues.
RESERVATIONS ACCEPTED
BEER AND WINE
MASTERCARD, VISA

Nob Hill Cafe ★

1152 Taylor Street
San Francisco
776–6915

The Nob Hill Cafe may be the swankiest counter restaurant in the City. It's the right restaurant for the neighborhood, offering most of the amenities of the nobs up the hill, but in its own informal, inimitable style. It is owned and run by a husband and wife, Gerardo and Michiko Boccara, and the mix of their European and Japanese backgrounds makes their restaurant unique.

They have fit together with jig-saw-puzzle precision four booths with tables covered with linen and then thick glass, six counter seats, and a kitchen into a space the size of a Nob Hill resident's closet. Cheery white walls to maximize the area, a clever paint job on ducts and pipes, natty navy blue trim and sidewalk canopy, good blue and white china, cloth napkins, fresh flowers, and the most sparkling-clean cooking area we've ever seen make the Nob Hill Cafe irresistible to passersby who peek in through the open dutch door.

The menu, written on a chalk board, looks French, but the truth of the matter is that the cooking is almost uncategorizable. Michiko does it all and her style is very much her own. She breaks most of the rules of French cuisine, incorporates Japanese technique, and progresses far beyond anything American, although her food has a directness and simplicity that satisfies conservative tastes.

Dinner begins with a cup of scalding hot *Soup*, such as smooth *Cream of Cauliflower*, deliciously full of fresh cauliflower flavor. The *Salad* looks Japanese in its careful arrangement of ingredients. Threads of carrot and red cabbage adorn a mound of butter lettuce, flanked by a perfect, ripe tomato wedge and hollowed-out cucumber slices, and with a tangy vinaigrette dressing drizzled on top.

Canard Orange arrives at the table untouchably hot. Its orange glaze, a copious slathering of bitter orange marmalade moistened with a little white wine, is caramelized on the darkly browned quarter duck. As it cools, it becomes gooier and gooier and finally quite chewy. At the point when it is just cool enough to put in your mouth, *Canard Orange* tastes like Peking duck, the glaze having tantalizingly melted into the skin.

Rack of Lamb Provençal is also unique, with a "breading"

164

that is really a garlicky paste and a sauce that tastes of red wine, tomatoes, and Japanese soy sauce.

For lunch, try the *Seafood Quiche*, a free-standing whole pie crust, glowingly brown, filled with a generous portion of moist scallops, crab, and snapper that had marinated in something delicious. It's topped with a Japanese egg custard that looks rubbery but is just the opposite. There was hardly any cheese in the pie, making it exceptionally light and alive with flavor.

We are equally enamored of *Provimi Veal Liver Lyonnaise*, a thin slice of liver from high-quality, milk-fed calves, sautéed until just firm and glazed with sweet, caramelized onions. Served with a pile of raw carrot threads and rice pilaf, it makes for an agreeably nourishing lunch.

We don't know if this restaurant would work on a larger scale, but in its present location, it's a gem. The charm lies in a small number of things done originally and well for the few lucky people that can get in each day.

PRICE RANGE: Moderate
HOURS: 11:00 A.M.–2:30 P.M., 5:30–10:00 P.M. Tues.–Sat.
     11:00 A.M.–4:00 P.M. Sun. (brunch)
RESERVATIONS RECOMMENDED
BEER AND WINE
MASTERCARD, VISA

Noble Frankfurter

1900 Polk Street
San Francisco
441–5307

The Noble Frankfurter in San Francisco serves the classiest *Hot Dogs* around—high-quality eastern sausages grilled to order and served on toasted sesame French rolls. You garnish them yourself at a counter that has excellent dill pickle relish, as well as sweet pickle relish, warm sauerkraut, finely chopped reconstituted onions, three different kinds of mustard of varying degrees of hotness, and Kosher pickles.

Drawbacks: The flexibility of self-preparation may not be an advantage for those who do not know the proportions necessary for the well-balanced dog. With a little practice, we suppose, most can figure it out. Also, you have to wait for your dog to grill. This ensures a hotter dog, but detracts from the purity of the fast-food experience. You can also get some excellent *Cole Slaw*, and a styrofoam cup of homemade *Chile*, rich with meat, beans, green peppers, and onions. The tastiest dog is the straight Kosher.

PRICE RANGE: Inexpensive
HOURS: 10:00 A.M.–1:00 A.M. Sun.–Thurs.
       10:30 A.M.–3:00 A.M. Fri.–Sat.

North Beach Restaurant

1512 Stockton Street
San Francisco
392–1587

There are a group of Italian restaurants in North Beach that have become San Francisco institutions. People jam into them night after night, appear to be having a good time, and recommend them to us constantly. One such place is the North Beach Restaurant. Everyone, it appears, loves the North Beach. Everyone, that is, but some food critics.

Over the years, we've eaten at the North Beach a number of times, and each time has been a disappointment. A few of the dishes have been excellent. The home-cured prosciutto, for instance, is as moist and tender as you can imagine for this king of hams. The pasta is cooked to just the right consistency; during basil season the pesto sauce is crunchy with flecks of fresh basil.

If we had to summarize the defect of the North Beach in one word, that word would be "dull." Nothing appears to be creatively seasoned; many of the dishes are dramatically under-seasoned, often lacking enough garlic, for instance, where garlic should predominate. There often appears to be a lack of concern about how the dishes come out. Vegetables, for instance, are frequently overcooked, and the veal more resembles beef than the tender, thin slices of milk-white veal we would hope for.

The North Beach is no longer the bargain it once was. The complete dinner, which includes antipasto, soup, salad, and pasta, now adds about $5 to the price of the entree.

What about those throngs of happy diners? If atmosphere means more to you than the quality of the food, you might have a fine time at the North Beach, where service is friendly and the spirit of lots of people eating lots of Italian food might become infectious. But we'd prefer to take our business to places like

166

Vanessi's and La Traviata, where people are also enjoying themselves, but, it seems to us, eating considerably better meals.

PRICE RANGE: Moderate
HOURS: 11:30 A.M.–midnight daily
RESERVATIONS ADVISED
FULL BAR
MASTERCARD, VISA

Oakland Museum

1000 Oak Street
(at 10th Street)
Oakland
834–2329

If you're visiting the Oakland Musuem, have lunch in the museum's airy, carpeted dining room, where you will be served three courses of wholesome, homey food like your mother used to serve at her bridge parties. It's brought to the tables by nice women volunteers in pinafores.

One afternoon we had a square of bright orange *Jello* studded with fresh honeydew and pineapple, a main course of *Baked Ham, Turkey Breast*, and *al dente* fresh *Asparagus* in a light cheddar cheese sauce, and a piece of homemade *Baklava*, composed of crispy layers of buttery filo-pastry, chopped nuts, and honey. On other days, you might get *Lentil Soup, Spinach Soufflé*, and *Chocolate Mousse*. The lunch changes every day. The coffee is excellent. The entire appealing meal is a bargain, and you must make a reservation for either the 11:45 A.M. or 1:00 P.M. seating.

For snacks, the museum also has a little counter where you can pick up the usual sandwiches, like that universal museum favorite, *Tuna Fish Salad*, a *Tossed Salad*, homemade pie or cake. The homemade desserts are available at the snack counter. Everything served at the counter is made on the premises, including the chile that gets slathered on their superb *Chile Dogs*, worth a trip to the museum alone.

PRICE RANGE: Inexpensive to moderate
HOURS: 10:00 A.M.–3:30 P.M. Tues.–Fri.
        Noon–4:00 P.M. Sat.

RESERVATIONS REQUIRED
BEER AND WINE
NO CREDIT CARDS

Ocean Restaurant ★★

726 Clement Street
(near 8th Avenue)
San Francisco
221–3351

Lots of people, ourselves included, tend to look with a bit of disdain at Cantonese restaurants. So often the standard Cantonese fare is a tasteless concoction in a thick, gloppy sauce filled with cornstarch. Little match for the more interesting, spicier creations of Szechuanese, Hunanese, and northern Chinese cooking.

That's what makes stumbling across a restaurant such as Ocean such a marvel. Another one of those plain-Jane Chinese restaurants out on the Avenues, you could walk by Ocean a hundred times and never suspect anything unusual is going on inside. But wait until you taste the food! Each dish is presented like the chef has been doing a painting—ablaze in colors of the crispiest of vegetables, seemingly carefully selected for how they contrast to each other in color, texture, and appearance. (The *West Lake Beef Soup*, in fact, is supposed to *look* like Hangchow, China's West Lake on a misty morning, and, indeed, the egg threads, coriander, carrots, and little shreds of beef combine to resemble a Monet painting.) The sauces are remarkably delicate and tasty, with virtually no use of thickeners.

One of the most interesting dishes here is the *Salt and Pepper Prawns*. The shrimp are baked in their shells on a bed of salt; the shells become so brittle that you can eat them right along with the shrimp inside. The shrimp are served unsauced, with just some lightly cooked green onion shreds for color. This is one of the most unique and delicious Chinese shrimp preparations we've ever had.

You also should try the spareribs, called *House Spareribs* on the menu. Instead of traditional ribs, you get baby pork chops in a delicate, nonsweet tomato sauce. The pork chops are remarkably tender and without a speck of fat, a far cry from the fatty, icky-sweet spareribs that are a staple of most Cantonese menus.

One of the few expensive dishes on the menu is the *Cold*

Chicken Salad, but it's well worth it. What makes it costly are the shreds of jellyfish skin that offer a crisp contrast to the smooth chicken. The dish comes in a sesame paste and hot chili oil sauce with loads of coriander, and is surely the most unusual cold chicken salad we've eaten.

Ocean offers thirteen soups (none of them won ton), a wide variety of interesting vegetarian dishes, and lots of fish and shellfish selections. Unless you have six or more people and can make a reservation, avoid the weekends, when the place is a madhouse. On weeknights, it's just comfortably jammed, but the wait is worth it for the combination of extraordinary food at very low prices.

PRICE RANGE: Inexpensive
HOURS: 11:30 A.M.–9:30 P.M. daily
RESERVATIONS FOR SIX OR MORE
BRING YOUR OWN BEER OR WINE
MASTERCARD, VISA

Original Hot Dog

1790 Haight Street
San Francisco
221–1511

Finding a great hot dog in the Bay Area is as hard as finding fresh asparagus in Alaska. They're simply not grown here. Our standard for the great hot dog comes from a place poetically named Flukie's on the north side of Chicago. Mr. Flukie is the Jean Troisgros of hot dogs. Through love and dedication to hot dogs and Polish sausage, he has created the flawless sandwich—a steaming hot Vienna dog on a warm poppyseed bun with carefully measured amounts of mustard, Kosher pickle relish, chopped onions, tomato slices, and two optional hot peppers. Chicagoans travel miles to wait in line for one of Flukie's masterpieces.

Recently, the Chicago-style hot dog has been appearing in the Bay Area, and the main purveyor is a new hot dog place on Haight near Cole, the same neighborhood that has brought you Memphis-style barbeque. The best dog to order at the Original Hot Dog is the *Original Hot Dog,* a fat Vienna dog on a soft poppyseed bun with almost classic fixings of mustard, chopped onions, sweet pickle relish, tomatoes, and pickle slices. The overall taste is authentic, but the hot dog itself is not hot enough,

169

the bun isn't warm, and the fries that come with it taste like old cooking oil. You can, however, substitute carrot sticks for the fries, a truly California option that we think is a stroke of genius, especially considering the fries.

PRICE RANGE: Inexpensive
HOURS: 11:00 A.M.–9:00 P.M. Sun.–Thurs.
11:00 A.M.–10:00 P.M. Fri.–Sat.

Original Joe's

144 Taylor Street
(near Market)
San Francisco
775–4877

Original Joe's, although well out of the Financial District, is nevertheless full by 11:30 A.M. The restaurant is in the heart of the Tenderloin and has its own set of colorful regulars, who have packed the restaurant for forty-three years. The seventy-six-year-old co-owner, Louis Rocca, sums up the success of the restaurant: "We feed good. We feed heavy. And we feed clean."

It is important, however, to go to Original Joe's in the right spirit and with one of those regulars who knows the vagaries of the long, diverse menu. Much of the food is indeed heavy, and the portions are huge. The restaurant is usually noisy, smoky, and crowded.

Our Financial District Lunch Advisor goes to Original Joe's on Tuesdays for the *Braised Short Ribs*. We can understand why. You get a plate full of tender, moist but not fatty beef short ribs that have absorbed the flavors of a well-seasoned tomato and red wine sauce. We were taken with Original Joe's famous *Hamburger Sandwich*, three-quarters of a pound of fresh-ground chuck, slapped with onions, and grilled to order. This giant piece of meat is served on hollowed-out sweet French bread, grilled, and buttered, a clever bit of cooking that allows you to get your mouth around the sandwich.

Another winner lurking in the list of twenty-four sandwiches is the *Fried Ham and Cheese*. Layer upon layer of good ham and melted cheese is piled on the soft French bread and served with fat french fries, which aren't crisp but soft and tasty. "It took us two years to find that one," the Lunch Advisor told us proudly.

170

Even the small *Salad* demonstrates Original Joe's flair for giving plain food a delicious edge. Torn romaine lettuce serves as a bed for chilled, cooked vegetables—cauliflower, zucchini, broccoli, black olives, and kidney beans, all in an excellent French or sour creamy blue cheese dressing.

Coffee is fresh and strong and tumblers of the red house wine, *Petri Napa Valley Burgundy*, go perfectly with the food, with no harsh aftertaste or cloying aroma.

Some suggestions: Always order the thick, delicious meat sandwiches like *Roast Pork* with a side order of *Au Jus*. Don't eat in the bar room. It's so dark you can't even see your food. And if you're going for lunch, get there before 11:30, or you'll have to wait a long time for a table.

The emphasis at Original Joe's is on simple, high-quality meats, and the more you order them, the better you'll eat—good, heavy, and clean.

PRICE RANGE: Inexpensive
HOURS: 10:30 A.M.–1:30 A.M. daily
NO RESERVATIONS
FULL BAR
NO CREDIT CARDS

Original Kasper's Hot Dogs

4521 Telegraph Avenue
(near 40th Street)
Oakland
655–3215

Harry Yaglijian has been selling hot dogs for thirty-eight years now out of a little wooden building on an island in the middle of Telegraph. Although they aren't Chicago-style, they may be the best in the area in terms of good, overall hot dog sensibility. Kasper's is like the corner store you grew up with in your neighborhood, run by kindly mom and pop.

You can get candy bars, potato chips, sodas, and one kind of *Hot Dog*, which is long and skinny and made especially for Kasper's. It comes on a matching bun and both are hot. Harry puts French's mustard, sweet pickle relish, sliced-to-order onions and tomatoes, and a sprinkle of celery salt on his dogs. They're softer and tenderer than most and delicious. Kasper's also carries

171

Yoo Hoo, a chocolate milk drink that comes in a glass bottle and tastes like a thin milk shake. Easterners will beat a path to Kasper's for these alone. The Original Kasper's is a gem out of the past. You had better get over there before Harry retires to go fishing.

PRICE RANGE: Inexpensive
HOURS: 11:00 A.M.–7:30 P.M. Mon.–Sat.

Orsi's ★★

375 Bush Street
San Francisco
981–6535

Orsi's has always been one of our favorite San Francisco restaurants. Tucked away in the Financial District with its interchangeable plush and banquette continental decor, the kitchen nevertheless turns out food that transcends stereotype. Orsi was a master Italian chef of Tuscan background, and his son, who now runs the kitchen, upholds his father's tradition.

Although the menu gives off a few hints of regional origin, for the most part, it's a list of continental dishes that stretches from *Lamb Chops with Béarnaise Sauce* to authentic Italian specialties like *Spiedini de Piccione*, grilled squabs cooked on a skewer with chunks of pork and fried bread.

The wine list is extensive and eclectic, with French, California, German, as well as excellent Italian sections. The Italian list offers such hard-to-find goodies as a soft, fruity *Carema, 1971* from Luigi Ferrando and a *Spana, 1964* from Campi Raudii.

The restaurant is geared to the American custom of everyone at table ordering different things. This means lots of tableside cart service where salads are tossed, meats carved, and pastas portioned out.

One of the best dishes at Orsi's is *Squid*, so tender it can be cut with a fork. It's breaded, sautéed, and sauced in a buttery pan reduction.

For pasta, have *Cannelloni* stuffed with a fine, prosciutto-pink forcemeat, one of the best we've tasted, and sauced with a balanced mixture of tomato and bechamel sauce. All the pastas are fresh, cooked *al dente*, and opulently sauced.

Etruscan Chicken is an Orsi's specialty. It takes a good half hour to emerge from the kitchen in its clay baking pot. A whole chicken is crisply browned and then stuffed with sprigs of fresh sage. It goes into the clay pot with fresh baby artichokes, turned potatoes, and mushroom caps, as well as garlic, wine, salt, and aromatic, lively pepper and herbs. Everything steams together.

Squab cooked on skewers are aged, tender, and juicy without being overdone. The veal dishes are never oversauced, allowing the tender scallops of white Provimi veal to shine.

For dessert, fresh *Strawberries* blanketed with a warm, made-to-order zabaglione with a nutlike flavor is about all you can eat after the rich food.

PRICE RANGE: Expensive
HOURS: 11:30 A.M.–11:00 P.M. Mon.–Fri.
      5:00–11:30 P.M. Sat.
RESERVATIONS ADVISED
FULL BAR
ALL MAJOR CREDIT CARDS

Palm Court

Sheraton-Palace Hotel
Market Street and New Montgomery
San Francisco
392–8600

The Palm Court is an opulently appointed Victorian dining room from San Francisco's past. It has an antique greenhouse ceiling that lets in the light needed to keep elegantly manicured palms, three stories tall, green and lush. In the grand hotel tradition, there are stately pillars, French doors and mirrors, and graceful archways. On Sundays, a reservation made early in the week gains you admission. Then, three banquet tables groaning with hot and cold dishes, desserts, and drinks fill the center of the room. They are gorgeous to look at but disappointing to eat. Cottage cheese in a silver bowl is still cottage cheese.

There are some half-hearted concessions to luxury (the brunch is not cheap) in the piles of *Smoked Salmon*, which is oily and resembles the kind you get prepackaged in the supermarket, and in the array of *Fresh Fruits*. The salads are of the canned kidney bean variety. Two punch bowls of watery *Bloody Marys* and *Screwdrivers* cohabit on a table with cake-mix-quality pastries and bland sweet rolls.

The hot table offers such items as *Lamb Shanks*, *Roast Chicken*, soggy vegetables, *Bacon*, *Sausage*, and *Eggs*. If you watch for an arrival of a fresh pan of eggs from the kitchen, you'll be doing yourself a favor.

At one time the hot table used to have *Baked Cod in Cream*, *Poached Salmon*, and *Scotch Kippers*, but not any more. The Palm Court brunch is coasting on its reputation, but it's still the most authentic grand hotel atmosphere in town.

PRICE RANGE: Expensive
HOURS: Seatings at 10:30 A.M., noon, and 2:00 P.M. for Sun. brunch
RESERVATIONS NECESSARY
FULL BAR
ALL MAJOR CREDIT CARDS

Panchito's Tiajuana Village

3392 24th Street
(near Mission)
San Francisco
647–1544

A burrito, for those of you who aren't sure, is a Mexican meal wrapped up in a flour tortilla and tinfoil. It consists of Mexican red beans, rice, cooked meat of some sort, *salsa*, which is a relish that may contain onions, tomatoes, and coriander, and something very hot. A typical burrito is shaped like a fat sausage, weighs anywhere from one-third to three-quarters of a pound, and feels warm in your hand. Perhaps its tactile appeal is one source of the burrito's popularity in San Francisco. Another must be that it is substantial, tasty and hot, inexpensive, quickly prepared, eaten without knife and fork, and sublime with cold beer, thereby making it the perfect fast food.

You can be as exotic or plain as you want to with burritos by choosing meat fillings that range from the ever-popular beef to truly ethnic beef tongue or pork tripe. There's always room for experimentation with different combinations, making burritos more interesting, say, than hamburgers.

Panchito's Tiajuana Village makes our favorite *Burritos*. First of all, Panchito's grills its beef over an open gas grid, which gives the meat a charcoal flavor. Second, it uses a moist bean mixture, which makes the burritos juicy. Third, its *salsa* of fresh tomatoes and chopped onions has lots of coriander. And, finally, Panchito's hot sauce is not out of the question. All this adds up to a burrito whose various elements melt together into the quintessential Mexican mélange, but that maintains a distinct Panchito character nonetheless. The proportions are right and each ingredient in itself has been carefully seasoned.

Panchito's *Burritos* cannot be eaten like a hot dog while you're driving an automobile. They drip and overflow onto the steering wheel, making it dangerously slippery and sticky. A few formica tables have been provided at Panchito's, but our feeling is that burritos should be eaten in the street or in a car or in front of a television with a bottle of cold Mexican beer. Eating burritos at a table is like eating a popsicle with a knife and fork.

PRICE RANGE: Inexpensive
HOURS: Noon–10:00 P.M. Tues.–Sun.
BEER

Panhandle Pantry

1603 Haight Street
San Francisco
861–9500

With its open kitchen and Italian-accented food, the Panhandle Pantry is like a poor person's Vanessi's. The eclectic menu offers pizzas, salads, soups, pasta, omelettes, vegetables, grilled hamburgers, and homemade pastries. They're all hearty, simple, and well prepared.

Pasta al Pesto is an important test for any restaurant. Here, coarsely chopped fresh basil, parsley, garlic, and imported olive oil provide a luscious, glistening coating for plump ricotta-filled ravioli. *Spaghetti* is cooked just right, always *al dente*, and tossed with your choice of a fresh-tasting tomato sauce, white clam sauce, or anchovy sauce.

The soup changes daily and is usually improvised from leftover ingredients. Don't pooh-pooh the method. On one occasion we had a sable brown melding of meat, poultry, and fish stocks with fresh tomatoes and black pepper that was superb. Another time we slurped up a delicious *Chicken Stew* with chunks of tomatoes, vegetables, and chicken in a golden broth.

175

Salads are assembled to order with the crispy greens dressed in a piquant lemon, garlic, and herb dressing. Plates of fresh vegetables can be ordered either steamed or sautéed in olive oil. Either way, they are always crisp and fresh.

Daily specials, filling and inexpensive, round out the menu. We forced ourselves to finish a homey-tasting *Lasagna* made with four different cheeses that oozed out between good noodles, garnished with a single huge meatball.

For down-to-earth, healthy, everyday eating, the Panhandle Pantry is a good place to go. The food has a home-cooked feeling about it. It's lighter and easier to digest than the typical North Beach Italian extravaganzas, but it still sticks to your ribs.

PRICE RANGE: Inexpensive
HOURS: Noon–9:00 P.M. Mon.–Sat.
NO RESERVATIONS
BEER AND WINE
NO CREDIT CARDS

Paprikas Fono ★

900 North Point
Ghirardelli Square
San Francisco
441–1223

Hungarian food, with its rich sauces, thick stews, and filling desserts, isn't exactly trendy in these days of *nouvelle cuisine*. But it's clearly one of the most innovative and interesting of European cuisines, perhaps ranking third, just behind French and Italian. Unlike them, however, Hungarian restaurants are sadly underrepresented in the United States; except for Hungarian neighborhoods in New York and a couple of big midwestern cities, they're almost nonexistent.

This is why San Francisco is so lucky to have Paprikas Fono, a very pretty and very authentic Hungarian restaurant located in Ghirardelli Square. For surprisingly moderate prices, you can eat on an enclosed patio offering a beautiful view of San Francisco Bay. The service is very friendly, the portions are large, and the food in general is expertly prepared.

In a number of visits to Paprikas Fono, we've practically gone through the menu, but we constantly find ourselves tempted to return to the veal dishes. The *Veal Paprikas* has never failed us; the chunks of veal are always tender, and the thick brown sauce is loaded with a marvelously aromatic paprika, the staple spice of Hungarian cooking. (Virtually *everything* at Paprikas Fono is loaded with paprika, yet there's even a shaker of it on every table—maybe for the coffee?) Another fine veal dish is *Mother's Palacsintas*, which offers one delicate crêpe stuffed with chunks of veal in a mushroom and herb sauce, and another crêpe filled with asparagus soufflé. In contrast to the tender and juicy veal, the chicken in the *Chicken Paprikas* tastes overcooked and dried out.

Be sure to start your meal with a cup of *Gulyas Soup* and some *Fried Bread*. The soup is a thick beef broth loaded with chunks of tender beef and potatoes. The bread is nothing less than a miracle; it emerges from the frying process light, fluffy, and without a speck of grease. You break open a clove of garlic and rub it on the bread—sheer ecstasy. The *Fried Bread* is so good it makes puzzling the choice of mediocre sliced rye that the restaurant serves with your dinner; if ever a cuisine required thick, crusty hunks of black bread, this is it.

Many of the main courses come with *galuska*, tender little egg-noodle dumplings that are perfect for sopping up sauces. If your entree isn't accompanied by a *Cucumber Salad*, order one the marinated cucumbers, topped with sour cream and a sprinkle of paprika, are superb.

The desserts tend to be overly sweet, a pity, since the *Sweet Cheese Palacsintas*—crêpes stuffed with cheese and raisins and topped with sour cream—would otherwise be lovely.

Our only major quarrel with Paprikas Fono is that year after year the menu is basically unchanged. No matter how good certain dishes are, you can tire of eating the same things visit after visit. Any restaurant that can demonstrate so much skill in the dishes it does could surely afford a little innovation from time to time.

PRICE RANGE: Moderate
HOURS: 11:00 A.M.–11:00 P.M. daily
RESERVATIONS ADVISED
FULL BAR
MASTERCARD, VISA

Pasand Madras Cuisine ★

Emeryville Market
Emeryville
655–9020

Pasand is one of those places so perversely unique, so chicly unchic, that a lot of people would be delighted to discover it even if the food were bad (fortunately, however, the food is terrific). The first problem is finding the place. Take the Powell Street exit to the east from Interstate 80, go up Powell Street, and look for signs pointing to the left to Emeryville Market. You'll go down a little winding street, across some railroad tracks, and into a huge parking lot that, if it's dinnertime, will contain about five cars. (No Ghirardelli Square this, no matter what its developers dreamed.) The second problem is to find which door in the big converted brick warehouse is open. No help here; it seems to change nightly.

Once inside, you'll see a counter against one wall marked "Pasand Madras Cuisine/Luigi's Italian Food." Don't ask for Luigi. The Indian family members behind the counter claim they can throw a pizza in the oven if anyone demands it, although we've never seen them taken up on this.

You order at the counter, sit at a nearby wooden table, and someone in the family (usually one of the children) brings you your food. For a few dollars, you can eat one of the best Indian meals in the Bay Area. Don't miss the *Masala Dosa*, the southern Indian vegetarian specialty we've seen on no other Bay Area menu. A giant crêpe the size of a dinner plate is filled with potatoes, onions, and carrots and fried until crisp. You get two separate sauces to put on it: a creamy, mild coconut curry sauce and a spicy tomato-based sauce. It makes for an extraordinary meal, particularly if you order the golden, thick, spicy *Lentil Soup* to start.

There are also some unusual appetizers called *pakora*. Vegetables are dipped into a chick pea batter and fried until golden brown. The batter comes out crispy and without a hint of grease. Try the *Eggplant Pakora* and, if you like roaring-hot food, the *Chili Peppers Pakora*.

Even the most mundane of Indian dishes are tasty at Pasand. The *Lamb Curry* is beautifully perfumed with an array of spices, while the *Vegetable Koorma* offers fresh vegetables, perfectly cooked, in one of those sauces that must contain at least a dozen exotic Indian spices.

178

Avoid the Pasand on Shattuck Avenue in downtown Berkeley. While it offers the same menu, for some reason the dishes taste precooked and not nearly as good.

PRICE RANGE: Inexpensive
HOURS: 10:00 A.M.–9:00 P.M. daily
NO RESERVATIONS
BEER AND WINE
NO CREDIT CARDS

Pasha

1516 Broadway
San Francisco
885–4477

Excellent Middle Eastern restaurants are not a novelty in San Francisco, and Pasha, a Moroccan restaurant, is one of the best. Its extraordinary food is matched by gentle, hospitable service and a good-looking belly dancer. Middle Eastern dining can be a slow, sensual experience. You eat at low tables, sit on the floor, and eat with your fingers. You finish over *Mint Tea* or sweet, muddy *Turkish Coffee*, sinking ever deeper into the soft cushions and velvety Persian carpets.

The dining room at Pasha is cavernous, but noise is softened by the fabrics that cover walls, floor, and ceiling, and the candle-lit darkness makes any corner of the room seem intimate.

Begin your dinner with *Mezza*, a tableful of hors d'oeuvres, including tart, rice-stuffed grape leaves, bright orange turnip pickles, and creamy *hommos*—chick peas pureed with sesame oil—which you eat with hot *pita* bread. You get cauliflower deep fried in delicious, sweet-tasting oil until it is golden brown but still crisp, and the best *falafel* we've ever tasted: little deep-fried patties of crushed beans highly seasoned with cumin and herbs. Then there is eggplant sautéed with zucchini, tomatoes, and onions, seasoned with cumin and coriander, and pureed to make a cold, spicy vegetable dip; and *tabbouleh*, chopped parsley, scallions, and bulgar wheat marinated in lemon juice to be scooped up with romaine lettuce leaves. Fat Egyptian broad beans come marinated in lemon and garlic, and in addition to all this, *Mezza* includes a plate of thick, creamed yogurt cheese arranged with cherry tomatoes and black olives.

Other tantalizing cold salads offered a la carte are *Shredded*

Cabbage dressed with garlic and lemon, or the utterly simple *Diced Cucumber and Yogurt Salad* seasoned with flakes of mint, one of the world's most refreshing dishes. An appropriately small portion of *Harira*, a rich Moroccan lentil soup, is another possible first course.

For main courses, their kebabs are superb. *Shish Kebab* brings the tenderest leg cuts of baby lamb, skewered with marinated eggplant, green peppers, and sweet white onions—all charcoal broiled to perfection. *Shish Taouk* are charcoal-broiled skewers of plump, juicy chicken combined with crisp vegetables.

Other specialties of the house are *tajines*: stews slowly cooked in covered crocks with spices and fruit. *Tajine of Hare in Paprika*, tender rabbit lavished with a deep red sauce, has a depth of flavor that only comes from long, attentive simmering. The muttony flavor of lesser cuts of lamb in *Lamb with Honey and Almonds* melts into a sweet sauce. *B'stilla*, chicken and almonds baked in filo-dough, is not as elegant here as it is at other Moroccan restaurants, but it's still a tasty example of this popular dish. *Couscous* comes garnished with marinated vegetables, no meat. Although rather plain, each grain of semolina is tender, moist, and feather light, just as it should be. Pasha's *Mousaka*, unlike the molded Greek version, is a delicious casserole of eggplant, cheese, ground beef, tomatoes, and white sauce.

Most entrees come with a seasoned rice pilaf studded with toasted almonds, and fresh green beans and carrots. Unlike most other Middle Eastern restaurants, the wine list offers a number of French and California wines at reasonable prices.

One is hard put after a meal of *Mezza* and *Shish Kebab* to try the *Baklava*, but the crisp filo-dough pastry is irresistible with *Turkish Coffee*.

PRICE RANGE: Expensive
HOURS: 6:00–11:00 P.M. Tues.–Sun.
RESERVATIONS RECOMMENDED
FULL BAR
ALL MAJOR CREDIT CARDS

Perry's ★

Perry's is one of those amazing restaurants that never fails. You, however, may fail in the process of actually getting something to eat. Don't even think about finding a parking place and walking over together with your party. Rather, drive up in front and let someone out to put your name on the waiting list and to stake out a little area, where you can stand for the forty-five minutes or so it takes to be seated, if you are lucky. This scout should not be a gregarious woman, for she may disappear into the throng of drinkers inside before you can meet up with her.

The bar area gets so congested, smoky, and loud that the outdoor corridor, though drafty, is the best place to wait. So be sure to wear something warm. From this vantage point you can look through the windows at the activity inside if conversation has run out. Send someone tall to the bar for drinks—it's easier for them to get through, and cocktail waiters are few and far between. Come armed with conversational topics that will last a long time—hotels around the world, gardening, and the state of the arts in San Francisco have all worked well for us.

Do not become impatient. The blue-blazered host positioned near the sidewalk is a model of fairness. He will show you the waiting list if you ask. He remembers each party by sight and will personally fetch you when the big moment has arrived.

If you are still standing and coherent, request a table in the back, an area separated from the bar, and all that that implies, by a long corridor. There you will get a quiet, blue-checked, linen-clad table with a fresh flower and a polite, efficient waiter. Now you've got the thing licked.

You order from a list of items displayed on the walls. Perry's serves the best pub food in town, so anything you choose from the menu of salads, grilled meats, and fish will be hearty, fresh, and carefully cooked.

We always begin with a *Green Salad* of chilled, dry, mixed greens topped with at least a quarter of a pound of crumbled imported Roquefort and tossed in a well-balanced vinaigrette dressing.

The old standby of broiled *New York Steak* always hits the spot. The New York strip is cut in half lengthwise, trimmed of all fat, and then served in narrow, luxuriously thick pieces. *Fried*

181

Chicken, so often abused, attains new heights of crispiness without getting dried out. Each small piece, from small, flavorful chickens, is lightly and evenly breaded and fried just to the point at which the meat has firmed. A seasonal special, *Broiled Salmon Steak*, is as fresh a specimen as you can find in the best fish houses.

Each entree comes with crisply steamed buttered vegetables and either piles of golden, greaseless potatoes or brown rice pilaf.

Some feel that Perry's *Hamburgers* are the best in town. They're huge rounds of lean ground chuck served with slices of tomato and onion and Perry's homemade cottage-fried potatoes, which taste like thick potato chips. Our favorite dish is the *Calves Liver* smothered in fried onions and thick strips of bacon.

Like every other detail of Perry's operation, the small list of predominantly California wines is a model of solid taste and fair prices. Chardonnays from Phelps, Chateau Montelena, and Freemark Abbey, and cabernets from Liberty School, Chappellet, and Phelps, give you an idea of the range.

What astounds us most about Perry's is the management. Everything stays under control even during the most bacchanalian times. The waiters never rush you or show the slightest signs of weariness. They're calm, courteous, friendly, infinitely patient, and totally professional.

We have found a way to get a table at Perry's without waiting. Go for breakfast. Light streams in through the skylight in the back room, and for the first time you notice the pots of flowers, the old photographs on the walls, and the fabulous ventilation system that gets rid of the smoke and alcohol smells from a few hours before.

Try the *Eggs Blackstone*, two poached eggs cooked with split-second precision and placed on English muffins, tomato slices, and freshly cooked crumbled bacon. It's all afloat in light lemony hollandaise sauce—another small Perry's masterpiece.

PRICE RANGE: Moderate
HOURS: 9:00 A.M.–midnight daily
NO RESERVATIONS
FULL BAR
AMERICAN EXPRESS, MASTERCARD, VISA

Pig-by-the-Tail ★

1512 Shattuck Avenue
Berkeley
843—4004

A restaurant critic's refrigerator is truly a dismal place. A couple of old eggs, a soft carrot, some cartons of leftover Chinese dinner—typical of someone on the run. Our solution is to drop by Pig-by-the-Tail, the *charcuterie* in Berkeley, pick up a *Coq en Pâte Franc Comtoise*, otherwise known as the most glorious chicken pie you've ever set fork to, open a bottle of chilled white wine (an item that doesn't spoil), and invite some lucky friend over to enjoy it.

"How did you ever find time to do this?" they ask as they break through the buttery crust into a paradise of chicken breast, sweetbreads, ham, crêpes, brandy, and cream. We just smile and take credit for knowing where to buy something wonderful.

Pig-by-the-Tail is chock full of exquisite, difficult-to-make foods that you can serve at home. You can choose a first course from a selection of fresh-herbed *Pâtés*, *Duck* and *Chicken Liver Mousses en Gelée*, or a beautiful mosaic *Galantine of Turkey with Green Peppercorns*. Serve them with *Red Peppers Sautéed with Garlic and Oregano*, *Broccoli in Mustard Dressing*, or a crisp *Ratatouille* redolent of garlic and fresh thyme. The *Red Potato Salad* with homemade mayonnaise is what you wish every potato salad could taste like.

We are particularly fond of the Pig's homemade sausages, especially the delicate *Boudin Blanc*, made with chicken breast and pork, and the garlicky *Toulouse Sausage*, coarse and seasoned with three kinds of pepper. You can distinctly taste the wine in small *Champagne Sausages*, good for breakfast or for stuffing in quail. The *Garlic Sausage* has fennel and *jalapeño* peppers, and *Crêpinettes*, flat pork sausage with spinach wrapped in lacy caul fat, are delightful barbecued over charcoal.

In addition, Victoria Wise, who opened her shop six years ago when it was the only *charcuterie* in the United States, has perfected a number of stunning take-home dinners, such as *Cassoulet with Comfit of Duck*; *Choucroute Garnie*, sauerkraut combined with house-cured ham and Toulouse sausages; and rolled, butterflied *Leg of Lamb* stuffed with garlic and Provençal herbs; and she promises to keep coming up with new dishes. She makes one each weekend, or you can call to order in advance.

If you can't wait to get home, Victoria will put anything you choose between slices of crusty baguette. Try the *Red Pepper Salad* with *Prosciutto* or the *Céleri Rémoulade* with the *Chicken Liver Mousse*. You can devise some of the classiest sandwiches from Pig's array of salad, pâtés, and sausages.

PRICE RANGE: Moderate
HOURS: 10:00 A.M.–6:00 P.M. Tues.–Fri.
       10:00 A.M.–5:30 P.M. Sat.
NO CREDIT CARDS

Poor Red's ★

Main Street
(off Highway 50, near Placerville)
El Dorado
916/622–2901

Whenever we are anywhere in the vicinity of Poor Red's, which means within an hour's drive, we make our way over with eager anticipation. No one has ever had a bad time at this Gold Rush vintage establishment. We happily join the throngs of locals throwing down Red's "milk shakes"—like the *Gold Cadillacs*, an ambrosial blend of Galliano, crème de cacao, cream, and ice—while we wait to get into the back dining room to eat Red's incomparable barbequed ribs, ham, and chicken.

Red cooks in a huge red-brick barbeque fueled with local hardwoods that sits right in the middle of the spartan dining area. You can feel the heat emanating from the oven, and the mouthwatering aromas of the smoking meats fill the air. The resulting barbequed meats are moist and full of real smoke flavor—the *Half Chickens* may be the juiciest we've ever tasted; the thick slices of *Ham*, the tenderest; and the lean *Pork Ribs*, the most succulent. The barbeque sauce that bakes into the meats, and also gets thrown on top, is a model of the right degree of spiciness and sweet-and-sour balance.

Poor Red's only concession to decor is a room-sized mural in the bar that depicts the local history of El Dorado with a lively, home-grown intensity, humor, and color, which becomes increasingly more so the longer you wait for dinner. The mural is an example of authentic folk art, just as Poor Red's is a vital, noncommercialized folk restaurant. If it were in even a small city, it would have expanded many times over. Luckily, it's in a

184

town with a single street in the foothills of the Sierras, and sometimes that's where you stand, waiting to get into this great local restaurant.

PRICE RANGE: Inexpensive to moderate
HOURS: 11:30 A.M.–2:00 P.M. Mon.–Fri.
      5:00–11:00 P.M. Mon.–Sat.
      2:00–11:00 P.M. Sun.
NO RESERVATIONS
FULL BAR
MASTERCARD. VISA

Rama Thai

863 Bush Street
(between Taylor and Mason)
San Francisco
441–1350

Going to the theater in San Francisco is often marred by the problem of where to eat. The choice is mainly to face mediocre, crowded restaurants in the Theater District, or go somewhere else and worry about finding parking at curtain time.

Rama Thai, a small, unpretentious, cheerful Thai restaurant three blocks up the hill from the Geary Street theaters, offers a pleasant alternative. You can get in and out fast, you don't have to face crowds, and, while you won't have the great Thai meal Khan Toke offers, you can eat pretty well.

Particularly good is the *Shrimp Lemon Soup*, which is bursting with the flavors of coriander, lemon, green onions, and flecks of red chili peppers, with lots of shrimp and straw mushrooms in a rich chicken-based broth. Any of several chicken dishes are also worth trying, especially *Mush-Sa-Man*, which consists of cut-up chicken pieces, including the bone, and potatoes, in a spicy curry-coconut milk sauce.

PRICE RANGE: Inexpensive
HOURS: 5:00–10:00 P.M. Tues.–Sat.
      5:00–9:00 P.M. Sun.–Mon.
NO RESERVATIONS
BEER AND WINE
DINER'S CLUB. MASTERCARD. VISA

Ramen-tei

458 Bush Street
San Francisco
981–6316

An American tourist who visits Tokyo can't help but notice how wildly successful the American fast-food invasion of Japan has been. The Japanese jam into McDonald's, Kentucky Fried Chicken, and other familiar names with seeming pleasure.

Now there is talk from Tokyo of Japanese businessmen planning to export that island's own version of fast food to the United States. If Ramen-tei, which calls itself a Japanese fast-food restaurant, is any example, we're definitely getting the better of the gastronomic exchange. In fact, if other places prove equally as good, you may see *ramen* and *gyoza* become almost as familiar words in America as taco and pizza.

Walking into Ramen-tei is something like walking into a Japanese Vanessi's. Behind a long counter, three men in chefs' outfits are furiously working at a series of gas burners, with some woks bubbling, some sizzling, and some spewing flames several feet into the air. Just like at similar restaurants in Japan, most of the customers are Japanese men dressed in gray suits. You can sit at the comfortable counter for a close-up view of the cooking action or at the handful of tables at the front and back.

If you think of fast food in the American sense, where almost everything is cooked in advance and put under heat lamps to congeal, you'll be surprised with a visit to Ramen-tei. Everything here is cooked to order. Moreover, there's no pressure on you to vacate your table; you have to ask for the check, and you can linger all evening over the sake if you want to. The only things really "fast" about the place are a small menu to choose from and very efficient service.

The most successful dish, and one of the best we've had in a Japanese restaurant anywhere, is mistranslated on the menu as *Fried Vegetables* (*Yasai Teishouku*). Two problems with the translation: the vegetables aren't fried, and there's a lot of pork in the dish. What you get is a huge portion of lettuce, bean sprouts, carrots, green peppers, and other vegetables delicately sautéed with slices of paper-thin, fat-free pork in a pungent sauce made from sake, soy sauce, and rice vinegar and flamed as part of the cooking process. The vegetables retain their crunchiness, the pork is perfectly tender without a hint of gristle or fat, and the sauce is unusually tasty for Japanese cuisine.

Gyoza are the Japanese version of a dish that seems to exist in almost every nationality, ranging from Chinese pot stickers to Jewish kreplach to Italian ravioli. In most Japanese restaurants, the *Gyoza* taste remarkably similar to pot stickers, but not ·at Ramen-tei. Here the skin is paper thin—much thinner than the Chinese variety—while the filling includes not only pork, but also some crunchy diced vegetables. The *Gyoza* are pan fried in a wok until the skin is a golden brown; at each table, you'll find vinegar and hot sauce to use for dipping.

The *Ramen*, a boiled noodle-in-soup dish that has already invaded American supermarkets in dried packages, tastes nothing at all here like what you'd get from a grocery store. The egg noodles are flat and thin, and the broth can be ordered in three different styles—soy sauce base, salt base, or miso and soy bean paste base—and the noodles and broth are topped with hard-boiled egg slices.

These dishes and others, like *Cold Noodles, Fried Noodles,* and *Fried Pork Cutlet on Curried Rice,* come at a price that makes Ramen-tei one of the cheapest meals in town. For instance, the addition of roast pork to our *Ramen*—they gave us four thick slices to the order—set us back exactly 40 cents!

PRICE RANGE: Inexpensive
HOURS: 11:00 A.M.–3:00 P.M., 5:00–9:00 P.M. Mon.–Sat.
NO RESERVATIONS
BEER AND WINE
NO CREDIT CARDS

Rising Loafer

160 N. Hartz Avenue
Danville
838–8800

Nothing tastes as good as freshly baked bread eaten warm from the oven. When you walk into the Rising Loafer, a cozy bakery and restaurant in a corner of a converted red brick firehouse in Danville, ten minutes south of Walnut Creek, the aroma of baking bread practically pulls you over to the counter. There you can get warm, thick slices of whole-grain breads slathered in butter right on the spot. What could be better?

The instigator of this oven-to-table ecstasy is Endy Stark, a woman who discovered the pleasures of baking and eating bread as a cook for Odiyan, a rural retreat for practicing Tibetan Buddhists. Although she studied more complicated French and continental cooking (she ran a gourmet cooking school at her ranch in Danville), the simplicity and wholesomeness of the Odiyan diet appealed to her. All the food she serves in her little restaurant tastes like it was just grown and cooked minutes before it's set on the table.

You may think that all sandwiches basically taste alike, but wait until you taste the Rising Loafers. They are made with the fabulous freshly baked breads, filled with simple combinations, and the proportions are right. *Guacamole and Melted Jack Cheese on Herb Bread with Mayonnaise* may sound like a bland health-food holdover from the early part of the seventies; but here it is a sandwich masterpiece.

The *Quiches with Salad*, with zucchini or broccoli folded into the custard and topped with tomatoes, have a velvety texture. The *Chicken Salad* comes alive with apples, celery, and cashews. Homemade *Soups* are thick, distinctively seasoned purees, such as *Cold Zucchini* with unbashful amounts of garlic, *Gazpacho* with fresh tomatoes, or hearty *Black Bean*.

Pizza on yeasty crust with mushrooms, green peppers, black olives, tomatoes, and onions, or *Spinach Cheese Pie* with filo-dough and Jack cheese are some of the other specialties.

You may not think you want dessert until you smell the *Chocolate Chip Cookies* baking in the back. When you finally get your hot whole-wheat cookie, the chips melted into the buttery pastry, you throw restraint to the winds. We washed them down with chiffon-light *Lemon Mousse*, made by Endy's daughter.

If you're anywhere in the area, this is the place to stop for lunch.

PRICE RANGE: Inexpensive
HOURS: 11:00 A.M.–5:00 P.M. Tues.–Sat.
NO RESERVATIONS
NO BEER OR WINE
NO CREDIT CARDS

Ronayne's

1799 Lombard
(at Laguna)
San Francisco
522–9060

In the last few years, an astonishing number of new fish restaurants have sprung up in various San Francisco neighborhoods, offering the natives an alternative to the tourist-jammed restaurants of Fisherman's Wharf. Unfortunately, as we've learned from one disappointing meal after another, in too many cases it's the same overcooked fish, the same gloppy sauces—only this time closer to home.

Ronayne's is a happy exception. While there are some disappointing things on the menu, most of the dishes are first rate. In addition, the restaurant is extraordinarily comfortable, elegant without being the least bit pretentious, and there's a large, pleasant bar if you come at a busy hour. The service is several cuts above that of the usual disinterested waiters at many fish restaurants, who blandly assure you that everything is fresh and simply want to get you out as fast as possible to promote a high turnover. On our last visit to Ronayne's, the waiter was as helpful as he could be, describing the preparations of different dishes in detail, warning us against ordering the *Fried Oysters*, and refilling the bread basket and butter dish without being asked.

A great way to start the meal is with the *Fried Calamari* in a basket. For a very modest price, you're brought a portion of squid so big it's almost a meal in itself. The calamari is tender, the breading unusually tasty, and the frying oil clearly fresh. Mediocre tartar sauce and passable cocktail sauce are brought for dipping; Ronayne's could clearly improve in this department.

If you're at all a fan of *New England Clam Chowder*, don't miss it here. The *Chowder* is not only the best we've had in San Francisco, but also compares very favorably with that of well-known fish restaurants in the East. No overthickening with flour here; the broth is delicate, creamy, and beautifully seasoned, and there are plenty of tender clams. By contrast, the *French Onion Soup* was disappointing, with a flavorless broth that tasted like beef bouillon.

In choosing your fish, you don't have to stick with simple grilling at Ronayne's to get a satisfying meal. The frying and sautéeing are done with a very light hand. The *Pacific Snapper Grenobloise*, sautéed in butter, wine, and mushrooms and garnished with lemons, capers, and croutons, has only the lightest of sauces, in no way masking the tender, delicate fish. The breaded *Baked Salmon* with béarnaise sauce served on the side was a very pleasant surprise, done with so much finesse that the delicacy of the salmon wasn't at all compromised. The béarnaise sauce was superb, unusually tangy with tarragon. *Grilled Tuna*, however, was disappointing; fresh tuna quickly resembles shoe leather if it's the least bit overcooked, and this wasn't taken off the grill quickly enough.

Two of the three desserts we had weren't up to the rest of the meal. The *Cheescake* was much too sweet and not nearly rich and creamy enough. A concoction called *Neopolitan Cream Pie* tasted like something you'd get in a high school cafeteria. The *Walnut Pie*, by contrast, was quite decent, and would have been sensational with a more buttery, crispier crust.

On my last visit, all the wines were under $10, although the list isn't very extensive. Corkage is $3 a bottle, but the waiter told us he was only charging $3 for the two bottles we brought, because he didn't believe in the concept of corkage.

PRICE RANGE: Moderate
HOURS: 5:30–10:30 P.M. daily
NO RESERVATIONS
FULL BAR
MASTERCARD, VISA

Rountrees

1919 Addison Street
Berkeley
841–3927

The atmosphere at shiny new Rountrees, recently installed in a modern office complex down the street from the new Berkeley Repertory Theater, is the opposite of many homey Berkeley places. It's the kind of sleek, high tech, hard-surfaced, wholly designed decor that you are more apt to see in San Francisco, the difference being that the food at Rountrees is more daring and, for the most part, more conscientious. It is being put out by a woman chef/owner who is using her own new restaurant as a training ground.

190

Rountrees' forte is salads, which makes it a better lunch spot than dinner house. We like very much the *Warm Spinach Salad*, with strips of Gruyère cheese and thick lardons of bacon. The perfect spinach leaves are nicely coated in a bacony sherry and wine vinegar dressing. We also gobble up an *Appetizer Salad* of cauliflower marinated in hot spices and yogurt, set on a bed of pickled onions and red peppers and served with *pakoras*, highly seasoned puffs of deep-fried pastry as good as any we've tasted in Indian restaurants.

Other salads do not show as strongly. A salad of *Canadian Wild Rice, Wheat Berries, and Long-Grain White Rice with Mushrooms and Toasted Hazelnuts* in a curried vinaigrette dressing, sounds more promising than it tastes. The grains are too dry, there aren't enough mushrooms, and all you can taste of the curried vinaigrette is the curry. Underdressing is also the downfall of *Shrimp Salad* with daikon radishes, cucumbers, snow peas, ginger, and pears, with a rice wine vinaigrette. Somehow, for all its interesting list of ingredients, the salad tasted like innocuous chunks of shrimp on naked vegetables. All the elements didn't come together.

Don't pass up the fabulous homemade *Espresso Ice Cream* with *Chocolate Rum Truffles*, Rountrees' specialty.

Rountrees needs some time to cull out their best dishes. Presently, there's too much emphasis on the lists of ingredients, and not enough on making them taste good together. But, the prospects look promising. All the ingredients are fresh, the raw food is not mishandled, and some of the combinations really do work.

PRICE RANGE: Moderate
HOURS: 11:30 A.M.–2:00 P.M. Mon.–Fri.
        5:30–9:30 P.M. Tues.–Sat.
RESERVATIONS ACCEPTED
BEER AND WINE
NO CREDIT CARDS

St. Orres

P. O. Box 523
Gualala 95445
707/884–3303

As we arrived at St. Orres after a two-hour drive that took us through the northern coast's mists and curves, we felt as if we had landed on the edge of civilization. Then, a produce truck from Stockton pulled up and unloaded crates of sunny looking valley produce, and we realized we might have found Northern California nirvana—romantic isolation, dramatic, natural surroundings, and good food.

The St. Orres Inn and Restaurant rises up out of the coastal terrain like a fantasy castle, an elaborate wooden structure with domes, turrets, stained glass windows, intricate facades and terraces. It looks like a cross between a Russian country house and a California craftsperson's dream project. Five years ago, a group of five architects and carpenters purchased the property two miles north of Gualala (which is a few miles north of Sea Ranch) and constructed their building on the foundations of the old Seaside Hotel.

The dining room takes up one of the three-story domed wings of the building. Light flows in through three tiers of windows, a jungle of foliage drifts down from second-story planters, and rough, 100-year-old structural timbers of huge dimensions contrast with finely finished wooden tables and wainscoting.

We began dinner with *Tiropita*, two flaky puffs of filo-pastry filled with kasseri, cream, and feta cheeses seasoned with minced scallions. Perfect. *Escargots à la Bourguignonne*, a dish for which we never have hopes outside of France, turned out to be tender, naturally spicy tasting snails served in the shell and lightly dressed with parsley, garlic, and butter, a model of restraint and good technique.

Entrees come with soup, salad, and aromatic home-baked wheat loaves served with orange butter. A *Salad* of crisp assorted greens tossed in a lemony, creamy textured remoulade dressing was proof that fresh produce can find its way to the coast.

Rack of Lamb Dijonnaise came succulently roasted to our medium-rare specification. Its mustard and bread crumb crust had properly sealed in the lamb juices, with a red wine deglazing of the cooking pan producing a sharply brown sauce.

The wine list rightfully emphasizes local Mendocino County wines of Edmeade, Fetzer, and Parducci.

You can take an overnight trip in the tradition of French country touring by driving up 101 to Highway 116, which takes you over to the coast along the Russian River and then allows for an exciting forty-five-minute ride north along coastal cliffs and beaches. The rooms are small and somewhat austere, but brightened by opulent homemade velvet quilts and finely crafted handmade hutches. The tiled, sky-lit bathrooms, one of which has a huge sunken tub, are down the hall. You can look forward to a *Continental Breakfast* set out on buffet with fresh melon and strawberries, pitchers of freshly squeezed orange juice, yogurt, and hot, home-baked coffee cakes.

PRICE RANGE: Moderate
HOURS: 6:00–9:30 P.M. Mon. and Wed.–Fri.
       6:00–10:00 P.M. Sat.
       5:30–9:00 P.M. Sun.
       Noon–2:00 P.M. Sat.–Sun. (lunch)
RESERVATIONS RECOMMENDED
BEER AND WINE
NO CREDIT CARDS

Sam's Grill

374 Bush Street
(between Kearny and Montgomery)
San Francisco
421–0594

Sam's Grill is one of the original "San Francisco Experience" fish restaurants. The ancient, wood-paneled dining room, the private cubicles for large parties with buzzers to ring the waiter, the loaves of sourdough bread, and the joking, informal service all create an atmosphere that tourists, as well as San Francisco regulars, love.

The atmosphere may be terrific and the prices reasonable, but the food has got to be chosen with care. In my experience, there's only one way to get a good meal at Sam's: Ask what fish is fresh, get that fish simply prepared (preferably charcoal grilled), and ask for it rare. Every kind of fish I've tasted at Sam's that's done in a sauce has turned out to be a disappointment. But the grilled fresh fish, if you make it clear you don't want it over-done, is almost always first rate.

To start your meal, consider a crispy *Romaine Lettuce with Red Bean Salad*, a plate of slightly soggy but still good *French-Fried Zucchini*, or, if it's in season, the marvelous *Cold Asparagus* with a tangy mustard sauce. Stay away from the *Clam Chowder*, though; this Manhattan-style chowder lacks enough of a tomato base and tastes heavily floured.

As a main course, the *Petrale Sole*, the *Boned Sand Dabs*, and the *Salmon* when in season are generally excellent. You also might consider the *Sweetbreads Sautéed in Mushrooms with a*

Red Wine Sauce—for this dish the sauce turns out to be skillfully prepared.

Getting into Sam's, unless you have a large enough group to make reservations, can involve a long wait at the small front bar. Although the restaurant claims to be open until 8:30, it's not a good idea to get there later than 7:00. One night, when six of us showed up at 7:30, we found ourselves being incredibly rushed at dinner by a waiter who bordered on rudeness in his efforts to get us through the meal as quickly as possible.

PRICE RANGE: Moderate
HOURS: 11:00 A.M.–8:30 P.M. Mon.–Fri.
RESERVATIONS FOR LARGE PARTIES ONLY
BEER AND WINE
MASTERCARD, VISA

San Francisco Museum of Modern Art

Van Ness Avenue and McAllister Street
San Francisco

The San Francisco Museum of Modern Art has a small cafeteria-type restaurant that's gaily decorated in bright yellow and silver mylar. It strikes us as the typical art student's hangout, and you see them next to Pacific Heights art matrons, all eating *Tuna Salad*. The tuna comes generously heaped on a plate of lettuce garnished with beet slices and hard-boiled egg wedges. It is very plain, just tuna, mayonnaise, and chopped celery, but good. There is a changing *Soup* of the day, such as *Potato and Leek*, and a number of good-looking *Sandwiches*, such as *Roast Beef*, *Ham*, *Liverwurst*, and *Pastrami*. If you want something hot, order the *Quiche*, really a cheese pie made with good imported cheese melted over a layer of fresh spinach or ham on a crumbly crust. It's microwaved and a little greasy, but tasty. Served with a bowl of romaine lettuce, the quiche is a lunch bargain, as is most of the hearty, functional lunch fare.

PRICE RANGE: Inexpensive
HOURS: 10:00 A.M.–4:00 P.M. Tues.–Sat.
NO RESERVATIONS
NO BEER OR WINE
NO CREDIT CARDS

Schroeder's

Schroeder's used to be a good restaurant for simple German food that appealed to your meat-and-potato cravings, especially when you didn't want to spend much time satisfying them. Schroeder's food, then, as now, was prepared in advance and dished out to order in such a systematic way that hundreds of people were served at one time.

It's been run that way for eighty-six years: Schroeder's is a Financial District institution. The prices are moderate, the service by tuxedoed waiters is efficient, and the ambience, a blend of German beer hall and old San Francisco, is pleasantly masculine. Women were not allowed to eat there during lunch until 1971 when they picketed and won admittance. After eating there recently, we wondered why they had bothered.

On the face of it, Schroeder's seems the same. The cavernous, dark-paneled dining room was packed full of businessmen. When we sat down at table, an assortment of chewy, fresh rye and pumpernickel breads awaited us, as did plates of vinegary cole slaw and delicious German potato salad. But when the main courses were plunked down in less than thirty seconds from the moment we ordered, we could only wonder if Schroeder's notoriously fast kitchen had spun out of control.

The *Sauerbraten* turned out to be two lukewarm, dry, tasteless pieces of nondescript, overcooked meat covered by a tepid, gelatinous brown sauce with the predominant flavor of Kitchen Bouquet. This was accompanied by two cold, dry, tough potato pancakes. *Smoked Tongue and Spinach*, the dish that had brought us back to Schroeder's over the years, was sadly overcooked, its usually firm texture a terrible mush. To add further insult to our favorite dish, it was unbearably salty.

Corned Beef and Cabbage and *Baked Chicken and Noodles* both displayed the devastation wreaked by prolonged stays on the steam table and then on a plate waiting to be ordered.

The *Lentil Soup* is still good: tomato-tinged, beefy, spicy, thick—a fine rendition. And some things, like meaty *Pork Spareribs and Sauerkraut*, braised to proper tenderness in a hearty dark brown sauce enhanced by tomatoes and perhaps a little wine, also seemed to hold up.

Excellent German beers on tap are enough to bring us in.

We feel shaky about recommending Schroeder's. How can a steady kitchen have slipped so disastrously? When speed and efficiency become more important than cooking, you might as well eat at McDonald's. At Schroeder's it's getting to be a rather fine line.

PRICE RANGE: Moderate
HOURS: 11:00 A.M.–9:00 P.M. Mon.–Fri.
NO RESERVATIONS
FULL BAR
AMERICAN EXPRESS

Sears Fine Foods ★★

439 Powell Street
San Francisco
986–1160

San Franciscans who have been losing themselves in Sears' *Deep Dish Pies* for the last thirty-nine years will send a few unkind thoughts our way for recommending this already popular Union Square restaurant, but Sears is an old-fashioned American restaurant that everyone should know about. It serves the kind of food we ate while growing up in the Midwest, when we motored out to the local farms for crates of peaches, buckets of hand-picked blueberries, and bags of young, sweet corn.

For those of you who were not taken to Sears by your mothers twenty years ago, the decor is haute coffee shop: carpeted, curtained, and acoustically tiled. You wait in line, not giving your name but identifying yourself by the number in your party, keeping your eyes peeled for the signal from far-ranging hostesses who wave their arms at you from the back of the cavernous room when they have found you a table. The line moves quickly; tables turn fast.

The clockwork movement of this restaurant depends on a team of professional waitresses with rouged cheeks in red uniforms who mean nothing but business. When one comes for your order, you'd better know it. There's no fooling around. Indecisiveness is greeted with disdain, probably because most customers have been ordering the same thing for decades. Once you order, the food gets to the table promptly and correctly.

The *Fresh Fruit Bowl* puts you back in childhood heaven. A large goblet brimming over with a gorgeous assortment of juicy

196

fresh cantaloupe, honeydew, pineapple, and strawberries, to name just a few of the fruits, is splashed with lemon-scented fresh orange juice, an elixir of refreshment. If you have particular rather than general fruit longings, you can get bowls of *Raspberries*, *Strawberries*, fresh *Orange Slices*, or a large *Baked Rome Beauty Apple with Cream*, freshly squeezed *Orange* and *Grapefruit Juices*, a fresh *Papaya*, or various melons. You can order fresh fruit with *Sears' Own Yogurt*, or on top of your choice of cereal, or in desserts, waffles, and salads.

Not only does Sears handle the fruit well, but all the breakfast classics are done to perfection. *Sears' Famous 18 Swedish Pancakes*, six baby stacks of pillow-light pancakes the size and thickness of half dollars, need only a drop of maple syrup. Like good bread or any good grain-based dish, they have a distinct, satisfying flavor enhanced by the cloud of whipped butter that easily melts into them. I never want to finish a plate of restaurant pancakes, but these disappear in a flash.

Sears turns out the best waffles we've ever had in a restaurant. Crisp, dark brown on the outside, tender and eggy inside, they're not even a close relative of the cottony, soggy waffles most coffee shops crank out. The *Strawberry Waffle* is submerged in whipped cream and fresh berries, with superfluous butter and syrup served on the side.

Sears' *French Toast* is also first rate. Sourdough bread is dipped in eggs and cream and served with a small cup of "Sears' Own Fresh Homemade Strawberry Preserves," really a barely sweetened compote.

Don't resist *Canadian Bacon*, "The Best Obtainable Anywhere," and no hollow boast. Three thick rounds with the flavor of smoky ham are browned on the grill. *Smoked Country Sausage*, made especially for Sears, is an even more generous serving of three thin patties of finely ground, spicy pork sausage cooked well done on the grill.

You must save room for dessert, for, once again, fresh, seasonal fruit steals the show. *Fresh Strawberry Shortcake* is what you dream of when you order this American classic, and deep dish pies come in their own glass cereal bowls filled to the top with baked fruit.

PRICE RANGE: Inexpensive to moderate
HOURS: 7:00 A.M.–2:30 P.M. Wed.–Sun.
NO RESERVATIONS
NO BEER OR WINE
NO CREDIT CARDS

Seven Seas

682 Bridgeway
Sausalito
332–1304

The Seven Seas is no new chi chi Sausalito restaurant. It's been around for years, serving huge tureens of California bouillabaisse and cioppino and large portions of fresh fish. Like most fish restaurants, you can wander astray by ordering sauced or frozen items, which are disappointing. But the Seven Seas always has a selection of outstanding fresh fish and seafood, and the efficient waitresses make no bones about telling you what's fresh and what isn't.

The *Cioppino* and *Bouillabaisse* are based on hearty fish stocks laced with tomatoes, bay leaves, and herbs, and are thick with crab, prawns, scallops, clams, local mussels, and big chunks of rock fish. They are cooked to order, so that each fish maintains its own identity. The steamed *Cherrystone Clams* are steeped in garlic and wine, their liquor served on the side. When you order fresh *Petrale Sole*, you get no less than three filets, egg dipped and sautéed and served with a good tartar sauce spiked with fresh onion. And you can't go wrong here with a dozen *Bluepoint Oysters on the Half Shell*. They are always well chilled and opened to order.

For the modest price of most of these dinners, you also get a salad made with unexceptional greens but enhanced by an excellent garlicky vinaigrette dressing.

While the Seven Seas is a large restaurant, it's so popular, especially during peak hours, that you will have to wait. There's a comfortable bar that serves reasonably priced drinks—another first for Sausalito. The dining area is actually an indoor-outdoor patio crammed with tree-sized plants and a glass roof that opens and closes depending on the weather. The patio is appropriately furnished with garden furniture. On sunny days you don't feel like a mole when you lunch at the Seven Seas. The sun shines right through the open roof, making it one of the best places to take visitors on those inevitable tours of Sausalito.

PRICE RANGE: Moderate
HOURS: 11:30 A.M.–midnight Sun.–Thurs.
11:30 A.M.–12:30 A.M. Fri.–Sat.
NO RESERVATIONS
FULL BAR
AMERICAN EXPRESS. MASTERCARD. VISA

Siam Cuisine ★★

1181 University Avenue
Berkeley
548–3278

In theory, the San Francisco Bay Area should be a mecca for lovers of spicy food. The dozens of Szechuanese, Hunanese, and Mexican restaurants together must put a substantial dent in California's output of chili peppers. All too often, as we've found time and again, these restaurants can be big disappointments. Either the spiciness is toned down to fit the cook's conception of the bland American palate, or else the various dishes offer only heat and no taste underneath.

Given that situation, the recent proliferation of Thai restaurants comes as nothing less than a godsend. If there is one type of cuisine in the Bay Area where you can pick a restaurant at random, walk in off the street, and be almost certain of a fairly decent meal at a reasonable price, Thai food is it. The use of fresh lemon grass, coriander, and lime juice, along with fresh chili peppers and other exotic seasonings, produces a bouquet of tastes that can make the most simply prepared dish seem like a marvel of sophistication.

One of the best examples of an unpretentious, family-run Thai restaurant is Siam Cuisine in Berkeley. Just be prepared for a slight shock when you walk in. Siam Cuisine inherited what was formerly a cocktail lounge, slapped up a couple of "Visit Thailand" posters, and opened for business, so you find vinyl banquettes and low lighting and a working fireplace!

The atmosphere might be American cocktail lounge, but the food is decidedly and uncompromisingly Thai. Many of the sixty-four dishes on the menu sing out with the heat of chili peppers and other seasonings. Even the most fanatic hot-food lover might meet his or her match in *No. 17: Chili Salad*. This dish consists simply of roasted hot peppers in a sauce of lime juice and fish paste. A box of Kleenex is an absolute necessity here.

The other hot dishes, while equally enjoyable, will nevertheless leave some of your sinus cavities intact. A variety of pork and chicken dishes are offered with sweet basil sauce, which combines green chilis, fresh basil, and other spices; or with curry sauces, which combine the piquancy of curry with the sweet, rich taste of coconut milk. The fresh *Calamari with Sweet Basil Sauce*

199

is particularly good; the blandness of squid makes a wonderful foil for Thai seasonings.

While it's rare to find any dish at Siam Cuisine that is less than satisfactory, several in particular stand out. The deep-fried, spicy *Fish Cake* served with cucumber sauce has been marvelous on all our visits. It's rare to find frying so delicate that the tenderness and juiciness of the fish isn't compromised. The cucumber sauce, consisting of ground peanuts, vinegar, sugar, chili peppers, and coriander, is a marvel.

The *Beef Sa-Tay*, beef marinated in coconut juice and Thai spices and then charcoal broiled, is another winner. The beef comes in a mild peanut curry sauce and is served with cucumber salad. One other standout on the mild side of the menu is *Angel Wings*, which are chicken wings stuffed with ground pork, deep fried, and served with cucumber sauce. The Thais do ingenious things with noodles, and *Paht Thai* is an outstanding example. We've rarely tasted a noodle dish more interesting in any kind of cuisine. Soft rice noodles are cooked with dried shrimp, ground peanuts, and a whole palette of seasonings. Then the dish is served with fresh bean sprouts on the side, so that the softness of the rice noodles is contrasted with the crunchiness of the bean sprouts. The result is a wonderful play of textures and flavors.

All this wonderful food is served by a Thai family whose friendliness makes you almost feel that you're eating in their home. Sometimes a small child will appear with a shy smile to take your dish away. The clan is presided over by a small, friendly man named Chai, who is constantly smiling and bantering with the diners.

PRICE RANGE: Inexpensive
HOURS: 5:30–11:00 P.M. daily
RESERVATIONS ACCEPTED
BEER AND WINE
MASTERCARD, VISA

Sorabol ★

372 Grand Avenue
Oakland
839–2288

In the Bay Area, despite the fact that so many people seem ready to jump at the opportunity to try a new type of Oriental cuisine,

Korean food has never really caught on. It's easy to understand why: Many of the Korean restaurants, apparently afraid of offending western palates, offer up only the blandest sort of broiled meat dishes, a far cry from the fiery food that's served in Korea itself.

Now, however, there's a real alternative. While Sorabol has the usual array of marinated broiled meats and fish (beautifully done, by the way, on a charcoal grill), there are also a number of Korean specialties on the menu, many of them zinging with the heat of chili peppers ground up into the sauces. Heading the list is a sensational preparation inadequately labeled *Squid with Hot Sauce*. What you get is a large portion of squid sautéed with onions, green peppers, carrots, and green onions, served in a thick, bean-paste-based sauce that will excite your taste buds at the same time that it sends you ordering a second bottle of beer. The sauce is totally unique, unlike any Chinese or Thai dish, and it's also offered on *Octopus, Scallops,* and *Prawns.*

You can also get several types of "casseroles" with hot sauce. When we ordered the *Fish Casserole,* it turned out to be a large chunk of rock cod, with lots of tofu and green onions, served in a broth tasting primarily of ground-up red chili peppers. If you like hot food, you'll love this dish, and the fish, like the squid, wasn't the least bit overcooked.

The condiments at Sorabol are also interesting. Dinner starts out with a deep-fried mung bean cake appetizer that for all the world tastes like a wonderful, greaseless potato pancake. The marinated spinach and bean sprouts that come with dinner are superb, as is the *kimchee*—the pickled cabbage that is the trademark of Korean food. Don't miss the unique tea, made with roasted rice hulls.

Although the prices are moderate, Sorabol is an elegantly decorated restaurant, with an open kitchen, beautiful wooden latticework ceilings, unusual cloth-upholstered chairs, and magnificent tile on the floors and in the restrooms. Set on one of the nicest blocks directly across from Lake Merritt, you'll want to stay for a large part of the evening. The menu also offers a few interesting-sounding higher-priced dishes, like *Cornish Game Hen with Ginseng Root,* which must be ordered twenty-four hours in advance.

PRICE RANGE: Inexpensive to moderate
HOURS: 11:00 A.M.–10:00 P.M. Sun.–Thurs.
        11:00 A.M.–11:00 P.M. Fri.–Sat.
RESERVATIONS ACCEPTED
BEER AND WINE
AMERICAN EXPRESS, MASTERCARD, VISA

South China Cafe

San Francisco
861–9323

The South China Cafe, a nondescript-looking storefront restaurant, seems totally out of place in the Castro District of chic, sleek, remodeled businesses. But once inside, you find the setting has a charm of its own. The interior has remained basically untouched since the turn of the century, and it boasts a decorative "pressed" ceiling in perfect condition and a number of entirely enclosed walnut eating booths. Even better is that two people can order dinner for under $10, tax and tip included. Two of us, on several different occasions, tried to spend more, but couldn't. The best news of all is that most of the Cantonese dishes served there are based on fresh ingredients that are deftly seasoned, cooked to order, and served steaming hot.

Our favorites are the simplest, like *Zucchini Beef* or *Green Bean Beef*, bits of tender beef and crisp vegetables in a hearty black bean sauce highly seasoned with garlic and ginger. *South China Chow Mein*, a huge plate of pan-fried noodles with bean sprouts, scallions, and smoked ham hock, avoids the usual chow mein pitfalls of sogginess or greasiness. In contrast, *Chow Fun Noodles* are wide, and purposely thick and buttery-soft in texture. They, too, are fine here.

South China's *Won Tons* taste like chips; they lack filling, and any of the northern Chinese dishes like *Potstickers* should be avoided. If you stick to meat or poultry with vegetables, and to the noodle dishes, you can't go wrong. As you look at your check with your fortune cookies, you realize that this is one restaurant where the good fortune truly belongs to the customers.

PRICE RANGE: Inexpensive
HOURS: 11:30 A.M.–10:00 P.M. Thurs. and Sun.–Tues.
       11:30 A.M.–11:00 P.M. Fri.–Sat.
NO RESERVATIONS
NO BEER OR WINE
NO CREDIT CARDS

Station House Cafe

Main Street
Point Reyes Station
663–1515

The Tomales Bay area, less than an hour and a half from San Francisco, offers some of the most beautiful coastal hiking trails and beaches in California. A little town nearby, Point Reyes Station, also offers a community restaurant that serves homemade breads, fresh vegetables, inventive vegetarian dishes, just-caught seafood, and home-baked desserts. The fare is perfect for before-or-after-the-hike repasts.

The Station House Cafe is in a brightly painted "salt-box" building decorated inside with children's drawings of whales, wildflowers, and stained glass work by local artists. The decor is as homey as the sweet crumbly cornbread placed on your table at the beginning of your meal. Then you get either a bowl of hearty vegetable soup or a nicely composed salad in a classic vinaigrette dressing. For main courses you can choose from a selection of fresh seafood (either dipped in tempura batter and deep fried or sautéed), vegetarian casseroles, or cheese fondues. The menu changes often.

Don't pass up dessert. They're made with a skillful, light hand. *Walnut Pie*, usually sticky and heavy, is buttery, nutty, and delicate here, capped with a fluff of real whipped cream. *Fresh Strawberry Shortcake* comes as a childhood dream of this classic dessert, with heaps of whipped cream and sweetened strawberries on warm white biscuits.

PRICE RANGE: Inexpensive to moderate
HOURS: 8:30 A.M.–9:00 P.M. Wed.–Mon.
NO RESERVATIONS
BEER AND WINE
MASTERCARD, VISA

The Swallow

University of California Art Museum
2626 Bancroft Way
Berkeley
841–2409

The Swallow, a cafeteria-type restaurant par excellence, is located in a basement wing of the University Art Museum in Berkeley, adjacent to the sculpture garden, where diners can sit on the grass on sunny days. The Swallow is run by a cooperative originally started by the same people who run the incomparable Berkeley Cheeseboard. Their stylish lunch offerings are never run-of-the-mill. The *Egg Salad Sandwich* has nuts; the *Cream Cheese Sandwich* is highlighted by dill; the *Roast Beef* gets anchovy butter; and they all come on fresh bread baked by Uprisings Bakery.

Other dishes include *Gazpacho*, a fresh, cold tomato broth laced with olive oil and chunks of green pepper; *Armenian Bean Salad*, firm, white beans with scallions, parsley, and a lemony dressing; and *Spinach Souffle*, really more like an Italian torta, a tasty mixture of fresh spinach, bread crumbs, onions, eggs, and cheese.

Our favorite Swallow dishes are the *Quiches*. No one does them better. The cheese and custard fillings are always tender and rich, the pastry flaky, and the various fillings, like creamy herbed eggplant, are a revelation. Often there is a reasonably priced hot dish, like *Chicken Breasts with Eggplant and Tomatoes*.

The desserts change frequently, although the regularly appearing *Carrot Cake* has achieved a fame all its own.

The food at the Swallow is remarkably varied, well made, and original. The cooks have an eye for color. They often serve opulent fresh fruit salads or assortments of raw vegetables vinaigrette, such as *Red Cabbage, Cucumbers, Carrots, and Broccoli*, that are as colorful as the paintings on the walls.

So there you are—eating art.

PRICE RANGE: Moderate
HOURS: 11:00 A.M.–5:00 P.M. daily
NO RESERVATIONS
BEER AND WINE
NO CREDIT CARDS

204

Swan Oyster Depot ★

The tourists who flock to Fisherman's Wharf for an "authentic" San Francisco fish restaurant would do far better to line up at Swan Oyster Depot. And line up you will, particularly if you come during the heart of lunch hour.

If you want to hear authentic, listen to this: Swan is the sort of place where about half the customers are greeted by name. It's the sort of place where, when you ask who smokes their salmon, they'll reply, "The same man who's been doing it for us for the last fifty years." And it's the sort of place where the fish tastes so fresh you might be tempted to peer out the window to see whether there's a fishing boat parked on Polk Street.

If you want some authentic atmosphere, at Swan's you've got it. The "restaurant" consists of about twenty rickety wooden stools that you pull up to a long counter. About half the counter has no knee room, so you either have to sit sideways or keep a newspaper on your lap to catch the drippings. At both ends of the counter is a retail fish market. All this in a room the size of some restaurants' kitchens.

There's no menu at Swan's. You have to scan the wall for signs indicating what they have that day. The basic staples are *New England Clam Chowder*, shellfish salads, and shellfish cocktails. To these are added whatever has come in that day—or whatever they feel like serving. (Some of the things sold at the fish-market part of Swan's, like their plump mussels, are almost never offered to the diners.)

The *Clam Chowder* makes a tasty start to the lunch. The broth is buttery, nicely spiced, and not thickened by flour, while the clams are both tender and abundant. After that, skip the salads and cocktails and go to the specials of the day. The *Salads* (*Shrimp*, *Crab*, and the like) are heaped on shreds of iceberg lettuce, then covered with Russian dressing that tastes like a mixture of ketchup and mayonnaise. (A huge jar of Best's Mayonnaise sits unashamedly on a shelf in full view of the diners.) The cocktails are served with a standard red cocktail sauce that does no justice to the shellfish. If you get a cocktail, skip the sauce and simply squeeze some lemon on it.

Other than the salads and cocktails, anything you get is likely to be outstanding. The *Bluepoint Oysters*, when they have them, are as fresh as you could imagine. The same goes for the perfect *Cherrystone Clams*, like the oysters, served on the half shell. During crab season, *Half a Cracked Crab* is a real treat, but again, pass up the mayonnaise and squeeze some lemon on it. If you're lucky enough to be at Swan's when they have freshly *Smoked Salmon*, you're in for a real treat. Several slices of rich, red salmon, delicately smoked, are served on sourdough bread with some shrimp salad on the side. That man who has done their smoking for fifty years really knows his craft. All these treats are offered at very moderate prices.

The always cheerful and helpful waiters who man the counter will even let you improvise. You can order some slices of raw fish, squeeze some lemon on it, and treat yourself to sashimi. On my latest visit, I noticed they were selling Washington State caviar by the jar. I asked for two dollars worth on a slice of sourdough bread, and they gladly complied, giving me a generous portion of some of the best caviar I've ever eaten. It's experiences like these, rather than a mediocre meal at Fisherman's Wharf, that make San Francisco so special.

PRICE RANGE: Moderate
HOURS: 8:00 A.M.–5:30 P.M. Mon.–Sat.
NO RESERVATIONS
BEER AND WINE
NO CREDIT CARDS

Tadich Grill ★★

240 California Street
(near Battery)
San Francisco
391–2373

Tadich Grill, a splendid fish restaurant that dates back to the Gold Rush days, is about as "Old San Francisco" as you can get. Even though it only moved into its current building in 1967, the abundance of dark wood paneling, the cracked plaster ceilings, and waiters who look and act like old veterans combine to make you think the whole ambience has been unchanged for decades. Like Sam's, the owners are Yugoslavians, and the tradition they brought with them of cooking over charcoal does wonders for the simple fish and meat dishes listed on the menu.

Don't be deterred by the mobs of people constantly jammed into Tadich. It's a pleasant place to have a drink while you're waiting for a table. If you get tired of waiting, you can usually be seated fairly quickly at the lunch counter, which, like Vanessi's, has an appeal all its own. The bartender is willing to move singles around to accommodate two of you.

Some of the simple charcoal dishes are among our favorites. The *Sand Dabs*, *Rex Sole*, and *Petrale Sole* are generally fresh and perfectly prepared, and the *Half Chicken* is a real treat. The waiters may discourage you from ordering the latter because it takes a half hour, but after the wait for the table, a half hour to you might seem relatively short. The *Grilled Swordfish* is always a thick, huge steak.

Perhaps our favorite dish is the *Calamari Steak Bordelaise*. The large pieces of squid have been pounded, lightly breaded, and sautéed, and are served with drawn butter. This dish is like a poor man's abalone—you'd be hard pressed to tell the difference. The *Fried Calamari* is excellent too, coming out tender and crisp.

What accompanies the main course is far less interesting than the main course itself. The french fries tend to be thick and soggy, and mixed vegetables taste like they had been frozen.

Desserts at Tadich Grill are definitely nothing fancy, more the sorts of things you'd expect to see in a cafeteria line. But don't let appearances deceive you; the *Rice Custard Pudding* is the best of its genre we've ever eaten, light and eggy rather than heavy and sweet. The *Baked Apples* are also excellent.

If you're in the mood to stand in line for a classic San Francisco fish experience, this is the place to go. What a difference from the plastic, touristy atmosphere and the overcooked fish of the restaurants on Fisherman's Wharf!

PRICE RANGE: Moderate
HOURS: 11:30 A.M.–8:30 P.M. Mon.–Sat.
NO RESERVATIONS
FULL BAR
NO CREDIT CARDS

Taiwan Restaurant ★

2071 University Avenue
(near Shattuck)
Berkeley
845–1456

Berkeley restaurant goers are a tough lot. They know about food because they cook for themselves. They're hard to please. They prefer the adventurous to the mundane. Decor and service are not as important as the food and they don't like to spend a lot of money.

The Taiwan Restaurant has won the loyalty of this hard-nosed group. The menu is an eclectic assortment of dishes from several Chinese provinces, prepared with Taiwanese accent, plus purely Taiwanese regional specialties that make use of such exotic ingredients as Taiwan pickled cabbage, taro root, pork chops, squid, eel, fish balls, and red wine sauces.

The kitchen excels in chicken and fish dishes. We have never had a morsel of overcooked fish or poultry here. The sauces may vary, but the timing is always perfect.

Crispy Chicken is proof of how succulent an expertly cooked chicken can taste. The bird is hacked into thick strips through the bones, a technique that keeps the meat particularly juicy, especially in contrast to the dark brown crispy skin. The spicy hot sauce is colorfully speckled with finely minced green onions and red peppers. It looks spectacular over the carefully arranged pieces, reassembled to look like a half chicken.

Another rich chicken dish is *General Tsuo Chicken*, a dish from Hunan, described as "Mao Tse-tung's hometown famous dish." It's the kind of food that could get the most lethargic army marching—chopped chicken in a hot, red sauce.

Lemon Fish Filets may be the best fish bargain in town. A large portion of firmly fleshed white fish, sometimes rock cod, other times snapper, is cut into thick pieces, battered, deep fried, sauced with an almost transparent emulsion, and garnished with paper-thin slices of fresh lemon. *Squid* is also beautifully presented here. It is scored so that when it cooks and curls it looks like an exotic flower. With hot pepper sauce, it takes on a musky, smoky taste. Sautéed with crunchy celery, it becomes a hot salad.

We always order barely wilted *Wok-Fried Spinach*, unabashedly sprinkled with diced garlic. Sometimes the garlic is crisp, sometimes raw, but either way, this is a wonderful way to eat spinach. It resembles the spinach in Italy, where garlic and oil are also applied with a free hand.

Don't neglect the *Wok-Fried Bean Sprouts*, so crunchy and palate refreshing they can easily slip into the most overordered dinner. Long, skinny Chinese beans are used in *Dry, Braised Green Beans*. Each strand is coated with oyster sauce and amply seasoned with chopped garlic and bits of pork. *Red-Cooked Eggplant* has been braised to a puree and makes a fine sauce for rice.

Pork a la Hunan combines thin slices of smoked pork that tastes like ham with Chinese cabbage. It's loaded with devastatingly hot, whole dried chilis that should be avoided by all but the iron-mouthed. Cabbage and pork are a classically good combination and the abundance of oil and fat in this dish enhances it.

At its best, the Taiwan offers some of the finest Chinese food in the Bay Area, at extremely reasonable prices. It's worthwhile, despite the always-present crowds waiting in line. However, eating at the Taiwan over a number of months, we've found it peculiarly uneven. What is wonderful one day will be much less expertly prepared the next.

Be sure to try the Taiwan's northern-style Chinese brunch on weekends. Almost totally unlike the Cantonese *deem sum*, it features *Soy Bean Soup*, long, nonsweet *Fried Donuts*, *Sesame Cakes*, *Turnip Pudding*, and many other dishes you'll find on few other Chinese menus.

PRICE RANGE: Inexpensive
HOURS: 11:30 A.M.–9:20 P.M. Mon.–Fri.
       10:00 A.M.–9:20 P.M. Sat.–Sun.
RESERVATIONS FOR LARGE GROUPS ONLY
BEER AND WINE
AMERICAN EXPRESS, MASTERCARD, VISA

Taqueria Morelia ★

4481 E. 14th Street
Oakland
261–6360

If you are anywhere near Taqueria Morelia, we recommend that you stop in, because this immaculately clean, efficient kitchen makes the best *Quesadillas* and *Chorizo Burritos* we've ever tasted.

Taqueria Morelia is a true fast-food operation of the highest order. You place your order at the cash register, choosing from a limited menu posted above the kitchen. Then you find a table or a booth, go next door to the connecting bar and buy some beer, and by the time you're back your food is ready.

By all means start with the *Quesadillas*, rolled corn or flour tortillas stuffed with melted Jack cheese and chopped tomatoes and onions. They are superb. Then, get a *Chorizo Taco* or *Burrito*. The *Mexican Sausage* at Morelia is aromatic with cloves, cumin, garlic, and spicy hot chilis. It's not the least bit greasy. Mixed with whole beans and the *salsa cruda* used in the *Quesadillas*, it makes for the best tortilla filling imaginable.

Almost as exciting are the *Chile Verde*, *Tacos*, and *Burritos*; also lean *Pork* simmered with hot green chilis, onions, tomatoes, and coriander; and *Carnitas*, long-cooked pork without the chilis, which tastes like suckling pig. You would find it difficult to find pork prepared as well as this in restaurants that charge four times the price.

Although the menu is small, all the items are made so well that you never tire of them. The food has real vitality. We stop by for snacks or meals or just about anytime we can. Taqueria Morelia is a great local restaurant.

PRICE RANGE: Inexpensive
HOURS: 10:00 A.M.–10:00 P.M. daily
NO RESERVATIONS
FULL BAR CONNECTED NEXT DOOR
NO CREDIT CARDS

Taqueria Tepatitlan

2198 Folsom Street
San Francisco
626–1499

Taqueria Tepatitlan is a burrito restaurant of serious proportions. It reminds us of restaurants in Mexico City, taking up the whole bottom floor of a large, yellow stucco building decorated with Mexican murals. Once inside, you are faced with the largest choice of fillings for burritos and tacos in the city, including lamb, guacamole, beef, chorizo, pork, chicken, and tongue.

We order the combination *Chorizo Burrito*, spicy Mexican sausage with guacamole and orange-colored cheese, for a major meal. Noncombination burritos are smaller. They're all very moist; the ones with creamy guacamole practically flow out of their tortillas like melted ice cream out of a cone. You have to use lots of napkins.

The *salsa* here is a green chili type with raw, chopped onions, and the hot sauce is red and fiery.

Tepatitlan also sells enchiladas and is known for its hot, freshly fried *Corn Chips*, which are sold by the bag to take out.

PRICE RANGE: Inexpensive
HOURS: 9:00 A.M.–8:00 P.M. Mon.–Fri.
          9:30 A.M.–7:00 P.M. Sat.–Sun.
NO RESERVATIONS
BEER
NO CREDIT CARDS

Teresa's Place

1235 Jackson Gate Road
Jackson
209/223–1706

Teresa's Place, a sixty-three-year-old restaurant in the heart of the Gold Country, began as a boarding house for miners. It has not changed much over the years, although the bunkhouse in the back is now an antique store and the miners have been followed by loggers and ranchers. Huge platters of hearty food are served family style in an old, pine-walled dining room. If you have worked up an appetite exploring this historic area of California, Teresa's is the best place to go.

For starters, there is an inviting *Antipasto Plate* of ice-cold fresh vegetables—marinated cauliflower, red peppers, and artichoke hearts, as well as slices of salami and olives. This is followed by a tureen of good *Minestrone with Grated Cheese*. A *Salad* with lots of tomatoes in a lemony dressing comes next. Then you get a choice of either a huge slab of medium-rare *Prime Rib* or a *Combination Plate of Roast Chicken and Thin-Sliced Beef*. They are accompanied by both ravioli and spaghetti in a meat sauce and superb stuffed zucchini, hollowed out and filled with a forcemeat of mushrooms, veal, and cheese.

Wash all this down with a bottle of quaffable *Zinfandel* from nearby D'Agostini vineyards, and have dessert later in the form of an *Amaretto and Cream Drink* concocted by Teresa's son.

Sitting in the front bar room by the fireplace in this old, Gold Rush structure, listening to the locals talk, you feel like time has stopped.

PRICE RANGE: Moderate
HOURS: 11:00 A.M.–2:00 P.M. Fri.–Sat. and Mon.–Wed.
 5:00–9:00 P.M. Fri. and Mon.–Tues.
 4:00–9:00 P.M. Sat.
 2:00–9:00 P.M. Sun.
NO RESERVATIONS
FULL BAR
MASTERCARD, VISA

Tien Fu ★

1395 Noriega Street
San Francisco
665–1064

We first visited Tien Fu, a Hunan and Szechuan restaurant several people had recommended, with our China Expert, Barbara Tropp, a tiny western woman with a musical voice and a passion for Chinese cooking. It turned out that Barbara and the current owner of Tien Fu were old friends. What followed was one of the best Chinese meals we have ever eaten and one that even impressed our critical China Expert.

Having dinner with Barbara at Tien Fu was like being taken on a guided tour of China. The menu opened up for us, and we were able to get past the potstickers and the hot-and-sour soup to dishes we would not have thought of ordering. Tien Fu is just the place to bring a knowledgeable Chinese epicure. Its menu is complex with the many unusual Szechuan and Hunan preparations. No matter how strange some of these sounded or looked, they were invariably delicious, totally acceptable to the western palate.

As an initial test, we devoured a plate of *Potstickers* made with homemade noodle dough pressed around a sausagy pork filling; and we followed this with a bowl of *Hot-and-Sour Soup* thick with strips of tree ears, pork, bamboo shoots, and eggs. An added splash of vinegar from the bottle on the table brought its hot-and-sour contrast to just the right pitch.

Then we moved on to the more unusual *Smoked Fish in Pieces*, a cold appetizer of marinated rock cod that had first been deep fried, then pan fried in caramelized sugar, all of which made it taste like uncommonly juicy smoked fish.

The *Green Onion Pancakes*, thick, tender flat breads, came with a hot peanut and sesame paste. We could have made a meal of them if they hadn't disappeared so fast. Then *Bon-Bon Chicken* made its way to the table and we were able to get more of that intriguing hot sauce, this time on strips of tender, cold poached chicken served on a bed of cucumber. What a showcase of contrasts between hot and cold, soft and crunchy, bland and spicy.

Hot Sauce Beef with Spinach surprised us with the slippery, buttery texture of the meat, the chewiness of the barely wilted spinach, and the exotic flavors of the Chinese barbecue-type sauce. Without Barbara, we could never have known that *Steamed Pork, Hunan Style* would be the Chinese version of *choucroute garni*. Slices of fresh bacon attained a melt-in-your-mouth texture from hours of steaming. They were served over velvety, steamed purple cabbage that was awash in a hot, delicious, spicy ebony sauce.

Another rib-sticking dish, *Hunan Fish and Bean Curd Stew*, came bubbling to the table in a clay casserole. Somehow the large chunks of rock cod fish and bean curd stayed firm, while absorbing the flavors of yet another sable sauce seasoned with whole cloves of garlic and red pepper.

We were expecting the boom to fall any minute from the happy billowed sails of our meal. Yet, dish after dish impressed us with the freshness of ingredients, the finesse of the sauces, and the clearly defined balance of flavors. We were all excited by our discovery.

A crispy *Fried Chicken* dazzled us with crackling crisp skin barely attached to creamy meat. *Eggplant in Szechuan Sauce* was a model of its kind. Plump, sweet, slippery fingers of eggplant absorbed a spicy-hot, sesame-tinged sauce. *Dry, Pan-Fried String Beans* were notable for their tenderness and a savory coating of finely minced pork, garlic, dried shrimp, and pickled kohlrabi. How the chef wrested such a perfect texture from our currently stringy, tough Kentucky Wonder beans sent the China Expert to the kitchen on a research expedition.

We could have continued all night. We had only begun to explore the 132 numbered offerings on the menu, each a distinctive dish in its own right, but our appetites gave out.

Our excitement over Tien Fu was confirmed. This one-chef operation assures consistently superb Szechuan and Hunan fare. The incredibly long hours and culinary dedication of Tien Fu's chef-owner should bring him much deserved success.

PRICE RANGE: Inexpensive
HOURS: 10:00 A.M.–10:00 P.M. daily
RESERVATIONS ACCEPTED
BEER AND WINE
MASTERCARD. VISA

Tommaso Famous Pizzeria ★

1042 Kearny Street
(near Broadway)
San Francisco
398–9696

Every city with a large Italian population seems to have a predominant pizzeria, both famous and jammed. In Chicago it's Pizzeria Uno; in New York, Fats Goldberg's; and in San Francisco, Tommaso. The reported occasional presence of Francis Ford Coppola as a Tommaso pizzamaker, the constant bustle of Augustino, the proprietor, as he greets old customers with one hand and clears tables with the other, and the long lines in front willing to endure almost endless waits do nothing to discourage the Tommaso reputation.

If the wait isn't endless, it certainly seems that way. Unless you're willing to arrive very early or very late, plan to spend a good deal of time on the front steps, bathed in the neon glare of the nearby peep shows. You can, however, pass the time drinking reasonably priced although hardly distinguished Italian and California wines from Tommaso's wine list.

Once seated, you'll find yourself in a restaurant that appears unchanged for decades. Faded murals of Italian scenes line the walls, and brick contact papers and lanterns on the ceiling give the impression of a high school drama troupe trying to recreate Venice on a shoestring budget.

In short, the wait is trying but the place is definitely fun. But what about the food? Never have we seen such contrasts under one roof. If you stick to pizza, you'll be doing well. If you order *Calzone*, the pizza "turnover" literally folded in half to form a huge pizza "sandwich," you'll be eating one of the finest dishes in San Francisco. But, if you venture away from the pizza to other items on the menu, you may find that the quality has dropped precipitously.

For example, one of our recent meals started with a *Zucchini a la Vinaigrette*, which left everything to be desired. The zucchini was way overcooked and tasted charred, as if it had been burned in the pan. The vinaigrette dressing had far too much oil and far too few spices; garlic and black pepper weren't even detectable. The bread that accompanied it was a most unsatisfying sweet "French" bread.

Then came two pastas that, while passable, were nothing we'd ever order again. The *Stuffed Manicotti* tasted leaden, instead of light and fluffy, and the *Linguine with Clams and White Sauce* had virtually no flavor, except for the extreme saltiness of the chopped clams.

With the arrival of a *Pizza Super De Luxe*, things began to look up considerably. Anyone who has had pizza in the East and frowns on the quality of San Francisco pizza should try it at Tommaso before complaining. The crust is outstanding—the best we've had anywhere. Perhaps because of the effect of the wood-burning, brick pizza oven, the crust comes out totally crisp all the way through, even underneath. There was plenty of cheese and tomato sauce, although many eastern pizzas have cheese that is somewhat runnier and sauce with considerably more spice. Tommaso's version, nevertheless, tasted great, except for anchovies that were so salty they could hardly be eaten.

Finally, a *Calzone* was brought to the table, and here Tommaso has no peer. That same wonderful pizza crust is folded over to enclose ricotta and mozzarella cheeses and thin slices of pro-sciutto ham. The ricotta, something we would hardly expect to see in pizza, works a miracle, blending perfectly with the spices and other ingredients. The crust tastes even better than it did with the regular pizza, perhaps because the folding process allows it to get even crispier. Suddenly that long wait became a distant memory.

PRICE RANGE: Moderate
HOURS: 5:00–10:45 P.M. Wed.–Sat.
          4:00–9:45 P.M. Sun.
NO RESERVATIONS
BEER AND WINE
MASTERCARD. VISA

Ton Kiang ★

683 Broadway
(at Stockton)
San Francisco
421–2015

Ton Kiang calls itself a Hakka restaurant, and it's one of the few in the United States. The Hakka are non-native Cantonese who immigrated from northern China, retaining their own dialect, costume, and cuisine. The accomplished chef at Ton Kiang cooks with equal finesse a wide variety of Hakka, Cantonese, and some northern Chinese dishes on a huge menu.

The decor is typical bare-bones Chinese—a square, storefront dining room, plastic tables, and stark lighting. Most of the customers are Chinese, but the waiters are helpful to newcomers. They patiently describe the odd-sounding menu items and identify dishes on neighboring tables, always a good way to order in a Chinese restaurant.

We recommend the Hakka specialties, strange though they may sound, grouped together in their own menu section. *Pan-Fried Beef Balls with Tender Greens* have a pleasant gelatinous quality and a surprisingly intense beefy flavor. They look like gray tulips on their verdant bed of Chinese broccoli. *Salt-Baked Chicken* has a salty yellow skin that seasons the succulent white flesh of the bird, along with garlic and fresh coriander. *Ton Kiang Bean Curd Stuffed with Meat* is fat squares of soy bean cake stuffed with a sausagy pork filling and served with a lovely, aromatic sauce decorated with delicate wisps of scallions and coriander leaves. Finally, don't pass up *Deep-Fried Fish Balls*, which are puffy, crisp, and chewy all at the same time. They make the perfect appetizer.

Ton Kiang's menu is a challenge. We always taste something new there and almost always like it. The food is authentic, complex, and unusual for western palates, but it is prepared with such skill that it has universal appeal. It's the kind of restaurant you can find only in San Francisco or maybe in New York, and it's one of the reasons why San Francisco has a reputation as a great dining-out town.

PRICE RANGE: Inexpensive
HOURS: 11:00 A.M.–midnight Fri.–Wed.

Trader Vic's

20 Cosmo Place
San Francisco
776–2232

Trader Vic's is a Bay Area phenomenon that has become an American institution, with nineteen branches in nineteen different cities and a line of packaged food products. When Trader Vic's at Cosmo Place opened thirty years ago, we can see why it was a sensation. The mélange of Chinese, Polynesian, and Indian foods, the exotic drinks, and the Kon Tiki decor must have seemed inventive. Today, with excellent, authentic ethnic restaurants all over the City and an ever-growing patronage of traveled, sophisticated diners who frequent them, Trader Vic's now seems to us like a parody of itself. The decor is hokey, the price is high, and both the level of service and the quality of food are too variable.

There is one area, however, in which Trader Vic's is unsurpassed, and that's the bar. Trader Vic's tropical drinks use three different kinds of rum, specially made syrups and fresh fruit juices. They're expensive, but they can't be beat. We particularly admire the *Honi-Honi*, the *Gun Club Punch*, and the *Scorpion*, and we've thrown down one too many *Mai-Tais* without even realizing it. One too many, by the way, is more than one. Even to get into the bar men must wear a jacket and tie, so you have to plan ahead for this one.

With drinks, it's a good idea to order Trader Vic's hot hors d'oeuvres for grounding. The better of the two assortments is the *Cosmo Tidbits*, which includes deep-fried shrimp, spareribs, crab-filled won tons, and smoked pork. The *Malayan Tidbits*, including *rumaki*, chicken livers and water chestnuts wrapped in bacon, and curry puffs, are always overcooked when we've had them, except for the *Cheese Bings*, which are so good that you should order them separately.

After drinks and tidbits, your meal at Trader Vic's will be mostly downhill, with a few exceptions. *Bongo-Bongo Soup*, a velvety puree of oysters, spinach, and cream, and *Cosmo Salad Marie*, a delightful combination of chopped celery, fresh mush-

217

rooms, and artichoke hearts in a mild mustard dressing, are two dishes that deservedly helped to make Trader Vic's famous.

Meats cooked in the Chinese oven—two huge, enclosed vats fueled by hardwood logs, which you can see behind a window as you enter the dining room—can also be good. The meats are suspended in the ovens and cook through circulating heat and wood smoke. The *Triple-Thick Lamb Chop* fares the best. You can get it rare, and its slightly smoky flavor does not obscure the naturally sweet taste of the high-quality lamb. *Indonesian Lamb Roast* is ruined by a cloyingly sweet marinade. And the sweetened peanut butter and canned peach garnish do nothing at all to help it. More delicate items like *Mixed Grill, Calcutta Style*, with filets of beef and pork, veal sweetbreads, and kidney, get completely dried out from the ovens. Do, however, order *French-Fried Onion Rings*, another Trader Vic's tour de force.

Coffee tastes as weak as dishwater and espresso isn't much stronger. The straight ice creams without sauce are dense and creamy, but the sauces, like the *Praline Sauce* served with *Rum Ice Cream*, are toothachingly sweet.

Most of the basic raw materials are first rate at Trader Vic's, but the methods of preparation are not up to the standard of the main ingredients. Too many things taste like they come from cans and bottles, and everything is oversweetened and overcooked. Tastes have changed. *Better Homes and Gardens* cooking is not what you expect anymore at an expensive restaurant. When you're paying the kind of money that Trader Vic's commands, you shouldn't have to wade through a huge menu to find the two or three good dishes.

Finally, if you're not a Trader Vic's regular or a celebrity with access to the comfortable and pleasing dining room, the Captain's Cabin, the service and amenities do not match the prices.

The best way to approach Trader Vic's is to go there for cocktails and hors d'oeuvres, and then move on to a better restaurant for dinner.

PRICE RANGE: Expensive
HOURS: 11:30 A.M.–2:30 P.M. Mon.–Fri.
　　　5:00–midnight daily
RESERVATIONS NECESSARY
FULL BAR
ALL MAJOR CREDIT CARDS

Tung Fong ★★

808 Pacific
(near Stockton)
San Francisco
362–7115

If you had to eat just one lunch in San Francisco, *deem sum* (Chinese tea pastries) would definitely be the route to go. This is a cuisine unique to only a handful of cities in the world—cities with large Cantonese populations—and only Hong Kong rivals San Francisco for the variety and excellence of its *deem sum* parlors.

Deem sum is also terrific fun. You sit in a jam-packed restaurant as young women emerge in a steady stream from the kitchen, offering you an astonishing variety of little delicacies, steamed, deep fried, baked, sautéed, and everything else. If you've never eaten *deem sum* before, only the egg rolls will look familiar. Otherwise, every bun, dumpling, or pastry you bite into will offer a totally unique taste treat. The more people you have, the more fun it will be, since you'll be tempted to grab one of everything off the passing trays.

In our view, Tung Fong stands out as the best of San Francisco's *deem sum* parlors. Because it's small, it lacks the ambience that many Cantonese are fond of—mobs of people in a huge room, with everyone watching everyone else, but the food tends to be a little more delicate, the baked crusts a little flakier, the meat fillings a little less fatty than at the larger *deem sum* houses.

First, the protocol. A waitress will come to your table immediately and ask what kind of tea you want. No Lipton (or oolong) teabags here. You get a choice of seven different Chinese loose teas, many of them unbelievably fragrant. We'd recommend either a mixture of *Half Jasmine and Half Chrysanthemum* (yes, these are the dried flowers, which puff back to life when water is added), or else *Dragonwell*, a green tea that the Chinese claim aids digestion.

Then you sit back and choose from the passing trays. Don't worry about the price. At the end of the lunch someone will come to your table and count the empty plates, bowls, and steamers, and, by a formula it would take a computer to figure out, add up your check. Just be assured you can stuff yourself to the gills for a few dollars.

Every *deem sum* parlor has a number of specialties that really

219

stand out, and at Tung Fong the list is long. The *Har Gow*, little balls of shrimp wrapped in a thin dough and then steamed, pass a key *deem sum* test: The wrapping should be as thin and delicate as possible. The *Char Shu Bow* looks like a steamed white roll the size of a doughnut; inside are tender, juicy, fat-free pieces of pork that have been cooked in a rich, brown sauce with a hint of sweetness. Tiny succulent *Spareribs* come either in a black bean sauce or an unusual, tangy garlic and plum sauce.

There is some exotic fare, too. The *Steamed Turnip Cake* will make you into a turnip addict, even if you've never had dealings with this surprisingly interesting vegetable before. The deep-fried *Taro Root Balls*, which look something like tiny chicken croquettes, present a texture and taste that probably come closest to wild rice. The *Marinated Bean Sprout Salad*, and the *Bean Sprouts in a Cold, Rice-Pastry Wrapper* offer a plesantly crunchy contrast to the rest of the dishes. The *Deep-Fried Bean Curd Stuffed with Shrimp* demonstrates how ordinarily bland tofu can be made to sing with flavor if properly prepared.

If you want to impress out-of-town guests, or simply impress yourself with a wonderful alternative to the usual omelette brunches, you can't do better than to head to Tung Fong.

PRICE RANGE: Inexpensive
HOURS: 9:00 A.M.–3:00 P.M. Thurs.–Tues.
RESERVATIONS FOR LARGE PARTIES ONLY
NO BEER OR WINE
NO CREDIT CARDS

U.S. Restaurant

431 Columbus
San Francisco
362–6251

A close second to Little Joe's for tasty, inexpensive Italian food is the nearby U.S. Restaurant. By ordering carefully you will come away with some good, hearty food for even cheaper prices.

The U.S. has expanded its two rooms by adding an amusing triangular space that gives you a view of both Stockton and Columbus Street sidewalks. A minuscule kitchen in full view of customers has not been enlarged.

The U.S. runs out of daily specials, as well as many items on the regular menu, so it's best to come early. Our favorite dish is the *Veal Parmigiana*, large scallops of breaded veal with melted cheese on top and a little moistening of tomato sauce. It's quite different from the wet and saucy parmigiana at Little Joe's, more of a Milanese type of preparation, striking for the crunchiness of the grilled veal.

The choice of accompaniments will leave you disgruntled. The vegetables are so overcooked they're gray and mushy—a crime, because they started out fresh.

On various occasions, we've enjoyed such daily specials as *Baked Rib of Beef*, thick slices of tender, fat-marbled meat taken from near the bone, and *Calve's Liver with Onions*, thin slices not overcooked, that are smothered in caramelized sautéed onions.

Other good specials are *Coteghine*, boiled Italian sausage served on Wednesdays until they run out; *Stewed Rabbit*, on Fridays; or *Osso Buco*, veal shanks, on Saturdays. If you stick to the meat dishes you won't be disappointed.

The *Cheeseburger with Everything*, a North Beach favorite, is a huge hunk of ground beef, cooked to order, served on French bread. It's a feat to get your mouth around it.

The U.S. is not as good as Little Joe's, but the physical facilities are more comfortable, though still spartan. If Little Joe's weren't up the block, you'd have good reason to think you had really discovered the best little Italian restaurant around.

PRICE RANGE: Inexpensive
HOURS: 7:00 A.M.–8:30 P.M. Tues.–Sat.
NO RESERVATIONS
BEER AND WINE
NO CREDIT CARDS

Vanessi's ★

498 Broadway
San Francisco
421–0890

Vanessi's is a restaurant that may be getting sabotaged by its own success. Open since 1936, Vanessi's could always be depended on to serve food that never dropped below a certain solid, culinary level, but during the past five years or so, the volume has tripled. What was usually a full restaurant is now a packed restaurant.

After several recent visits, we find that the food and service are simply neither as good nor as dependable as they used to be. The pace is too harried, the kitchen too pressed. Dishes that always used to be exceptional are now hit-and-miss, thrown together by cooks whose major responsibility is keeping up with orders. Plates of food that used to be fresh from the kitchen are waiting too long for the waiters to pick them up. You know what's going on, because you can see it when you sit at the counter in front of the cooking line. Everyone is just racing to keep the thing together.

Many of the reasons why Vanessi's is so popular continue to be true. The atmosphere is quintessential North Beach and the place is hopping well past midnight. There are no pretentions about the food or service. You feel comfortable in evening dress or blue jeans. The menu is so large that you can eat a different meal every day for a month, and you can order a little or a lot without feeling pressured.

What's most important about Vanessi's is that the basic quality of food has always been high. The restaurant uses excellent beef, which it ages itself, white Provimi veal, really fresh fish when it's available, pastas made that day on the premises, and fresh vegetables. Portions are large and prices more than reasonable, especially on the meats, which undercut practically everyone in the City. The cooking style is broad Italian—not too rich, not too distinctive, but tasty and hearty. Given all this, the crowds at Vanessi's are certainly deserved.

The problem these days is how the multitudes are treated. After you've waited an hour at the bar, as we've done even with reservations, you feel you deserve Vanessi's best efforts. In this regard, we feel cheated.

Here are some examples of what we've encountered on our latest visits:

Linguine and Clams, an old favorite, was a disaster for the first time. One portion had all the clams, while the other was naked. Even the saucy portion tasted flat and winey; the proportions of this usually creamy, garlicky sauce were all wrong. The charcoal-grilled *New York Steak*, ordered rare, came medium. The daily fish special, this time *Rex Sole*, ended up being cold by the time it was picked up, boned, and served; a starchy tartar sauce didn't improve it. *Calve's Liver Steak* was ordered rare and came raw; it had been cooked too quickly on the hottest part of the fire, so that it was singed on the outside and cold inside.

Other dishes were as good as we've had them in the past. *Herring with Sour Cream* came mounded high on the plate, the sour cream fresh and thick and the herring of good quality. The *Caesar Salad*, made with real anchovies, egg yolks, imported olive oil, and vinegar, was excellent. The *Chicken Cacciatora*, sautéed to order with tomatoes, mushrooms, and crisp bell peppers, was also as good as ever. The same with the *Fish Stew*, a San Francisco classic loaded with chunks of bass, snapper, chewy calamari, and clams in a thick tomato broth full of cloves, garlic, and oregano. And the *Minestrone Soup* just can't be beat; thick, rich, and tasty, it was jammed with vegetables.

At this juncture, it seems that the best time to eat at Vanessi's is at lunch or early dinner when the menu is smaller. In the evenings, things get too crazy, and being served a good meal becomes a matter of luck. We suppose if you order carefully, avoiding the pasta station, sticking to sautées, and insisting that you want your meats or fish grilled a certain way, you'll do all right. But it makes us sad to see one of our favorite restaurants taking steps that have led other great dining establishments into mediocrity.

PRICE RANGE: Moderate
HOURS: 11:30 A.M.–1:00 A.M. Mon.–Sat.
          4:30 P.M.–midnight Sun.
RESERVATIONS ACCEPTED
FULL BAR
ALL MAJOR CREDIT CARDS

Vegi Food ★

1820 Clement Street
San Francisco
387–8111

Just when a lot of our friends have already lived through some trying nutritional phases, most of which involved giving up meat, we have found the restaurant they all would have loved: Vegi Food, a Chinese vegetarian restaurant. Not only does this little restaurant put out satisfying, well-balanced vegetarian meals, but it also ranks high as a Chinese restaurant in a town that is full of good ones.

Vegi Food exudes modesty. The prices, the decor, the awful names of the dishes have no pretensions. For some reason, they've put yellow light bulbs in the fixtures, which makes everyone look jaundiced. Some people who eat there look like the types that chew each bite fifteen times, and many, I'm sure, were vegetarians before it became faddish. But the bottom line is that the food is not only delicious, but also more interesting than most, because careful attention is paid to seasoning, texture, and (despite the lighting) appearance. Basically, the same ingredients are used over and over again in most of the dishes, but each one tastes distinctly different. Chinese cooking in general depends on the liberal use of vegetables. After eating at Vegi Food, you realize that the addition of meat may be superfluous.

The most lovable dishes turn out to be vegetarian versions of popular meat dishes. *Vegetarian Mu Shu Pork*, served with square pancakes that look like hankies, is every bit as savory as the version with egg and meat. You spread salty plum sauce on the pancake, pile it with ribboned mushrooms and vegetables, fold it up, and enjoy it.

Fried Walnuts with Sweet-and-Sour Sauce duplicates the finer renditions of sweet-and-sour pork, except that the whole walnuts dipped in batter and deep fried are far superior to the gristly pieces of pork that usually end up in this dish. Here the sweet-and-sour sauce is a symphony of contrasts, its texture silken and the seasoning sharp; and the fried walnuts themselves may be one of the most delightfully rich morsels of food we've ever eaten.

Fried Won Ton here have a marvelous black mushroom filling. They're deep fried to ultimate crunchiness. *Spring Rolls*, however, are mundanely filled and greasily wrapped, tasting like a lot of spring rolls on tourist menus in Cantonese restaurants. A small disappointment.

Fiery *Hot-and-Sour Soup* makes sweat break out on your brow. Highly seasoned with soy sauce, hot oil, and vinegar, and full of julienned black mushrooms, it is more powerful and satisfying than those you get in most Mandarin restaurants. The real find in the soup section is *Corn Porridge with Vegetables*, a thick, richly brothed corn chowder studded with kernels of crisp, fresh sweet corn, crunchy water chestnuts, bright green peas, and those meaty black mushrooms. It's one of the best soups we've had in any restaurant.

Some of the dishes are a little too unusual for omnivores, who can get protein from nonvegetable sources. *Lo Han Jai Mixed Vegetables Deluxe*, an assortment of about fifteen very odd, unmingling ingredients, is probably a vegetarian's dream dish, with various fungi, tree ears, soy beans, seaweed, bean curd, and fried gluten. But you have to be a very pious vegetarian to eat it. However, *Gluten Puffs*, though they have a terrible ring, are not as bad as they sound. Gluten is pure plant protein, and these far-from-puffy pieces of it slide inconspicuously into several different preparations.

There's no beer or wine, but perfumy *Jasmine Tea* is a nice accompaniment.

PRICE RANGE: Inexpensive
HOURS: 11:30 A.M.–3:00 P.M., 5:00–9:00 P.M. Tues.–Fri.
11:30 A.M.–9:00 P.M. Sat.–Sun.
NO RESERVATIONS
NO BEER OR WINE
NO CREDIT CARDS

Vienna Coffee House

Mark Hopkins Hotel
California and Mason
San Francisco
392–3434

When mother comes to town she stays at the Mark Hopkins. This allows her at least one meal a day at the Vienna Coffee House, a plush little den of iniquitous pastry on the bottom level of the hotel. She tries to stay away from the *Swiss Nut Rolls*, the *Cheese Strudel*, the *Apple Turnovers*, the *Viennese Chocolate Cake*, the *Cherry-Custard Tarte*. Instead she demurely orders the tender, finely textured *Blueberry Muffins*.

The small room, tucked away in a secluded corner of the hotel, is a room for ladies in the old-fashioned sense. Everything is soft, round, and overstuffed, with plush red carpeting and cafe-curtained, frosted glass doors that open onto a pastry cart of Sacher Hotel proportions. A bevy of pleasant young waitresses in starched pink uniforms, watched over by a matronly woman at the cash register, recite the daily-changing pastries by heart.

We've sampled almost everything on the breakfast menu, which can be ordered at any time of the day, and it all comes from the kitchen hot and carefully prepared.

Along with the pastries, our favorites are *Danish Ableskivers*, tiny raised turnovers stuffed with apples. Smeared with whipped butter and drizzled with blackberry syrup, these tender little puffs rank with *Sears' Famous 18 Swedish Pancakes* as the best in town.

You can also get a large portion of hot, smooth *Oatmeal* or plates of juicy *Kiwi Fruit* or fresh berries in season.

You can tell that the staff at the Vienna Coffee House is used to particular requests from its patrons, many of whom stay at the Mark because they want attentive service. You pay for this, of course, as you do in most hotel dining rooms, but at the Vienna

Coffee House you don't feel put out. It's a unique room with some genuinely special offerings. As mother says, "If you're going to eat pastry, it might as well be the best."

PRICE RANGE Moderate
HOURS: 7:00 A.M.–midnight daily
NO RESERVATIONS
FULL BAR
ALL MAJOR CREDIT CARDS

Vivoli's ★

2115 Allston Way
Berkeley
845–6458

1229 Ordway
Berkeley
524–8760

Vivoli's is named after the famous ice cream store in Florence, where for a few thousand lire you can taste no less than twenty different flavors. We have recently done just that, and frankly feel that the Italian ice cream made by Vivoli's in Berkeley is better. (See Gelato for a description of Italian ice cream.) Berkeley Vivoli's ice cream is richer and denser in texture and the flavors are natural. No artificial syrups or colorings are used.

The most spectacular ice creams in the Bay Area are Vivoli's seasonal fresh-fruit flavors. The *Melon Ice Cream* sometimes tastes like cantaloupe and at other times like honeydew, depending on which are the best in the market, and it has an amazingly luscious, fruity quality that's rarely achieved in homemade ice creams. The *Strawberry*, the color of palest pink, has captured the very perfume of the berries. Fresh *Blueberry*, likewise, is infused with berry flavor.

We are also fans of Vivoli's *Espresso Ice Cream*—a friend of ours claimed it keeps him up all night—and *Amaretto*, thick with toasted almonds and a subtle splash of the liqueur. The *Vanilla* is speckled with pulverized vanilla beans, and the *Lemon* reminds us of old-fashioned lemon custard.

The women who own Vivoli's commissioned craftswomen to build handsome wooden tables and counters, and the stores are personably decorated with works by local artists. An eclectic collection of records plays in the background, and the atmosphere is more that of a convivial coffee house and meeting place than a takeout ice cream store.

HOURS: Allston Way location:
Noon–11:00 P.M. Mon.–Fri.
Noon–midnight Fri.–Sat.
Ordway location:
10:00 A.M.–11:00 P.M. daily

Vlasta's European Restaurant

2420 Lombard
San Francisco
931–7533

It sometimes seems that you can name almost any country in the world and come up with a minimum of a dozen restaurants in San Francisco specializing in that cuisine, but there's at least one major gap in that formula—Central European food. It's a cuisine that can be beautifully done, inexpensive, and uniquely satisfying, but that is sadly under-represented. That's why a place like Vlasta's, which would be one of a crowd in New York City, is a gem in the Bay Area.

Vlasta's menu offers an amalgam of Czech, Hungarian, and German dishes, all at moderate prices. The main courses can be spectacular. A good test for any restaurant of this sort is the *Duck*, and Vlasta's passes with flying colors. You get half a roasted duck in a light sauce, with the skin perfectly crisp and the meat juicy and tender, and no hint of fat or grease. (Roasting a duck might seem like a fairly simple task, but consider the number of restaurants at which it comes out so greasy it practically slithers off your plate when you cut into it.)

The *Sauerbraten* is simply the best we've had anywhere. All too often, sauerbraten comes in such a cloyingly heavy brown sauce it's enough to send you for the Alka-Seltzer. At Vlasta's, the *Sauerbraten* is done almost in *nouvelle cuisine* style. The beef is marinated in wine and vegetables for several days, and then roasted with herbs and spices. Then, the vegetables are pureed with some cream and served as the sauce. The beef not

227

only emerges beautifully seasoned, but also so tender you can cut it with a fork.

Unfortunately, with the exception of a satisfying thick *Beef Vegetable Soup*, the accompaniments at Vlasta's tend to be a disappointment. The dumplings taste tough and stale, the rye bread is bland (why not chunks of Eastern European black bread?), and the homemade *Apple Strudel* has mushy apples and a soggy crust. The wine list is very reasonably priced, and Vlasta's offers a selection of excellent German and Czech beers.

PRICE RANGE Moderate
HOURS: 5:30–11:00 P.M. Tues.–Sun.
RESERVATIONS ACCEPTED
FULL BAR
ALL MAJOR CREDIT CARDS

Warszawa ★

1730 Shattuck Avenue
Berkeley
841–5539

Eastern European food was fortunately invented well before people started counting calories. Thick, hearty soups, huge platters of meat with sour cream and dumplings, and whipped cream-laden desserts aren't exactly the stuff of which *cuisine minceur* is made.

On the other hand, a well-prepared Eastern European meal can be enormously satisfying. And "well prepared" is exactly the description to fit Warszawa, a Polish restaurant so authentic that some of the waiters barely speak English. When you walk in, you might have your doubts: Warszawa is housed in a building whose decor, if anything, looks Early American (and which, oddly enough, was formerly an Italian restaurant). But when you begin your meal, you know it's being prepared by truly skilled Eastern European cooks.

The hot *Borscht* is nothing less than miraculous, easily a rival for the world-famous borscht of the Russian Tea Room in New York. It's filled with thick slices of beets and chunks of tasty sausage and herbs, in a rich beet and sour cream broth. The *Pea Soup* is also first rate, with lots of tender slivers of smoked ham imparting its flavor to the thick puree of split peas. Don't miss the homemade *Herring in Sour Cream Sauce*, either; it puts to

228

shame the herring sold in jars in supermarkets, and makes a perfect accompaniment to the crusty black bread you get with your dinner.

All of the entrees made with pork or beef are delicious. Our particular favorite is *Hunter's Stew*, a thick, pungent blend of beef, pork, sausage, bacon, and sauerkraut. Stews are something you don't see often anymore on restaurant menus, and you can easily forget how tasty a stew can be if prepared well. Another outstanding dish—one considerably lighter than most of the entrees—is *Nalesniki*, two crêpes filled with a blend of chopped meat and mushrooms and served with sour cream and lightly sautéed vegetables. The crêpes are unusually light and fluffy. The *Stuffed Cabbage* might not be light, but it's expertly done in a tangy paprika and sour cream sauce. In fact, among all the entrees, our only quarrel is with the *Duck*, which sometimes comes out greasier than we would prefer. You do, however, get an entire half duck, roasted with apples and prunes and served with dumplings.

All the desserts are excellent. Our particular favorite is the homemade *Rum Walnut Torte*, which looks like a regular frosted cake, but tastes heavenly. It isn't cloyingly sweet, as tortes sometimes can be, and the batter is crunchy with bits of walnut and soaked with rum.

Don't bring your calorie counter to a meal like this; just bring a hearty appetite and you won't go away disappointed.

PRICE RANGE: Moderate
HOURS: 5:30–10:00 P.M. Sun.–Mon. and Wed.–Thurs.
       5:30–11:00 P.M. Fri.–Sat.
RESERVATIONS ACCEPTED
BEER AND WINE
MASTERCARD, VISA

Wim's ★★

141 Columbus
San Francisco
421–3481

Wim's, a little counter restaurant, a converted Zim's, is a hangout for the Francis Ford Coppola film crowd who work in the triangular building above it. The food is absolutely top-notch, simple though it is.

Wim's serves one of the best *Hamburgers* in town. Chuck is ground daily, formed into six-ounce burgers, and grilled over a charbroiler to your specified degree of doneness. It comes on tender egg rolls with lettuce, tomatoes, and pickles, with potato chips on the side. If you order your hamburger rare, you'll get it rare, and the quality of the beef is so good at Wim's that you can feel okay about eating it that way. Imported blue cheese or bacon and cheese can be ordered on it.

The crisp *French Fries* are made with fresh potatoes, skins on. Real old-fashioned milk shakes are thick with ice cream and come in tall silver shake containers that fill two glasses. You can drink a large glass of freshly squeezed *Orange Juice* or real *Coca Cola*, a correctly balanced mix of syrup and soda water, a delicacy these days.

On Friday, have the daily special of *Fisherman's Chowder*, made with clams, turbot, carrots, potatoes, and mushrooms in a creamy, unthickened broth. The vegetables are still crisp, big meaty chunks of fish are still firm, and the broth itself is redolent of clams and herbs.

Another Friday special might be a huge *Filet of Snapper* in an egg batter, grilled golden brown on the outside but moist on the inside. It comes with french fries and a medley of quickly sautéed vegetables in garlic and butter. It's an all-time bargain lunch.

For dessert, have *Rebecca's Homemade Apple Pie*. It's the kind of apple pie you wish your mother could have made—flaky brown crust and thinly sliced fresh apples seasoned with just the right amount of sugar and lemon juice. *Espresso* and *Cappuccino* are strong and aromatic, up to the best North Beach standards.

Frankly, we are amazed by the exceptional quality and low prices of this little restaurant. Is it subsidized by the film industry? A possible drawback is that there is only one table, usually occupied (sometimes by celebrities), so you have to sit at the counter. Also, it can get a bit stuffy, what with the hot grill and french frier, but that's a small convenience for the great food.

PRICE RANGE: Inexpensive
HOURS: 7:30 A.M.–7:00 P.M. Mon.–Fri.
NO RESERVATIONS
NO BEER OR WINE
NO CREDIT CARDS

Wine and Cheese Center ★

2111 Union Street
San Francisco
563–3606

At the Wine and Cheese Center, you can taste seven or eight different California and French wines, and then have a glass of your favorite at 25 percent of the retail price of the bottle. Or better yet, you can drink any bottle of wine in this excellent wine shop for retail price, thereby taking advantage of the best wine list in town.

The opulent cold lunches served here at five or so tiny tables set up between the wine crates live up to this enlightened wine policy. Every week there is a special, like a cornucopian platter of *Ripe Melon Draped with Prosciutto; Rice Salad Made with Ham, Fresh Peas, Raisins, and Artichoke Hearts*; and a still-life bunch of *Concord Grapes, Bright Green Baby Artichokes, and Fresh Figs*. The next week there might be a plate of *Cold Roasted Chicken Seasoned with Fresh Rosemary, Cubed Cucumbers and Feta Cheese Sprinkled with Virgin Olive Oil*, and *Calamata Olives and Spicy Stuffed Grape Leaves*.

If you enjoy sampling cheeses as well as wines, you can order a board of three, which you choose from the overflowing cheese counter. They're all in perfect condition and are showcased to best effect by fresh baguettes and fresh fruit.

For dessert there are rich homemade desserts and full-bodied coffee.

Erudite, chatty Dave Crane presides over all the tasting. He's one of those people for whom wine is a passion. By the time you leave his congenial little shop, you'll probably be carrying a case of that seventh bottle you tasted.

PRICE RANGE: Moderate
HOURS: 11:00 A.M.–2:00 P.M. Tues –Sat.
NO RESERVATIONS
WINE. WINE. WINE
MASTERCARD. VISA

Yenching ★

939 Kearny
(near Columbus)
San Francisco
397–3543

Yenching is the sort of restaurant you could walk by a hundred times and never notice. The yellow storefront facade is nondescript. Chinese movie posters are scotch-taped on the windows. The sign gets lost in the Chinatown jumble of old buildings. If you peek in, you see one of those bare, overly lit rooms painted orange and packed with plain tables. How would you guess that one of Chinatown's premier Mandarin chefs lurks within?

The food is fantastic, the prices reasonable, and Yenching features one of the best Mandarin dishes we've ever tasted: *Princess Prawns*. Large battered shrimp are deep fried just until the blush of rawness fades, and are served in a complex sweet, sour, and garlic sauce laced with flecks of hot pepper. This isn't the only first-rate dish: The *Mu Shu Pork* appears on every Mandarin menu, but Yenching's is a model of what it should be. Shreds of vegetables, pork, and scrambled egg maintain their individuality, and the pancakes prove tender but sturdy.

The vegetable dishes are particularly good, too. *Dry Cooked String Beans* are tender but crunchy, having absorbed their cooking liquid. The hotness of *Garlic-Flavored Eggplant* seems to grow as you eat it, a vegetable dish with the substance of meat.

Yenching is not exactly elegant dining. The restaurant is so noisy it poses a scream-or-give-up situation. Crying infants frequently add to the din. But your evening will be saved by the food. Who need to talk, anyway, when your mouth is so full?

PRICE RANGE: Inexpensive to moderate
HOURS: 11:30 A.M.–10:00 P.M. daily
RESERVATIONS ADVISED
FULL BAR
MASTERCARD. VISA

Yoshida-Ya ★

2909 Webster Street
(near Union)
San Francisco
346–3431

Some recent dining-out experiences at Yoshida-Ya, a stunning, comfortable Japanese restaurant, confirmed the bothersome notion that the day of the week and the hour you eat at a restaurant make a considerable difference in the quality of the meal you will get. Come here on weeknights, when the food preparation and the service don't break down under the crush of diners, and you'll have a relaxing, first-rate dinner in an elegant setting.

What makes Yoshida-Ya unusual is the wide selection of *yakitori*—various choices of meats, fish, and vegetables that are marinated, grilled on skewers over charcoal, then brought to your table and kept warm on individual clay braziers. You get two skewers in each serving, and they're relatively inexpensive, so you can order several different kinds and share them, just as in a sushi bar. (*Yakitori* restaurants are extremely popular in Japan, but for some reason haven't caught on here.)

Some of the tastiest *Yakitori* include *Scallops, Mushrooms Stuffed with Ground Chicken, Asparagus Wrapped in Sliced Pork*, and butter-tender *Filet Mignon*. Each different food radiates its own essence, making you feel as if you were eating only the choicest morsels. The mundane becomes a delicacy.

There are several interesting appetizers. We particularly like the *Yama Kake*, thin slices of Japanese mountain potatoes served with slices of raw tuna and seaweed. The potatoes, served raw, are snow white, crunchy, and slightly sticky, and don't resemble American potatoes at all. Another excellent appetizer is *Atsu-Age*, large, creamy cubes of breaded and deep-fried soy bean curd in a strong broth seasoned with grated radish and ginger. The deep-fried bean curd took on the qualities of a light, creamy cheese.

Eat upstairs, where you're ushered into a quiet, multilevel, softly cushioned and carpeted dining room with traditional Japanese seating. If you avoid the weekend crowds, the experience can be lovely.

PRICE RANGE: Moderate
HOURS: 5:30–10:30 P.M. daily

RESERVATIONS ADVISED
FULL BAR
AMERICAN EXPRESS. MASTERCARD. VISA

Zuni Cafe ★

1658 Market Street
San Francisco
552–2522

The 1600 block of Market Street looks like a chunk of New Mexican desert transported to the city, flora intact. On the corner lies the Red Desert, a fascinating cactus store with a botanical garden of spiky barrels, yuccas, and spears growing in its front windows. Nestled next door is what appears to be an Indian pueblo, otherwise known as the Zuni Cafe. It is high ceilinged and sky lit, with whitewashed stucco walls, tables that look like they are carved out of stone, and benches covered with authentic Indian weavings. Most important, it has a bright, airy atmosphere that seems sunny on even the gloomiest of days. We've spent afternoons at the Zuni feeling like we were in the middle of New Mexico.

While the decor is southwestern, the food is an eclectic assortment of skillfully made salads, soups, cold plates, and pastas with a French feeling, like a slice of spicy *Rabbit Pâté* garnished with Dijon mustard and cornichons, or a *Lentil Salad* seasoned with scallions and a good vinaigrette dressing. You can get a freshly made *Chicken Salad* with diced celery and fresh basil, or creamy *Egg Salad*, or loosely textured slices of *Meat Loaf* seasoned with thyme.

The green salads are served in big glass bowls, which allows you to toss them in the vinaigrette dressing without scattering leaves across the table. A bowl of *Spinach* or *Mixed Red Leaf and Butter Lettuce*, each leaf perfect, is the best way to begin your meal. With the salads come crusty slices of rye and a crock of sweet butter.

For dessert there's a dense, chocolaty *Reine de Saba* or an uncloying *Pecan Tarte* and excellent *Colombian* or *French-Roast Coffee*.

As you eat, you can gaze at an ever-changing exhibit of paintings by interesting local artists, all of which is enhanced by the good natural light in this clever little neighborhood restaurant.

PRICE RANGE: Inexpensive to moderate
HOURS: 11:00 A.M.–6:00 P.M. Mon.–Sat.
NO RESERVATIONS
BEER AND WINE
NO CREDIT CARDS

Restaurants
by Nationality or Type
and
by Location

RESTAURANTS BY NATIONALITY OR TYPE

American
Alfred's ★ ★
Andalou
Burton's
Cadell Place
Cafe Potpourri
Capri ★
de Young Museum Cafe
Diamond Sutra
Fourth Street Grill ★
Great American Meat & Potatoes ★
Greens ★ ★
Hoffman's Grill
Jack's ★
MacArthur Park
Mary's
Millard's on Fillmore ★
Oakland Museum
Panhandle Pantry
Perry's ★
Rising Loafer
Rountrees
San Francisco Museum of Modern Art
Seven Seas
Station House Cafe
Swallow
Vienna Coffee House
Wine and Cheese Center ★
Zuni Cafe ★

American—Barbeque
Firehouse Station No. 1
Hog Heaven
KC Bar B-Q ★
Leon's Bar-BQ
Poor Red's ★

American—Breakfasts & Brunches
Alta Mira Hotel
Café Lido

Doidge's ★ ★
Lois the Pie Queen
Mama's ★
Mama's Royal Cafe ★
Palm Court
Sears ★ ★

American—Fish
Hayes Street Grill ★ ★
Ronayne's
Sam's Grill
Swan Oyster Depot ★
Tadich Grill ★ ★

American—Hamburgers
Bill's Place ★
Clown Alley
Fat Albert's
Hamburger Mary's
Wim's ★ ★

American—Hot Dogs
Noble Frankfurter
Original Hot Dog
Original Kasper's

American—Ice Cream
Bud's
Double Rainbow ★
Gelato
Joe's
McCallum's
Vivoli's ★

Basque
Auburn Hotel

Chinese
China First ★
Chin Szchawn ★ ★
Golden Eagle
Happy 6
Hunan
Kum Moon ★
Maggie Gin's

Mandarin
Mike's ★
Ocean ★ ★
South China Cafe
Taiwan ★
Tien Fu ★
Ton Kiang ★
Vegi Food ★
Yenching ★

Chinese—Deem Sum
Asia Garden ★ ★
Louie's
— Tung Fong ★ ★

Colombian
Chibchas

Cuban
— Cuba

Eastern European
Paprikas Fono ★
Vlasta's
Warszawa ★

French
A La Carte ★ ★
Bay Wolf
Cafe at Chez Panisse ★ ★
California Culinary Academy
Carnelian Room
Chez Panisse ★ ★ ★
City Hotel ★
— Cocolat
— Delice de France ★
Ernie's ★ ★ ★
La Bourgogne ★ ★
La Chaumiere ★
La Mirabelle ★ ★
— Le Candide ★
— Le Central ★
Le Chalet
— L'Olivier

Maurice et Charles ★ ★ ★
Miramonte ★ ★ ★
Nadine
Nob Hill Cafe ★
Pig-by-the-Tail ★
St. Orres

German
Schroeder's

Indian
Gaylord ★ ★ ★
Moti Mahal
Pasand ★

Indonesian
Java

Italian
Abalonetti ★
Basta Pasta
Bruno's
Cafe Riggio ★
Caffe La Botte ★
Caffe Sport ★ ★
Ciao
E'Angelo
Giramonti ★
Il Pirata
La Pergola
La Traviata ★ ★
Little Italy
Little Joe's ★
Modesto Lanzone's ★ ★
Napoli
North Beach
Original Joe's
Orsi's ★ ★
Teresa's Place
U.S. Restaurant
Vanessi's ★

Italian—Pizza
Arinell Pizza
Caffe Roma

242

Frank's Extra
Milano Pizza
Tommaso ★

Japanese
Akasaka ★ ★
Edokko
Hana ★ ★
Ichigo
Kichihei
Mifune
Misono
Ramen-tei
Yoshida-Ya ★

Japanese—Sushi
Ino Sushi
Kinokawa ★ ★

Korean
Hahn's Hibachi
Sorabol ★

Mexican
Cafe Central
La Rondalla ★
Murillo's ★ ★

Mexican—Burritos
La Cumbre ★
La Fiesta Market
La Taqueria
Panchito's
Taqueria Morelia ★
Taqueria Tepatitlan

Middle Eastern
Agadir ★ ★
Caravansary
Pasha ★

Polynesian
Trader Vic's

Russian
Archil's ★
George's ★ ★

Salvadoran
El Tazumal ★ ★

Spanish
Alejandro's ★ ★

Thai
Khan Toke ★ ★ ★
Rama Thai
Siam Cuisine ★ ★

Vietnamese
Cordon Bleu
Golden Turtle ★
Mai ★

RESTAURANTS BY LOCATION

Castro & Outer Market & Noe Valley
Bud's
Burton's
Diamond Sutra
Little Italy
South China Cafe

Chinatown
Asia Garden ★ ★
Louie's
Ton Kiang ★
Tung Fong ★ ★
Yenching ★

Civic Center
Hayes Street Grill ★ ★
San Francisco Museum of Modern Art
Zuni Cafe ★

Downtown & Union Square
Delice de France ★
La Bourgogne ★ ★
Original Joe's
Palm Court
Sears ★ ★
Trader Vic's

East Bay
A La Carte ★ ★
Arinell Pizza
Bay Wolf
Cafe at Chez Panisse ★ ★
Chez Panisse ★ ★ ★
Chin Szchawn ★ ★
Edokko
Fat Albert's
Fourth Street Grill ★
Golden Eagle
Great American Meat & Potatoes ★
KC Bar B-Q ★

Lois the Pie Queen
Mama's Royal Cafe ★
McCallum's
Nadine
Oakland Museum
Original Kasper's
Pasand ★
Pig-by-the-Tail ★
Rountrees
Siam Cuisine ★ ★
Sorabol ★
Swallow
Taiwan ★
Taqueria Morelia ★
Warszawa ★
Vivoli's ★

Excelsior District
Caffe La Botte ★

Financial District
Akasaka ★ ★
Carnelian Room
Ciao
Clown Alley
Ernie's ★ ★ ★
Hoffman's Grill
Jack's ★
Kinokawa ★ ★
Le Candide ★
Le Central ★
L'Olivier
MacArthur Park
Orsi's ★ ★
Rama Thai
Ramen-tei
Sam's Grill
Schroeder's
Tadich Grill ★ ★
Wim's ★ ★

Ghirardelli Square
Gaylord ★ ★ ★
Mandarin

246

Modesto Lanzone's ★ ★
Paprikas Fono ★

Haight Street
Hog Heaven
Original Hot Dog
Panhandle Pantry

Japantown
Ino Sushi
Mifune
Misono

Marin County
Alta Mira Hotel
Andalou
Giramonti ★
La Chaumiere ★
Maurice et Charles ★ ★ ★
Moti Mahal
Seven Seas
Station House Cafe

The Marina
Caravansary
Cocolat
E'Angelo
Greens ★ ★
Ichigo
Kichihei
La Pergola
Ronayne's
Vlasta's

The Mission & Portrero Hill
Bruno's
Cafe Central
Cuba
El Tazumal ★ ★
Il Pirata
La Cumbre ★
La Fiesta Market
La Rondalla ★
La Taqueria

La Traviata ★ ★
Panchito's
Taqueria Tepatitlan

Nob Hill

Cafe Potpourri
Nob Hill Cafe ★
Vienna Coffee House

North Beach

Agadir ★ ★
Alfred's ★ ★
Basta Pasta
Cadell Place
Café Lido
Caffe Roma
Caffe Sport ★ ★
Frank's Extra
Hunan
La Mirabelle ★ ★
Little Joe's ★
Mama's ★
North Beach
Tommaso ★
U.S. Restaurant
Vanessi's ★

Northern & Central California

Abalonetti (Monterey) ★
Auburn Hotel (Auburn)
Chibchas (Hwy 140)
City Hotel (Columbia) ★
Happy 6 (Modesto)
Le Chalet (Guerneville)
Murillo's (Vacaville) ★ ★
Poor Red's (El Dorado) ★
Rising Loafer (Danville)
St. Orres (Gualala)
Teresa's Place (Jackson)

The Peninsula

China First ★

Polk Street
Cordon Bleu
Double Rainbow ★
Noble Frankfurter
Pasha ★
Swan Oyster Depot ★

The Richmond
Alejandro's ★ ★
Bill's Place ★
Cafe Riggio ★
de Young Museum Cafe
Firehouse Station No. 1
George's ★ ★
Golden Turtle ★
Hahn's Hibachi
Java
Joe's
Khan Toke ★ ★ ★
Kum Moon ★
Mai ★
Mary's
Mike's ★
Napoli
Ocean ★ ★
Vegi Food ★

South of Market
California Culinary Academy
Hamburger Mary's

The Sunset
Gelato
Hana ★ ★
Milano Pizza
Tien Fu ★

Union Street & Pacific Heights
Archil's ★
Doidge's ★ ★
Leon's Bar-BQ
Millard's on Fillmore ★

Perry's ★
Wine and Cheese Center ★
Yoshida-Ya ★

Wine Country
Capri ★
Maggie Gin's
Miramonte ★ ★ ★